Hank Harrison

The

CAULDRON

and the

GRAIL

Ritual Astronomy

and the

Stones

of

Ancient Europe

The Archives Logo

The Archives colophon is a circular magical formula, used for meditation by monks and alchemists from the Dark Ages. Its current form is derived from the *Monas Hieroglyphica* of John Dee, the renaissance magus and mentor to Queen Elizabeth I. The earliest source of this signet, according to Dee, is a woodcut in a handwritten copy of *De natura rerum* of Isidore of Seville (AD 560-636). In that work the signet accompanies a quotation from the *Hexameron* of Saint Ambrose (III. xiv) describing the interrelation of the four alchemical elements: fire, air, earth and water, with their complimentary perceptual qualities: hot, cold, dry and moist.

Elaborate cabalistic formulas, such as that depicted in the logo, were common in Europe from the fifth century until the end of the Renaissance. In the tenth century John Scotus Erigena, an Irish monk, expanded the idea to a larger platform by adapting the vast memory systems used by the Celtic bards and Greek orators. Erigena named his system *ars naturae*: the art of nature. He also added Aristotelian structure to the schema and found proofs of the natural paths to God in the folk traditions of the Irish, Welsh and Greeks.

The basic cosmic conception symbolized by the "knot" can be traced to the earliest Shamanism. In this scheme the Earth is linked to water by the common quality of cold. Water is linked to air by the quality of moisture. Air is linked to fire by heat and fire is linked to earth by dryness. The signet also represents the eight yearly festivals which inspired archaic humans to record natural laws in stone.

The Archives Press

San Francisco • London • Amsterdam • Dublin

ii

About the Cover

The stone cauldron is archaeologist and astronomer Martin Brennan's rendition of the Grail stone in the east passage at Knowth, a huge Neolithic stone mound located in the Boyne Valley about twenty-five miles north of Dublin, Ireland. This passage admits a lightbeam which strikes the cauldron on Spring Equinox each year.

The carved stone emerging out of the cauldron is Brennan's exact rendering of the controversial sundial stone also from Knowth. Both stones are part of a still active calendric computer system built more than six thousand years ago. But however magnificent Knowth may seem it is only one node in a vast network of such machines located on both sides of the Atlantic.

The Archives Press
334 State Street
Los Altos, California 94022

Designed by BookProcessor

Library of Congress
Cataloging-in-Publication Data

Harrison, Hank
The Cauldron and The Grail:
Ritual Astronomy and the Megaliths of Atlantic Europe.
Vol.1 The Grail Trilogy —

1st Edition

Includes bibliography, footnotes and index

ISBN Hardcover: 0-918501-17-2

1. Holy Grail 2. King Arthur 3. Quest literature
4. Archaeology 5. Anthropology
6. Witchcraft 7. Occult 8. Celtic Mythology 9. Astronomy

I. Harrison, Hank II. Title
LC#: 91-071189

University of London Warburg Institute and
British Museum Categories

In Memory of
Dame Frances Yates, O.B.E.

Acknowledgements

The author would like to thank the following people and places for their unstinting support in the preparation of the Grail Trilogy: Don Skirving and Beth Grossman; Candida Denadio; Maude Elizabeth Johnson; Lloyd Saxton; Omar Del Carlo; Nelson Algren; Elaine Markson; Tom Constanten; Marylin and Patty Kitchell; Rodney Albin; Peter Albin; Peter Rowan; Ichiro Kodaka; Elizabeth Leader; Janette Jackson; Shirley Abicair; Jim and Lynn Gillam; Dan Aeyelts; Crystal Aeyelts; Christopher Rudmann; Helene Kopejean; David Leiberman; Bill Franklin; Wolfgang Bielefeld; Sandy Bazett-Cox; David and Carolyn Eyes; Ted Eyes; Dan Mcleod and all the folks at the Georgia Straight; Kay Hoffman; Dan Rossett; Tony Bove and Cheryl Rhodes; Ekhardt and Persis Gerdes; Anata Riddle; Abbey Johnston; Paul Kluwer; Simon Vinkenoog; Joffra Boschart; Diana Vandeburg; Dr. M. Sickez; Phil Lesh; John Michell; Jerry Garcia; Bob Hunter; Alan Triste; Joan O'Sullivan; Karen Melquist-High; Gerry Ganter; Futzie Nutzle; Henry Humble; Spinny Walker; Dan Kottke; Harry Ely; LaVerne Leroy; Dan Poynter; Danny Moses and Sierra Club Books; Randy Flemming, Chuky Winton, Mike Winton, Bill Hearst, and all the people at PGW; Dave Hinds and Celestial Arts; Randy Beek, the Lizard Lady and all the folks at BookPeople; all the folks at Inland Books; Montalvo Center; Martin Brennan; Jack Roberts; Brian Martin; Nancy Cummings; Ron McKernan and family; John and Jane Challas; Keith and Merrill McFarland; Triona Watson; Bob and Terry Weder; Wiloughby Pudley II, Bubba White Toes, Amber, Brenda; and Courtney Harrison-Rodriguez-Menely-Love-Child.

I would especially like to thank the manufacturers of Norton motorcycles for developing a machine guaranteed to clear one's mind. Finally, I would like to thank Ira Einhorn and Ben Moore for saying it couldn't be done.

The Grail Trilogy

The Cauldron and The Grail:

Ritual Astronomy and the

Megaliths of Atlantic Europe

The Ace of Cups:

The Grail in the Tarot and Cabala

The Secret Grail:

An Initiation

By the same author:

The Dead Trilogy
Pig Pen and the Blues
The Shamrock and the Swaztika
Cocaine and the Fourth Reich
Apple Sixteen
Hamburger Zen
Glass Country
Head Keeper
The Scarlet Shamrock
Quest for Flight
Computer Smut
The Initiation of Fuego Deo
The Dream Place

Contents

Appendices

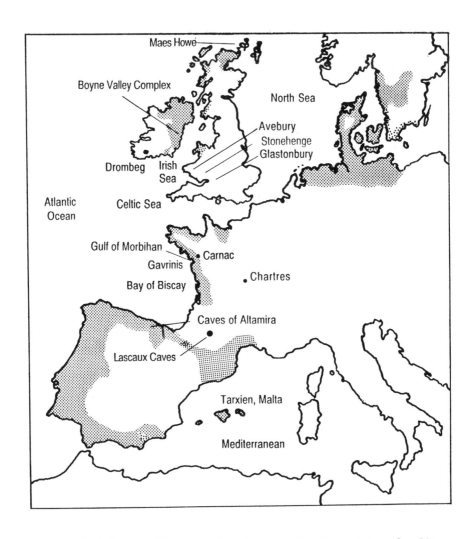

Maes Howe

Boyne Valley Complex

North Sea

Avebury
Stonehenge
Glastonbury

Drombeg Irish
Sea

Atlantic
Ocean

Celtic Sea

Gulf of Morbihan

Carnac

Gavrinis

Chartres

Bay of Biscay

Caves of Altamira

Lascaux Caves

Tarxien, Malta

Mediterranean

Map of Atlantic Europe showing major Star Temple Sites.

The
CAULDRON
and the
GRAIL

There are probably no lost civilizations —
only academic blind spots

FOREWORD

This is the first volume in a trilogy dedicated to the exploration of the Grail myth as it evolved from the megalithic temples of Western Europe. I thought no one would be interested in how this trilogy got started, yet a large group of trusted friends urged me to provide a sketch. It is to them, and my mentor, that this book is truly dedicated.

My quest began around 1949, when I was nine. I was a library troglodyte by that date. There was no Indiana Jones to wrest The Holy Grail from the clutches of the fictional Third Reich because the real Nazis were still around, in various forms. On more than one occasion I was caught worming my way through the adult stacks searching for brain food. With the exception of *Classics Illustrated* comic books, I was bored to tears with the typical children's literature of the era. By the time I was ten I knew the difference between hard science and the wilder shades of fiction. I guess my parents sensed I was on to something because they bought me an advanced academic book on ancient sites as a birthday gift. In it, in a black and white half-tone still etched in my mind, stood Stonehenge. Beneath the picture the cut line read: "Mysterious stone circle in England. Origin unknown."

I didn't give much thought to Stonehenge until it came back in full color fifteen years later. I was in graduate school studying for a pharmacology final in an empty lecture hall when the room began to fill with professors. I was impressed because the entire faculty was gathering to preview a newly acquired, and unscheduled, film about

Stonehenge made by the Columbia Broadcasting System (CBS) The film showed the ball of the sun apparently rising over the heel stone at Stonehenge on June twenty-first, the Summer Solstice, proving, at least to my satisfaction, that places like Stonehenge hold the key to other, more complex, mysteries. I was sure archaic peoples were advanced beyond previous estimates.[1]

The one-hour documentary was based on the research of Professor Gerald Hawkins, an astronomer, who was definitely bucking the establishment by asserting that Stonehenge, and by association other megalithic structures, was designed to make astronomical observations. This set off a controversy because, at the time, the art products of the New Stone Age were considered primitive while monuments like Stonehenge were considered pagan sanctuaries. Astronomy was out of the question. The assumption at work here was that any culture without a written language and metallurgy was backward. Anyone who would connect the Stone Age with intelligent activity, was wrong *a-priori*. Many academics pooh-poohed Hawkins, his theory, the sensationalism surrounding the film and the best-selling book it was based on, but I thought the core idea was worth exploring. And I was curious about the mysterious people who built Stonehenge. Even today we know very little about them.

The builders of Stonehenge used sundials, often called gnomons, to search for star, moon, planet and sun alignments in the Stonehenge structure as was suggested by the astronomer Sir Norman Lockyer in the late nineteenth century and by the antiquarian John Aubrey (1626-97) who worked out moon correlations in the outer ring at

---

[1] I say "apparently" because the sun does not rise. To be a true heliocentric, one must take an enduring vow to point this out as often as possible.

Stonehenge. The "Aubrey Holes" at Stonehenge are named after him. Hawkins simply used a modern computer to "test" an ancient computer.

More importantly Hawkins was able to explain Stonehenge to the American and European public for the first time without the hocus-pocus. Almost overnight Stonehenge grew into a spawning ground for science fiction writers and quickly became a topic of heated academic debate. Dozens of books and short stories appeared. Pseudo-science soon collided with academia. The science fiction faction took an immediate, " I told you so" posture. The academic community, frightened to align with anything based on fiction, regrouped under an even more conservative banner, both lost ground. Obviously a new science was forming. Stonehenge is not fiction.

In spite of the on-going media debate, or perhaps because of it, I went on active lookout for more information about the megalith builders. The astronomy wasn't as important to me as the reconstruction of their cultural milieu. Since there are thousands of other rings and standing stones dotted around the Atlantic seaboard, many of them far more spectacular than Stonehenge, it made sense to look away from England for clues. Although each megalith seemed different to the experts I saw the similarities and assumed, rightly as it turned out, that there was a widespread and uniform, religion prior to Christ in those areas. 2

I stopped reading science fiction. At last reality was outdistancing fiction. Unfortunately there was very little non-fiction pertaining to the megaliths. The questions of "what" and "why" were well documented but only a handful

---

[2]Reconstruction of the religion would be a likely place to start if one were interested in building an ethnological profile.

of studies shed any light on the "who" question. Who built Stonehenge? Were they like us? What language did they speak? What was their religion like? Were they precursors of the Irish and Welsh or were they strangers from a far off land? And, as a secondary consideration, were they our direct ancestors?

I compiled enough material by 1973 to begin addressing some of these questions. I began work on a book comparing the ancient stone circles to electronic computer systems. It was tentatively titled *The Mandala Technology*. To my mind, Stonehenge was both an early computational device and a religious mandala. When looking at an overhead shot of Stonehenge, I saw a similarity to the radial hand-cranked device called a Difference Engine designed by Charles Babbage and programmed by Ada Lovelace in the nineteenth century.

Aerial views of Stonehenge also reminded me of C.G. Jung's "mandalas," which he defined as universal radial symbols of the human psyche. I began to think that the focal mandala for our era is the extended computer system, which can be viewed as a radial star network and that the ancient systems were similar, in a functional and cultural sense, because they were used to standardize celestial observations and measurements.

From what I could gather, the original rationale for Stonehenge seemed to be the need to permanently store and retrieve observations of cosmic events over long periods so they could be ritualized and made into ceremonies, ceremonies designed to track animal and crop cycles so as to harmonize the human race with the cosmos.

Until Hawkins produced proof that ancient peoples were capable of precise math models, the whole of western science was under the impression that Aristotle was the first to institute scientific methods such as the exclusion of variables, testing against standards, applied logic, and observation of behavior under controlled conditions. Now we see that tribes of goatskin clad hunters, living in the mists of the Atlantic islands, were able to calculate the orbit of Venus and the exact moment of Winter Solstice thousands of years before Aristotle. [3]

The most exciting aspect of this insight was the probability that people haven't changed much over the past six millennia. We still wear leather and goatskin jackets and, in spite of rapid advances in medicine and technology, we remain awestruck by the cosmos and are obsessed with tracking every possible celestial, lunar and planetary event. Our entire global shipping schedule, virtually the entire worlds commerce, depends on accurate time and tide tables. Stock markets crash or rocket skyward on the news of a flood or other natural event. Why should we assume the tenders of Stonehenge were any more or less enamored of the celestial mysteries?

By the time I finished the first draft of *Mandala Technology*, the self-cure movement was upon us in force. Timothy Leary, Werner Erhardt, L. Ron Hubbard, Chuck Deidrich, the Reverend Sun Moon, and many other gurus — not the least of which was the Valium guzzling Sri Rajneesh — were eventually exiled or jailed. These quick cure snake-oil marketeers were sucking money out of the lost tribes of suburbia like a horde of industrial strength vacuum cleaners. Living gurus weren't enough. The late black magician Alastair Crowley and other satanists made a comeback in the sixties promoted by such luminaries as

---

[3]If it can be established that the people who built Stonehenge were attempting to test hypotheses (no matter how magical they may seem) they must have been engaging in an organized quest for knowledge, if not for the sake of knowledge, then for its applied results, viz. to harmonize society and reduce anxiety.

Mick Jagger of the Rolling Stones and the film maker Kenneth Anger. Their influence was widespread.

Conveniently and quite by coincidence, Crowley's private papers and memorabilia were housed in a secret basement storeroom in a famous London library — and my scholars pass gave me a chance to visit the closed collections. My first reading of Crowley's books — *777* and *The Equinox*, a multi-volumed set of foolscap and scribbles; and his comments on Rodin — were adequate to reveal his superficiality. As I was in the library almost everyday, I was able to observe a cross section of Crowley's minions as they shuffled past the security desk. They came in all sizes, shapes and descriptions. Humble hippies on semi-sincere quests and evil entrepreneurs came in droves when the whereabouts of the collection was revealed by an underground paper. Most of these day trippers were not above slitting pages out of his books with concealed razor blades so, fortunately, the collection was placed off limits to the public. When one of the visitors told me that Charlie Manson and Ozzie Osborne were Crowlyites I got the picture. Crowley never was a simple and misunderstood fool, he was rather a psychopathic genius revered by other psychopathic geniuses.

As if Crowley wasn't sufficient travail to any writer or publisher trying to get new insights to press, the mid-1970s ushered in a renewed interest in the so called "New Age" and the books of various trance mediums and glossolalic channelers including ranking proto-facists like Madame Blavatsky, late of the Theosophy movement. I noted that most of the channelers were ex-*est* holes and unrequited Scientologists still looking for a "Theta Clear" or "IT" in all the wrong places. As a result of their publishing efforts no new data was being presented to the public, except in Europe. The North American publishing establishment was not supporting honest fresh research. Reprints of books out of copyright, were the rage. Psychic healing was replacing Psychology. Stonehenge was not a computer, it was a flying saucer landing pad. Erik Von Daaniken's ideas about early spacemen visiting Earth became *de facto* truisms. My mandala hypothesis paled by comparison and the New Age genre was not about to bottom out until circa 1990.[4]

I continued gathering as much original data as possible but the literary waters were muddy. It was essential that data from C.G. Jung, Marcia Eliade and Joseph Campbell be separated from the hocus-pocus and speculation of Madame Blavatsky, Crowley and Von Daaniken so I began the process of panning for gold in a turbulent river. During the two year period, between 1971 and 1973, I noted that Hermetism, Tarot, Cabala, Alchemy, Gnosticism and numerous other streams, originated and ended in the chalice or cauldron motif. More significantly, I noted a rich and unexplored connection between the megaliths of Western Europe and rituals surrounding the Holy Grail as presented in medieval prose epics such as *Sir Gawain and the Green Knight*. How was the Grail, once a pagan chalice ritual known by many names, incorporated into Christianity? Was the computational nature of Stonehenge at the center of the Grail myth? Was Stonehenge a prototype for King Arthur's Round Table? [5]

---

[4]L. Ron Hubbard, the founder of Scientology, has been connected with black magic and the Order of the Golden Dawn, a Crowley foundation group. See: "Later Crowley Derivatives" in Warburg *Institute*, 1973.

[5]The reader's attention is directed to the works of the late Professor John Allegro, the foremost *Dead Sea Scroll* scholar. In his controversial best seller, *The Sacred Mushroom and the Cross,* he postulated that Jesus was under the influence of mushrooms when crucified.

The Maltwood Treasure

I discovered the new direction the research would take in February, 1973, after visiting the Maltwood museum in Victoria, British Columbia. This was the repository of the estate and papers of Mrs. K.E. Maltwood, a woman of considerable wealth coupled with ability in both art and science.

During a long illness, which she sensed would mark her last days, Maltwood prepared a black linen bag filled with her most important papers to be opened by scholars upon her passing. She sealed the bag with a small safety pin and a little piece of notepaper which simply identified the parcel as: "The Black Bag." This parcel was placed in a file cabinet in the special collections reading room of the University of Victoria library. The Grail Trilogy took form the moment I peered into that bag. What I discovered compelled me to dig further into the work of Katherine Maltwood, an amazing intellectual and a lesser-known member of the Bloomsbury Circle in London after World War I. Unlike Virginia Wolfe and the Huxleys, Maltwood saw the world through the eyes of an architect which she expressed in sculpture and archaeological research. Her visionary writings were inspiring because, if she was correct, the entire topic of the Grail would have to be reinvestigated. Maltwood claimed to have discovered a huge, and very ancient, radial effigy system sculpted into the landscape, which she called *The Round Table of King Arthur* or alternatively *Glastonbury's Temple of the Stars."* This effigy system, which stretched across the farm and village lands of Central Somerset county in southwestern England, was measured by her survey team and was found to be twelve miles in diameter. This is significant because one part of the radial effigy pattern includes Glastonbury Tor and

Glastonbury Abbey which lie on a straight thirty-mile line to Stonehenge. These ancient lines are called Straight Tracks and were used for navigation and cattle trails by Neolithic farmers and builders. [6]

Maltwood further speculated that the monks of Glastonbury Abbey knew about the effigies and maintained them. She was convinced the monks conspired to insert heterodox information about the huge circle in the text of certain books, mainly the *Perlesvaus*, a well-known Arthurian source book of uncertain authorship, written around AD 1150. To this day the existence of the effigies has not been accepted by archaeological authorities. Indeed they may not be Neolithic, but they do exist.

Hundreds of experts with sterling credentials have traced out Maltwood's maps and have drawn the same conclusions. In the final volume of this trilogy I set forth my thoughts on who built them and what they represent. Still, it is undeniable that extensive activity took place in the Neolithic era in and around Glastonbury. Settlements at Chedder Gorge and Wookey Hole, located about ten kilometers from the modern town of Glastonbury, date back at least twenty five thousand years.

If Maltwood's little-known research was my only source I would have gone off the deep end. Luckily, I balanced my preliminary reading with *The Grail Legends,* the widely acclaimed work of Emma Jung, the wife of C.G. Jung, who dedicated her life to Grail research. The result of Emma Jung's scholarship was a definitive — for her era — psychological tour through the manuscripts of the Middle Ages. Archaeology was not an issue. Interestingly, there seemed to be a conflict between Maltwood's findings and

---

[6]Maltwood, K. E.*Glastonbury's Temple of the Stars*. London: James Clark, 1964.

Jung's. Frau Jung and her editors ranked the *Perlesvaus* near the bottom of the list of major works on the Grail, preferring the writings of Chretien De Troyes and Wolfram von Eschenbach. [7]

The older literature, generally based on excavations conducted in the 1960s and before, were patently sexist and racist. I was sure there was a bias operating in the assumption that the megalith builders were savages. I was not alone. North American archaeology was progressive and objective. Younger minds schooled in ethnography and astronomy were interpreting old data. These fresh scientists were not traumatized by their discoveries. Those that I interviewed were pleased to find a degree of sophistication in the artifacts they unearthed. [8]

In 1974, another seemingly insurmountable problem arose. It became obvious that no single discipline was adequate to cover the panoply of topics touched on by the new definition of the Grail emerging in my research. So, as Maltwood suggested in her diary, I stepped up my trips to the actual locations mentioned in the Arthurian literature. This required a full three years living in Europe. To my astonishment every major Round Table locus mentioned in *The Perlesvaus* was built over a pre-Celtic, henge, mound or megalithic ring, each with ritual significance and dedicated to the practice of astronomy.

After visiting Kercado in France and Glastonbury Tor, Avebury and Stonehenge in England, I too was convinced

---

[7]Jung, Emma.*The Grail Legends*. New York: Putnam's, 1970. The *Perlesvaus* is crude in style compared to Chretien and Wolfram, but it has a depth that seems connected to the Dark Ages. Chretien, Wolfram and Robert de Borron claim they possessed an earlier manuscript as a guide and *The Perlesvaus,* or an earlier version of it, may be that manuscript.
[8]Struever, Stuart & Felicia Antonelli Holton. *Koster: Americans in Search of Their Prehistoric Past*. New York: Doubleday, 1979.

the Grail was inextricably wrapped in nature worship and connected to these very old and unexplained stone monuments. I was also sure the Grail legends were traceable to an ancient form of healing, a quest for emotional and psychological balance, an ancient and undocumented quest for initiation into the secrets of the cosmos as known to the megalith builders.

I reasoned that the romance literature — covering both Arthurian and Grail motifs — is Medieval, but that the original Grail saga is almost unimaginably older. There was, however, a link. According to Maltwood the information was transmitted from generation to generation. In the earliest literature the main arena for the Grail drama is not a shining castle, as many romantics are led to believe, but a megalithic ritual site and the sky above it. I was stunned by the implications of this insight with more to come.

In 1976, I was granted a chance to study with the late Dame Frances Yates at the Warburg Institute near the University of London. Yates, the author of a number of definitive works on the Renaissance, was greatly celebrated for her research techniques and writing style. She stood about five foot ten in her stocking feet, I know this because she often took off her shoes in her office. In spite of her eccentricity, exemplified by chain-smoking and a preoccupation with leopard-skin pill box hats, I was fairly sure I was in the presence of genius. Anyone who attended even one of her lectures will know what I mean. I have no idea why she selected me but, as she told me privately, I was the kind of American she liked. She didn't like my preoccupation with "secret societies" and "hocus-pocus," but she thought I was fresh and at least on the right track. She confided eventually that she expressed a distaste for American academics, finding them even stuffier than the British.

Dame Frances could speak three live, and two dead, languages interchangeably. She could drain you of your last intellectual breath one minute then pick you up and race you to the heights of intellectual quest the next. This was obviously good for me. She gave me an insight into the discipline I would need to go all the way with this Grail research and encouraged me to continue. I regret she could not see the finished work.

Between 1970 and 1982 I managed to visit and film most of the sites covered in the academic literature, at least once. I was sure I was observing traces of an organized archaic religion — possibly traces of a global Paleolithic religion — that could prove to be the oldest on Earth. I could clearly see that the origins of the Round Table myth were not Christian, at least not originally. This realization led me into a wandering state of shock, something everyone, tangled in the Grail web, must experience.

Because I went through the zen monastery system in California, I realized the exhilaration I was feeling was a kind of peak religious experience. This in turn caused me to apply a higher standard to my work. By 1974, the book was writing itself but I couldn't cram all of the discoveries, all of the dredged up data, into one book. The library research and the archaeological connections between the megaliths, the cathedrals, the Tarot and the Cabala, begged to be presented separately and yet the Grail, as an ikon, acted as a unifying theme. A trilogy was taking shape.

Questions arose in the form of sweaty little daydreams. If the Grail quest ritual was a product of cultures older than Christ, which culture should I focus on? How many Atlantic Rim pocket cultures existed seven thousand years ago? Who gave the ritual to the Celts and how did the Celts give it to other cultures to the east if they possessed no writing? Are petroglyphs a form of writing? Was the cauldron ritual a product of the New Stone Age, about 5000 BC, or was it older, possibly part of the ritual of the Cro-Magnon cave painters of the Upper Paleolithic in France some twenty thousand years ago?

The worship of a bowl or chalice, symbolic of the womb of the Great Goddess, wherein the primordial cosmos was created, is pre-Christian, but I was not aware that the concave ritual objective might also be part of a North American polar group, which I learned, much later, was called the Maritime Archaic Culture. I found this out only by accident when researching the relationship between Shamanism and red ochre pigment in ritual. I realized the flying saucer explanation was tame compared to the idea that the Grail legend, and certain elements within Christian worship rituals, might be more than one hundred thousand years old. I was amazed and a bit petrified that I wouldn't be understood, and yet I found support for the basic idea in high places.

At the insistence of the late South American playwright Omar Del Carlo and Elizabeth Leader of RILKO in London, I digested Hamlet's *Mill* by Giorgio Santillana. Joseph Campbell's *Flight of the Wild Gander* helped guide me to the mysterious Dawn People, although Campbell was a diffusionist thinker inextricably bogged down in the racist Indo-European world view. While working for Greenpeace in Vancouver, another friend drew my attention to the research of Alexander Marschack in *National Geographic*. Marschak discovered a hand-held bone calculator, tied to lunar cycles, dating from the Middle Paleolithic period. I wasn't alone. [9]

---

[9]Marschak, Alexander "Exploring the Mind of Ice-Age Man." *National Geographic*, CXLVII, January, 1975.

The Cauldron and The Grail

It was like searching for a phantom, a virus or a quark. I knew the key to the Grail was there, but I couldn't really hear it or see it. New detection instruments needed invention. Where was the missing puzzle piece between the copper cauldron of the Bronze Age and the concave grinding stone (Hamlet's Mill) of the cave shaman? What was the link, if any, between the bell beaker of the Bronze Age and the Chalice supposedly used by Christ? Was the worship of the skull in the Neanderthal cave connected in some way to the symbol of the chalice and bowl at the crucifixion on a mound in Jerusalem: "The Place of the Skull?"

Between 1976 and 1980, in frustration, I shelved the Grail book, at least the active writing phase of it, wrote a novel and a children's book, taught school, went back to the practice of industrial consulting, lived on a houseboat, continued traveling, did some hang gliding and learned to ride to hounds. I remained fascinated with microcomputers. While in Holland I was introduced to Diana Vandenberg and Joffra Boschart, the leaders of the Hermetic Symbolist school of painting. Their guidance and wisdom helped me develop a third dimension in my writing, something they called "psychic perspective." During those trips I corresponded with many writers including Richard Leigh, co-author of *The Holy Blood and Holy Grail* and Simon Vinkenoog, editor of the Dutch occult magazine *Bres*. I also held many meetings with the British mystic John Michell, who horrified the entire academic world in 1970, with his second book *The View Over Atlantis*. Michell argued that the ancient landscape was well organized and that the people who built the megaliths may have also designed straight roads. These ideas were not his originally, but he popularized them. Many academics were disturbed by Michell's books because they rallied forces against the long seated and racist idea that the megalith builders were numskulls and

xxvi

mud grubbers. We now know they were anything but primitive and that they were attempting to create or preserve an earthly paradise.

In 1980, I took what I thought would be a leisure trip to Ireland. I was assured by many British scholars, including Dame Frances, that there was little of import in the Neolithic stratum in Ireland, Wales or Scotland. To Yates, especially, the main cross current of historical import in Ireland rested with a mysterious monk named Duns Scotus Erigena, from the ninth century. This proved to be a narrow view. With the possible exception of Brittany, which is smaller in area, Ireland is by far the most exciting Neolithic province on Earth. It is a bilingual country peppered with ancient monuments, each described in a vast archaeological literature in many languages. Even so, I could not have known how deep the Irish waters were until I discovered for myself, and quite by accident, the exact nature of the megaliths in Ireland. [10]

My reason for being in Ireland had nothing to do with megaliths. I was invited to discuss my earlier works on American cultural anthropology on Irish National Radio (RTE) where I met with other authors and archaeologists. This gave me a chance to compare notes and to look into a few good book stores in Dublin. While ploughing through Greene's on Clare Street, one of the oldest bookshops in the town, I discovered a book of photographs depicting megalithic sites in Ireland. I asked my friend and RTE guide Joan O'Sullivan, where some of the mounds were located, chiefly those with carved stones. I was still laboring under the assumption that the carved stones were sculpted with

---

[10]Contrary to the comments on scarcity encountered in *Smithsonian* for February, 1985 (p. 105 f.), Gaelic speaking storytellers known as Shanachies are on the rebound in Ireland. They can be men or women, and each village has at least one.

copper or bronze tools and could not have been Neolithic.
Before coming to Ireland I labored under the further mistaken impression that most of the Neolithic mounds were
tombs and that they were located adjacent to each other in
the Orkney islands about five hundred miles to the North in
Scotland. I pointed to a picture of Newgrange, a massive
grass-covered mound built from cyclopean stones, and said,
"I'd sure like to visit that one." Joan blithely said, "Oh, well
that's only about twenty miles from here, near Drogheda!"
We drove to the Boyne Valley immediately, stopping only
for lunch.

Imagine my surprise when I first visited the Boyne
complex and realized how old and beautiful the carved
mounds were. The missing link turned out to be hidden in
plain view. The Grail Stone, which is discussed throughout
the present book, was located in the middle of Newgrange,
in the interior chamber. I could see immediately it was part
of the original ritual although the tour guides took umbrage
at any such suggestion. [11]

It dawned on me that the basin stones of the temples, the
concave stones found inside the mounds in precise settings,
are early forms of the Holy Grail. I went into an academic
reverie. The sheer beauty of the temple and the spirit of
place is astounding. I wandered around Ireland for weeks
seeing mound after mound. I missed my plane and was
forced to adjust the tickets several times. My social visit to
Dublin turned into a full time study. I leased a Georgian
house on the Boyne River one mile from Newgrange, directly across from Dowth and close to a famous bend in the
Boyne called Ros na Rig which has spawned the following

---

[11]The Boyne Valley Star Temple complex is located twenty-seven miles
north of Dublin and is easily accessible by car or bus.

Foreword

rhyme, said to be the last words of the great Medieval king Bryan Boru:

"*Bury me at Ros na Rig with my face toward the sun.*"

As it turns out Ros na Rig is aligned with the entrance of Newgrange. For me it was like living in the mounds themselves.

I proceeded to test every known hypothesis. It didn't take long to agree with other modern authors that the so-called "Passage Tombs" were primarily celestial, lunar and solar observatories, designed to track cycles, probably for animal husbandry or even human cycles. Like any tabernacle or temple, church or chapel, they were used as places of assembly, baptism, oaths and marriages. To call them tombs is to miss the cultural importance of their design. In reality they are temples to astronomy, the first true scientific instruments of the human race.[12]

Earth Balance

Most of the sites mentioned in this trilogy are imperiled by exposure to weather, human bacteria and body salts to say nothing of slipshod restorations. The megalithic circles and mounds may be flying saucer launching pads or tombs for the high kings, it matters little which explanation one accepts... they will be gone soon. Conservationists should therefore preserve these ancient sites to raise consciousness about the unresolved issues in human evolution. The temple and the environment are one entity. One cannot save a temple in the Yucatan without saving the rain forest surrounding it. Stonehenge could not be preserved without

---

[12]The closing of Lascaux cave has produced excellent results and the restrictions to public access at Stonehenge seem to be helping archaeologists, even though a police riot often occurs in observance of Summer Solstice.

rescuing the ecology of Salisbury Plain. Newgrange cannot be rebuilt without a plan to stop pollution in the Boyne river. Saving the temples and art products of the Stone Age is as essential as cleaning up a beach or preventing an oil spill.

SUB-THESIS

The present work is a speculative study. The thrust of the argument is that we should start appreciating the megaliths and other artifacts left to us by ancient societies. They are, after all, the treasures of our ancestors, vital clues to their life and times. There is an urgency to this argument. We have failed as custodians because we no longer worship nature. I fear we have inherited the curiosity of the ancients, their mental skills, but not their sense of preservation of the Earth.

H.H.

...the distinction between past,
present and future
is an illusion,
although a persistent one.

Albert Einstein

INTRODUCTION

The Holy Grail, known to romantics as the glistening chalice sought after by the knights of King Arthur's Round Table, is supposedly also the goblet used at the Last Supper and the container used by Joseph of Arimathea to receive the blood from the wounds of Christ. Unfortunately this belief is bathed in superstition. No one has proven any specific vessel to be genuine, and yet many claimants believe they possess the true Grail.

The trustees of the Chalice Well in Glastonbury, England, have a glass bowl which they think is the actual Grail. This object is set on a table in the attic of Chalice Well House along with place settings for the return of the twelve disciples and Jesus. A family in Wales claims to have the wooden cup of the Abbey Strata Florida which is supposedly made from the true cross. Others suggest the medieval French sect known as the Cathars possessed the true cup called *le Graal*. Not to be outdone, the Neo-Nazis claim they have the talisman and that it once was buried with a cache of Hitler's gold and other treasures in a mountain lake in Bavaria. [13]

---

[13]The erroneous legend of Nazi control over the Grail was re-popularized, in a 1989 film titled: *Indiana Jones and the Last Crusade.* Although fine as entertainment, the film did little to shed light on the true origins and meaning of the Grail.

Then comes the idea that the chalice of the last supper was wrapped in the Shroud of Turin — also known as Veronica's Veil. Although the chalice has never been recovered, the shroud has been tested by radiocarbon dating and proved to be a thirteenth century forgery. Bogus or otherwise, this shroud and a silver chalice of some kind were put on display throughout Europe in the Middle Ages and many claims of miraculous healings were made for them. [14]

The *Sacré Cantino* of the Knights Templars, brought back from the occupation of the Holy Land, is also a contender for the Holy Grail title. Said to be carved of malachite with emerald inlays, it too was shown with the Shroud, or the head of Lazarus, or the sword that beheaded John the Baptist, or other relics of the crusades — most of them ersatz. Eventually Napoleon, in his struggle to wrest power from the church, proclaimed these "so called" relics to be frauds. [15]

The chalice of the Abbot Suger, on display at the National Gallery in Washington, D.C., is perhaps the most fascinating claimant. This chalice has been used in the coronation of all French Queens since Eleanor of Aquitaine, the queen of the troubadour movement.[16] (Plate i)

---

[14]Currer-Briggs, Noel *The Shroud and the Grail*. London: Weidenfeld & Nicolson, 1987. Currer-Briggs traces a specific chalice from Jerusalem to France and Germany, and although the hypothesis may be particularly accurate with reference to certain medieval owners and relics, it is bogus in that the Grail of the medieval myth is not a cup but an initiation symbolized by a cup. The shroud has long been suspect, but certain families did inherit these objects and thought they were authentic at the time.

[15]Angebert, P. *The Grail and the Third Reich*. New York: Macmillan, 1976. Angebert's book is without question the easiest to read and most edifying compendium of facts relating to the Grail, the Nazi's and the Albigensians.

[16]Generally, it is known as the chalice of the Abbot Suger, after the administrator of the Gothic abbey of Saint Denis near Paris from 1222 to 1155.

Introduction

Finally, just prior to World War II, John D. Rockefeller, Senior, a well known eccentric and thirty-third degree Freemason, made claims for the Antioch Chalice, a beautiful silver and gold filigreed goblet now in the Cloisters in New York, but this cup is also suspect.

If any of these contenders were proven to be the real chalice used by Christ it would be nothing more than a curiosity piece. It would certainly not be the Grail mentioned in *Parzival* by Wolfram von Eschenbach, who defined it as a red stone. Nor could it be the Graal mentioned in the works of Chretien de Troyes, who defined it as a book, possibly a book titled *The Holy Grail.* No, like all voodoo objects, a chalice, no matter how authentic, would only be vested with magical powers for those who believe in such things. Still, most people persist in the belief that the Grail is the chalice of the Last Supper. So the elusive object remains hidden from view. But we must define it before we can find it. Calling it a mere chalice is missing the point. It

---

The famed chalice was used in the consecration ceremonies of the new altar chapels on June 11, 1144, making the handles and base at least seven hundred years old. The inner cup is probably older by far. Suger was a Benedictine and a brilliant politician. He served as regent of France during the second crusade and was both a devout Christian and a high ranking member of the Knights Templars. He was also a troubadour initiate and as such was aware of important esoteric movements in France, Italy, England and Germany. He was probably one of the most powerful clerical figures in twelfth century France, yet he was known as a humble and pious man. Although the story may not be true, Abbot Suger was sure that the inner part of this chalice was the actual cup used by Christ at the last supper. It is carved from sardonyx, familiar to North Americans as jasper. This inner part of the cup is impossible to date. The silver and gold *repoussé* base, dated to the twelfth century, reveals a significant message. The reference, "I am the Alpha and the Omega," symbolizes immortality and spiritual transformation. The cup is also adorned with bunches of grapes (representing Dionysian precursors to Christianity) and wheat sheaves representing the communion host and the fertility of the Goddess of the harvest as well as the body or flesh of the crucified Jesus. The rim of the inner cup is worn from the many communions served in it.

3

may prove to be more than a chalice, it may turn out to be a ceremony of unequalled spiritual power, conducted throughout the ages by a specific group of enlightened guardians.[17]

Although the concept of the Holy Grail came to literary expression in the Middle Ages, styled in one case as *Le Sang Graal*, the cup of Christ's blood transported to Glastonbury by his uncle, Joseph of Arimathea, it was an Occidental motif in oral tradition pre-dating Christ by thousands of years. We know it as a cauldron, a chalice and a baptismal font. In each case it is represented as a concave ritual object. In the pagan context it can be an inverted skull, a cup mark or other indentation ground in stone, a burial urn or a secret manuscript small enough to fit into a hermit's hand. It might also be a maze within a Gothic cathedral or the cathedral itself. [18]

The skull cup of the Atlantic shaman and the chalice of the Christian or Hebrew priest are similar in purpose. They

[17]Eisen, Gustavus A.*The Great Chalice of Antioch,* 2 vol. New York: Private Press, 1924. In 1910 workers digging a well in Antioch, Palestine, located a silver chalice. After passing through many suspicious hands it appeared in New York in the possession of one Fahim Kouchakji, who, by researching the object and hiring Eisen and his staff, contended that the inner part of the cup may well have been the actual cup used by Christ. The price of the object soared immeasurably and was purchased by John D. Rockefeller for the Metropolitan Museum. It is now on display in the Cloisters in Manhattan. This chalice can not be the original chalice as it is at least three hundred years too young, but it may have been an outer cover for some kind of relic. In spite of the publicity generated by the Monty Python group in the 1970s and the Indiana Jones films of the late 1980s, it is doubtful that any one cup can be established as the original chalice used by Jesus.

[18]Borron, Robert de *The Portuguese Book of Joseph of Arimathea.* Ed. H. H. Carter, Chapel Hill: The University of North Carolina Press, 1967. De Borron is the first to emphasize Joseph of Arimathea as the Grail bearer to the west. The story is extracted from legends of a Christian nature originating at Glastonbury before the Norman Conquest. Although Christian in tone, it retains elements of pagan rituals.

4

are prototypes of the Grail in the form of a goblet. But because the Celts maintained a tradition of the healing cauldron, the greatest of Grail traditions grew in Celtic territories, territories dotted with mysterious stone rings and temples like Stonehenge.[19]

In the Dark Ages Dionysian, Neoplatonic, and Christian elements came to play in secret troubadour manuscripts depicting a quest for a mysterious healing object called The Holy Grail. In every case, even in the later romanticized versions, the Grail is associated with ritual magic and initiation. Certain secret societies, the troubadours and Knights Templars among them, took up the task of maintaining the ideals embodied in the ritual and it is to these groups we must eventually turn if we hope to reveal the mysteries.

Since the Celts, or their ancestors, have inhabited the Western crossroads of the world since the dawn of history, they were able to absorb numerous exotic eastern traditions without dislodging their own beliefs. Because of their stability, the original forms of the Grail survived most directly in Celtic folklore and in Medieval and Renaissance writing of Brittany, Wales and Ireland. In Shakespeare, we find the Grail in *MacBeth* as the witches stir the cauldron. We also see the Grail ikon in a more fundamental sense in Irish, Scots, Welsh and Breton folklore as the cauldron of the Dagda or the golden bowl of the fairy faith.

---

[19]Hadingham, Evan. *Secrets of the Ice Age.* Walker, New York: 1979, p. 56 ill. The La Ferrassie cup-marked slab is the oldest sculptured stone known. It was used to cover a bear and human burial in a Neanderthal context dated some one hundred thousand years ago. I am convinced these cup and ring marks, the skulls used in the burial ritual, and the shamanism that directed them, are the prototypes of the medieval Grail myth. When they were translated into literature in the Middle Ages, the book, as a sacred art form, became the newest version of the skull cup or cauldron or cornucopia.

The Grail as a Metaphor of Creation

One way to define The Holy Grail is to see it as an ancient metaphor for the creation of the universe. Here the concave stone or cauldron holds the elements necessary to create the world in millions of iterations. The penetration of this mystery leads to a higher state of consciousness and the Grail ikon becomes the central object of a powerful and transformative initiation ceremony. Those who see the Grail as a simple material chalice, of the type encountered by Monty Python or Indiana Jones, will miss the point entirely. The quests conducted by the legendary knights of King Arthur's Round Table were not quests for an actual chalice. Instead they were quests for the cosmological information hidden in the symbolic Grail and for the psychological transformation promised to anyone who penetrates its mysteries. [20]

The writers of the Middle Ages suggest the Grail is many things. Each Knight and character in the saga held a different view of it. It could be a cauldron, a dish, a stone or a manuscript. It could appear on a cushion, accompanied by a procession of angels carrying a bleeding lance and a golden dish. It could be transported by maidens or be seen

---

[20]In America pumpkins are used but in England the lowly Turnip—quite similar to the size and shape of a human skull—does the job. For an overview of the survival of old customs see Wind, Edgar. *Survival of Paganism*. New York, Norton, 1976. Also: Chadwick, Nora. *The Celts*. London: Pelican, 1970. p. ix and Aveni, Anthony F. "Archaeoastronomy." *Advances in Archaeological Method and Theory*, vol. #4. Princeton: Academic Press, 1981. For the conservative view see: Herrity, M. *Irish Passage Graves*. Dublin: Irish University Press,1974. Also: Herrity M. and Eogan. *G. Ireland in Prehistory*. RKP, 1976. The worship of the concave stone, and its use in astronomy and navigation, seems to have grown from the cave cultures to the pastoral hunting and fishing cultures along the shores of the North Atlantic until it was formally housed within the fabric of astronomically aligned cairns and henges with integral arches and surrounding embankments.

floating, quite on its own, through a meeting hall. In Parzifal's case, the mere sight of the object was sufficient to send him into a spiritual reverie. Gawain encounters it as a a huge cauldron, but is not transformed. Lancelot catches a glimpse of it. In the court of the Fisher King it represents initiation. As a cauldron, it provides both edible and intellectual food. As a baptismal font, it represents rebirth. In King Arthur's court it was associated with the Round Table, where it became the focus of the quest for civil democracy.

We are stardust we are golden...
And we've got to get ourselves
back to the garden.

Joni Mitchell
Woodstock Nation
1969

RITUAL ASTRONOMY

A solitary figure is seated in the center of a stone circle in West Cork. The circle is situated so that it can be seen from the Celtic Sea and so that any participants in rituals held there can observe the sea and the distant horizon. This human being is an astronomer and a magician. He is preparing himself to enter the mystery world, a microcosm locked into the surrounding stones by his ancestors. The magician's face and arms are painted with red ochre. The figures on his body are identical to the figures carved into the stones. The magic spiral and diamond shapes glow in the sun and darken in shadow. [21]

The magician is an astronomer and a hunter. He senses the sun is at the center of the moving planets because he has observed certain vines seeking a fixed point in the sky as they wind themselves around a tree. He knows the moon shows the same face to Earth at all times. He knows the Earth is round because he has seen it measured at Newgrange, the great temple in the Boyne Valley to the north. On a clear day he can see the curvature of the Earth. His grandmothers taught him that the triangular tension between the Earth, moon and sun causes the tides to rise and

[21]Tierney, J.J. "The Celtic Ethnography of Posidonius." *Proceedings of the Royal Irish Academy*, X- C5, #60, Dublin, 1960.

fall. Eventually he will drink an hallucinatory potion from a small beaker — a drink of fermented apple cider mixed with honey and the ashes of a special mushroom shaped like a woman's breast. The cup he holds, an early version of the Grail, may be carved from stone or fashioned from shell or goat horn. The shadows moving across the stones will dial the exact moment for the beginning of the ceremony. When the time is right he will call up the spirits of the ancestors by spinning a moistened leather thong in the air, a thong strung with small crystal beads. The spinning thong will make the sound of a bull roaring and the spinning dance he must do will put him into a trance. In that trance he will be able to communicate with animals and the spirit world. He may even be able to see into the future. [22]

Through meditation and isolation the magician's trance will lead him to the core of the universe. If he is successful he will be reborn for that day or perhaps for his entire life. Each magical session will yield more psychic energy, more insight.When the magician is reborn the entire clan is regenerated. He is the shaman capable of great insights into people and nature. His female counterpart is a sibyl, capable of seeing the future. Together they unify and democratize the spiritual activities of their tribe or clan. Their prayers and rituals are the fundamental building blocks of the new civilization that will form around the monuments they have built. (Plate ii)

Toward the City of God

To the shaman or sibyl of six thousand years ago a void, knowable only through visions and ritual astronomy,

---

[22]Turton, Mary trans. Briard, Jacques *The Bronze Age in Barbarian Europe: from Megaliths to the Celts.* London: RKP, 1979. ill. p.182. For Western European use of *Papaver somniferum* see: Schultes, Richard Evans and Albert Hofmann. *Plants of the Gods.* New York: McGraw-Hill, 1979.

similar to the that described above, stood beyond material reality. It was not filled with monsters or with chaos as puritan antiquarians would have us believe.

As the shaman meditates a beam of light forms between a cleft in a rock and blinds him momentarily. In his hand he holds a small cup which he will use to decant the contents of the larger basin stone. The recumbent stone has two cup marks ground into it. A polished quartz crystal is placed in each cup. As the sun appears to set on the horizon, the beam splits between the crystals, striking the shaman, transforming him into the lightbeam itself. He has now seen the vision of his own creation; he is experiencing infinity. He is, in this state, the spokesman for his tribe at the court of the Goddess of creation. [23]

The ritual astronomy practiced by this skin-clad hunter was passed to the Bronze Age Bell-Beaker people, then to the Celts, then to the saints and prophets of the Middle Ages and finally, through them, to us. Nothing is lost because the stones are not lost. Through their carvings and their geometric layouts, the megaliths tell the story of creation as perceived by hundreds of generations of Atlantic rim hunter-gatherers. (Plate iii)

The Paleolithic belief in regeneration and resurrection, actually a doctrine of spiritual liberation from the fear of

---

[23]Eliade, Mircea. *Shamanism: Archaic Techniques of Ecstasy*. London: RKP, 1964. The use of the cauldron or inverted skull as a regenerative motif survived for thousands of years and became a central image in the pre-Celtic world. It influenced the Star Temple builders who dedicated rivers and entire sacred precincts to the Goddess. The Celts inherited this cosmology and adapted it. That an indole nucleate mushroom was used in ritual at Star Temples and ring monuments, can be checked quite easily. They grow in profusion in areas dotted by megaliths. See: Baille, Hugh. "Poisonous Fungi of South-Western England." *The Illustrated London News*, October, 1978; Furst, Peter T. *Hallucinogens and Culture*. San Francisco: Chandler & Sharp, 1976.

death and loneliness, found its way into the Aegean world at an early period. As culture evolved from west to east the Star Temples helped to modify Mycenean, Egyptian, Persian and Aramaic beliefs, as well as the traditional Hebrew verities both before and after Christ. By the time the Celtic tribes were converted to Christianity, the Atlantic and Aegean value systems were merged and most of the residual Shamanism, ritual astronomy, spiritual ethics and initiatory practice were subsumed under Neoplatonism, Mithraism and Gnosticism. Each of these doctrines practiced a cauldron or chalice rebirth ritual. Through the chalice — which brings heaven and Earth into contact — the old sacraments lived on and we find them today in Christianity at the root of the communion ceremony. [24]

A dream of an earthly paradise, wherein everything is in harmony, were sown across Western Europe by various secret societies. Christianity did not originate the idea. The pagan idea that the universe has been continually regenerated reached a golden plateau during the High Gothic era where it was eulogized in architecture by the cathedrals themselves. The oral traditions were transferred by roving poets and songsters of the post-Roman period who transformed the ritual for public consumption. The troubadours and the prose authors of the fourteenth century expanded on the idea of harmony through intervention of a divine Goddess, allowing the Goddess and the Arthurian and Grail literature to evolve into its present form. [25]

---

[24]Plato —*Timaeus and Critias.* Trans. Lee, H.D.P. London: Penguin Classics, 1971.
[25]Adolf, Helen. *Visio Pacis, The Holy City and Grail.* Philadelphia: Pennsylvania State University, 1960. For canonical reference see: Michelle, John. *City of Revelations.* Also: Cutts, A. *Works of Saint Augustine.* London: Austin, 1895.

Sometime in the twelfth century — in locations like Glastonbury Abbey, in Southwestern England, a place of extreme mystery and one rumored resting place of the Grail chalice — a form of raw visionary ecstasy, stimulated by abstinence, sensory deprivation, fasting and the constant hymns of one's fellow monks and nuns, became a hypnotic experience, not unlike a shaman's trance state. In this world the hermit might be transported into a reverie while engaged in something as mundane as scrubbing a floor or as profound as transcribing an illuminated manuscript such as the *Book of Kells* or *The Lindisfarne Gospels.* [26]

The trance-inducing drum beats and chants as well as the inspiration for many of the "Songs of Love," performed under the aegis of the troubadours might have come, indirectly, from Shamanism. The poetry and song of the Middle Ages in Brittany was transmitted orally from very ancient sources, and many of the legends are linked to the megaliths so it is possible that the rituals used to demonstrate certain principles were equally as old. [27]

The Star Temple Religion

Some six thousand years ago in Western Europe belief in the projective force of the stars evolved into an abstraction. Every totem animal owned a place in the star clusters twinkling overhead. Each played a stellar role in the sky legends. The animals, once feared, were no longer depicted in representational art. Now, the legends of the animals forming the constellations were directed into ceremonies

---

[26]Henry, Francoise ed. *The Book Of Kells.* London: Thames and Hudson, 1974. Also: Bale, J. *Illustrium maioris Britanniae scriptorium summarium.* Being a summary of the major British illustrated scriptoria as of the Tudor period. Ipswich: 1548. In mss.: Le Roux de Lincy Sur *le Abbay de Fecamp.* vol. I p. 292. Bodliean Library, Oxford.

[27]Kelly, Amy. *Eleanor of Aquitaine and the Four Kings.* New York: Praeger, 1988. See next.

aimed at harmonizing the human being with the cosmos. This astronomical splicing process was conducted in locations that can easily be called Star Temples, at least in the Western European context.

Star Temples are defined here as large stone covered mounds, cairns or stone rings (sometimes called "passage graves") dating from about six thousand years ago. They can be found on the Atlantic coasts of Western Europe and were clearly used for ritual purposes. The famed Stonehenge, in England, is both a henge monument, meaning a circle of stones surrounded by an embankment, and a Star Temple dedicated to the Summer Solstice sunrise and lunar cycles.[28]

But Stonehenge, dated to the beginning of the so-called "Bronze Age," is a relative newcomer on the Star Temple scene. There are thousands of more complex, interesting and older monuments dotted around the globe, especially in Western Europe and North America. Each megalithic structure seems to conform to a common unifying plan, each is linked to the others by a common understanding of the cosmos, and each displays clear evidence of ritual astronomy, yet no two are identical.

Close inspection of the geometry and layout of the Star Temples indicates that our species has been evolving a global religion since the dawn of humanity. A religion

---

[28]Evans-Wentz, W. *The Fairy Faith in Celtic Countries*. Universe, New York, 1967. p. 424. Wentz points out that Gavrinis in Brittany and Newgrange in Ireland are both cut from the same pattern and the mounds—in his opinion—were not exclusively tombs, but religious ritual abodes of some kind. This 1911 writing is the first mention of the mounds not being used as tombs that I have been able to find. It is not known how anyone, with the extensive credentials possessed by Evans-Wentz, could have been ignored. The term "sunrise and "sunset are superfluous and geocentric. When cornered I use " apparent sunrise' or " apparent sunset." In a poetic sense I might also suggest "dawn" and "twilight."

which has as its focus the reflection of the stars and planets in a concave object symbolic of the great Goddess and the womb of creation. (Plate iv)

The shaman of the ice caves saw a connection between the dome of the heavens in an inverted bear skull. The Buddhist focuses on the rice bowl, the Taoist sees the three-legged cauldron of bronze, the I-Ching, as an oracle which emerges from the void. The Jew passes the Seder cup which contains the knowledge of Cabala. The white witch consults the Tarot wherein the Ace of Cups contains the other aces and trumps. The Christian takes communion from a chalice thereby transporting the believer to a cosmic merger with Christ. Externally the rituals seem different and yet the human algorithm, hidden within the ceremony, is identical.

The first forms of this symbolic cup, the proto-Grail, evolved from the first phases of true human consciousness, in the earliest Ice Ages. The stone cup and inverted skull rituals, which have been speculatively reconstructed from the Upper Paleolithic about twenty five thousand years ago, are typically associated with Shamanism and cave paintings — like those at Lascaux and Altamira, in Western France and Northern Spain, paintings which hold clues to the mystery rites of the earliest truly human men and women based on the activity of the stars and planets.

The idea that the constellations project their images onto the Earth's surface in order to guide mankind is not unique to hermitism, astrology or modern mysticism. To the people of the late Ice Age the painted cave ceiling reflected the map of the night sky. Each of the animals retained a stellar counterpart and everything that was in heaven was reflected onto Earth, both through the light and the energy of the stars. When the Pentatuch tells us that God made man in his own image it is simply restating, in canonical form, what has been known by the shaman and sibyl for eons.

The most controversial form of the Star Temple is known as the passage tumulus or passage grave. There are about two hundred of these ranging from Northern Scotland to Portugal and from Ireland to France, and a few may be found in North America, although dates for the North American sites are not clear. These cairns are almost always built up with layers of stone and gravel as well as sod and rock and are often surrounded by a kerb line made up of huge elaborately carved stones. No metal objects were used in the construction of the earliest mounds, and yet they are trimmed to close tolerances.

It also seems apparent that Star Temple architecture evolved as each generation added to the basic concept. They are located in a wide lens around the Atlantic rim and virtually cover the coasts of Ireland. Many passage temples stayed in use into historical times and were probably instructive to any mariners, farmers or storytellers who happened upon them. Artifacts and offerings from Celts, Phoenicians, Eblites, Mycenaeans, Athenians, Romans, and Alexandrines have been found at various times around the mounds. Ironically, the Star Temples remain in use even today, precisely because we continue to study them and precisely because certain secret societies and mystery religions transmitted information about the Star Temples onward through each generation. See Appendix D (Plate v)

Krater Hermetis

It cannot be stressed too often that every religion in the Western world, and most Asian worship systems, possess a central ritual which focuses on a concave object. The Roman religion of Mithra, the Greek Bacchites and the followers of Neoplatonism and the Hermetic school, conducted rituals centering on a sacred cauldron called κρατερ: the *Krater*. In these mystery schools the earthly Krater was

15

represented by the chalice or drinking cup used to serve the sacred libation. In the cosmos the constellation Krater, located in the Northern sky near Hydra in the sign of Leo, echoed the mysteries on Earth. [29] (Plate vi)

In the rites of Eleusis it was called κψκιον, the Kykion. This smaller chalice was part of a bread and wine ritual which we also find in Christianity. The sacred wine was decanted from the Krater (vat) into the Kykion (chalice) thence to the cups of the waiting celebrants. Here God, or the Goddess, is the Krater; the priest or priestess is the Kykion, while the unredeemed souls of the world are the recipients. [30, 31]

The Celts were in close communication with the Greeks for many centuries. Ongoing studies indicate the Irish chiefdoms enjoyed liaison with the Attic and Mediterranean world through the port of Narbonne in the south of France. The monks who illuminated *The Book of Kells* using pigments imported from Africa are only one indication that Greek *attachés*, intellectuals and immigrants, were ferried back and forth to Ireland and Wales both overland and through the Gates of Hercules. The reverse was probably

---

[29]The largest Krater discovered in the Celtic sphere was unearthed at Vix in northern France, in 1977. It was highly decorated, held more than fifty gallons of wine and dated from the Gallo-Roman period, C. 400 AD. This huge ewer belonged to a wealthy courtesan, fond of holding celebrations dedicated to Dionysus. See: Wernick, Robert, "An unknown lady of Vix and her buried treasures." *Smithsonian*, March, 1986, pp 140-159.

[30]Lazzarelli, Ludovico. *Calix Christi et Crater Hermetis.* New York: Norton, 1968. Lazzarelli was one of the first to expose the direct literary and ritual connection between the Grail, Christ and Hermetism. Lazzarelli stipulates that the cup of Christian worship is identical to the Krater of the Hermetic school and his work is a key to the survival of the old mysteries up to modern times.

[31]Kahane, Henry, and Rene Kahane. *The Krater and the Grail: Hermetic Sources of the Parzival.* Urbana: University of Illinois Press, 1965.

also true during the Greek Golden Age, circa 500 BC. Irish legends speak of early visitors having descended from a Greek named Parthalon who established a small colony in the environs of Howth Castle on Dublin Bay. [32]

The Irish Star Temples

On December twenty-first each year, at the exact moment of Winter Solstice, a beam of light forms within the central chamber of a megalithic mound known as Newgrange. This mound, and its companions Knowth and Dowth, are possibly the oldest fully evolved stone buildings in the world. Newgrange is more than five thousand years old. Its companion mounds were built nearly six thousand years ago and yet the beam continues to shine, like clockwork, into a sixty-six foot long shaft. All three mounds are surrounded by carved stones, stones which reveal a hidden language, a language dedicated to the stars and to mankind. These miraculous mounds are real, anyone can visit them. They are located in Ireland some twenty miles north and four miles west of the Dublin airport in a sylvan setting along the Boyne River. Although Newgrange is beautiful to behold it is actually a scientific instrument, an observatory for planetary and lunar calculations and for the maintenance of sundials.[33]

As the lightbeam enters the inner chamber of the mound it intersects a carved basin stone. This stone is smaller than the elaborately carved stones at the entrance, but it too plays a role in the astronomy of the mound and the entire valley. As we shall soon see, this stone cauldron is a

---

[32]Joyce, Padraig Weston. *The Wonders of Ireland.* Dublin: Gill, 1911. Reprint, San Francisco: The Archives Press, 1992. p-21.
[33]Roberts, Jack. *Exploring West Cork.* Skibbereen: Key Books, 1989. There are many such ancient basin stones and quern-like objects throughout France, Ireland and England. In Gaelic they are called *Ballan* or *Ballune* stones.

prototype of the Holy Grail and its use as an astronomical instrument links the mystery religions of the New Stone Age or Neolithic era to the structure of the Gothic cathedrals and the deepest mysteries of Christianity as practiced in the Renaissance. (Plate vii)

Newgrange, reconstructed in the 1960s, is faced with many carved stones displaying zigzags, ovals and spirals. It is designed with a curved outer wall covered with glistening white quartz rocks hauled from many miles away. The ambience of the place is so breathtaking that the local farmers still believe it is inhabited by fairies. [34]

At Newgrange the stone basin is displayed in a perfect location to reflect light throughout the rather large chamber. When the large basin was filled with water, blood — or a red ochre liquid simulating blood — the markings on the ceiling stone would be reflected clearly. In this case the overhead stone "heaven" would reflect into the Grail stone "Earth." This is a perfect, and early, example of what we have come to know as the "Hermetic Paradigm." — heaven above is reflected in things on Earth. [35]

---

[34]The basin stone has been stacked upon another, even larger, concave stone in the east recess of the chamber. I am convinced that the smaller stone was originally located in the center of the chamber in the direct path of the lightbeam on Winter Solstice. George Coffey—the first objective researcher to come into contact with the stone—shows it in the center in photographs he took in 1912. may have been placed there as recently as 1966. If two crystals are placed in the two indentations— and the basin is placed in the center of the chamber—the beam will split into a cross shape, very much like a laser generated through a beam splitter. Mrs. Hickey's daughter and relatives—Hickey was one of the most respected early curators of the mound—swear they saw the Grail Stone at the center of the mound in 1952.

[35]Schultes, Richard Evans and Hofmann, Albert. *Plants of the Gods*. New York: McGraw-Hill, 1979. If there is a Neolithic continuity into Christianity then this ritual may be one source for the host in modern Christian communion. If an oblivious ecstasy were experienced at this point, it would suggest

Small clay cups and scallop shells, found buried in the soil along the apron of the mound, represent life on the human scale. In the context of the Greek mysteries which may have evolved from sites like this, the large basin or Krater is the macrocosmos, and the small shell or Kykion is the microcosmos. The large cauldron is heaven; the smaller, hand-held, scoop is Earth. The scallop shell is the microcosmos while the larger cauldron represents the molar universe. In the Christian example the chalice represents the human spirit while the baptismal font represents the eternal creator. Here again celestial activity is reflected in the mundane. [36] (Plate viii)

Reconstruction of the megalithic ritual derived from artifact collections is speculative, but it seems reasonable to conclude that the original ceremonies were focused on the basin stones within the central chambers. These chambers have been called tombs by archaeologists, but how could they be tombs when no skeletal remains dating to the original construction were found? [37]

The Empty Tomb

It cannot be stated too frequently that the mounds and cairns around the Atlantic rim are inaccurately referred to as

---

the use of a mushroom or refined ergot, made less toxic by exposure to an intense and coherent lightbeam.

[36] Vallancey, Charles.*Collectanea de rebus Hibernicis,* 6 Vols. Dublin: Government Printing Office, 1770-1894. No wonder later antiquarians, in particular Charles Vallancey in Ireland, thought of mounds like Newgrange as staging areas for the mysteries of the Roman god Mithra. Vallancey could not have known that the mound he was observing was constructed three thousand years before Mithraism, yet there are many similarities between the rites of Mithra and the mystery plays based on astronomy, which were probably performed at Newgrange.

[37] Stroup, Thomas B. *Microcosmos: The Shape of the Elizabethan Play.* Lexington: University of Kentucky Press, 1965.

tombs and "passage graves." Some of them were abodes for the dead in a secondary sense, but statistical evidence proves they were rarely built as graves. Their main purpose was to track celestial events such as eclipses, moon phases and equinox and solstice cycles on a monthly, annual or daily basis. In other words, they were used for astronomy. By constructing this vast hunting and mariner's log, and by worshiping at the site, the Star Temple people were practicing ritual astronomy and distributing their knowledge to a wide audience.[38]

By definition, each Star Temple is built within an elaborate precinct consisting of villages, cooking areas and meeting places, as well as other mounds and megaliths. Here the spirits of the trees and rivers could merge with the spirits of the stones and the sky. Each mound in the precinct features at least one cauldron with a reflective surface primarily designed to convert starlight, sunlight or moonlight into a coherent beam dial. [39]

In order to enter the chamber at Newgrange, the lightbeam must pass through a slit in a carved stone roof box which is decorated with eight "X" patterns signifying the eight festival days of the year. It may also be telling us that in this chamber the four quarters of heaven and the four

---

[38]Harrison, Hank. "A 6000 Year Computer." *Dr. Dobb's Journal-Software Tools*: December, 1982. These features were first reported on around the end of the eighteenth century by Vallencey and again in the late nineteenth century by Lockyer and others, but since their observations contradicted the conventional wisdom of the day, the astronomy aspect was dropped. "Electrical Timing of Human Ovulation." *American Journal of Obstetrics & Gynecology*, vol. 44 #223, 1942. Also: Huff, D. *Cycles In Your Life*. London: Gollancz, 1965. And: Brown, Frank. "The Clock Timing of Biological Rhythms." *Amer. Scientist*, Nov. 1972.

[39]De Valera. R and O'Nuaillain: *Survey of the Megalithic Tombs of Ireland* Vols. 1-3 Dublin Stationery Office, 1972. and Coffey, George, *Newgrange*. Original pub. 1912. Both De Valera and George Coffey noted the lightbeam. op cit. W. Evans Wentz: *Fairy Faith In Celtic Countries*. p 424.

directions of Earth are combined each year. Similar aperture arrangements can be seen at Kercado in Brittany and at Maes Howe in the Orkney Islands off the north coast of Scotland. [40]

During its sojourn in the temple the lightbeam becomes more focused until it crosses the exact meridian of the basin stone. It then touches the triple spiral petroglyph carved into the rear chamber and other basin stones in the side chambers. After seventeen minutes it begins to fade until it disappears from the mound. It may be wild speculation, but it seems plausible that various ceremonies were conducted at this site throughout the week of the Winter Solstice. This would explain the eight "Xs" etched into the roofbox. [41, 42]

The relationship between the lightbeam and indentations in the central stone, which probably once held crystals, is also observable twenty miles west of Newgrange at Loughcrew. It can also be seen at Dowth, about one-half

---

[40] O'Kelly, Michael J. *Newgrange: Archaeology, Art and legend.* London: Thames and Hudson, 1982.

[41] According to some authorities the solar aspect of the godhead was known as OG, Lugh, etc. The eight seasons of each year, when combined, were seen as a wheel and were known to the continental Celts as the Ogdoad. See: Kohane, P.*The Key.* New York: G. P Putnam, 1968. This is commonly seen in the Celtic Cross and in the Celtic Tarot.

[42] On December 20, 1982, the day before the official Solstice, this author conducted an experiment at Newgrange. A polished eight sided quartz crystal (originally a paper weight) weighing exactly sixteen ounces, was suspended by a plumb line from a level wooden rail lodged in the sides of the chamber above the exact point where the basin stone was originally located, eight inches above the present floor. This set up was justified because the small basin displays ovoid indentations set within a parabolic concave stone which may have held crystals or was at least filled with liquid which would reflect light. When the lightbeam struck the crystal the room burst into prisms of colored light. The stones that form the sides of the main passage at the tightest point of Newgrange are carved with ribs, which probably once supported bone or wood focal boards used to form an aperture for the beam, much like a modern laser beam.

mile east of Newgrange at the entrance to the sunset chamber. Nor is the relationship isolated to Ireland. The lightbeam and ring mark can also be found at Stonehenge on the altar stone and at almost every other recumbent stone circle in the Atlantic megalithic sphere. Prisms made from quartz crystals were set into the stones to mark the exact moment for worship.

During the Winter Solstice event the lightbeam inside the mound takes on the characteristics of a shimmering cross, four earthly points marked in stone, four heavenly points marked by the lightbeam — making eight points. The split beam may be the oldest known example of the illuminated cross. Again, elements of Christianity are in evidence in the Star Temple structure.

Obviously the mounds were constructed to stand the test of time. The weight of one of the kerb stones surpasses twenty tons. One visit to Newgrange will tell you that someone was keenly interested in building a permanent and stable platform here, not simply a tomb, but an observation chamber capable of capturing moonlight, starlight, sunlight and firelight, a chamber wherein a trained observer could watch and record planetary motion, lunar phases, star configurations and solar events with great accuracy. (Plate ix)

As amazing as this may seem, it is not science fiction. Newgrange, Knowth, and the other carved mounds in Ireland, Western Europe, and along the East Coast of North America were temples dedicated to observing, and worshipping, the light spectrum. Did the builders of these mounds understand the true nature of the lightbeam and its prismatic effect? Did they fathom the synchronous orbital relationship between the Earth and the moon? Could they navigate across seas, and if so, how far did they travel? Did they use the orbit of Saturn as a timing system? Whoever built them not only worshiped the planets, they worshipped the energy exchange between the visible and invisible universe, a complex relationship which is reflected in the petroglyphs. (Plate x)

How then were they different than ourselves? If a group of Neolithic architects could be transported to our modern era, they may not be able to support their arguments with strict reasoning, the etchings they carved into the stones are equations. Rigorous data collection methods, strict observation and reporting, the essence of phenomenology, is at work in their art. They might not be able to chalk talk their way through a canon of modern math models, but they were naturalistic observers and would have an intuitive sense of Gaussian statistics, frequency distributions and the exact periodicity of recurrent events. They would probably not be shocked to discover that the sun does not have an orbit or that the moon is as powerful as the sun in terms of tidal flux and that the Earth, being spherical, possessed a delicate ecology.

These monuments were not built by space invaders. They were built for people by people as a tribute to the earliest forms of democracy, the primordial unifying principles of light, darkness and dynamic change. [43]

---

[43]Brennan, Martin: *The Stones of Ancient Ireland.* San Francisco: Archives Press, 1991. Brennan has pointed out that the lightbeam is more than a simple morning event. It can also be an evening event and can be related to the moon or Venus. Unbeknownst to archaeologists, the beam enters another, even older chamber at apparent Sunset at Dowth, another huge mound, about one mile to the east. As the sunbeam enters the mound it passes through two huge cup and ring marks which may have held quartz crystals in the original setting. The same procedure takes place at dozens of locations throughout the Atlantic biome. The lightbeam forms through apertures and/ or crystals, enters a dark recess and lingers for a few minutes before it leaves the cavern. During the time the beam is moving through the cavern, it is illuminating various writings on the walls. This same phenomenon has been observed in Chaco Canyon in Arizona, although it is not known if the two locations are linked directly.

A Simple Red Stone

It is well established that red ochre, a fine red oxide powder mixed with animal fat, was used to paint walls as well as the human face and body in rituals. This mysterious substance has been found in hundreds of locations on both sides of the Atlantic and is often associated with the megaliths.

Could red ochre be one of the keys to the secrets of the Grail? The ritual used in manufacturing the pigment was to mimic the grinding motion of the celestial sky as it appeared to revolve around the pole star. Grain was also turned into a fine flour by milling in rotary and saddle querns, but red ochre seems to have been used to symbolize blood and immortality in specific birth and death rituals. [44]

The *matatae* or grain quern, used for grinding nuts and berries, was one obvious prototype for the Grail. The quern probably replaced the skull as the concave ritual extended itself into settled agrarian communities along the Atlantic coastline. Saddle querns and grinding stones were also used to prepare various dyes and pigments for body dressing and ritual purposes. One could speculate that it was this body painting or tattooing ritual that connected the food and fertility ceremonies of the tribe to the idea of blood and immortality, or blood and flesh transposed to bread and wine in the final manifestation of the rite.

Colin Renfrew, the visionary British archaeologist, reports that Maes Howe, in the Orkneys, displays a beam dial on Mid-Winter sunset, like Dowth, confirming the orientation observations of Brennan and Thom. The prevalent theory, which is hopefully fading, is that these mounds are not linked to one another except as burial chambers and have no astronomical significance.

[44]No claim is made that red ochre is the Philosopher's Stone so long sought by the alchemists, but similarities in its use over five millennia tempt comparisons.

There can be little doubt that the barley grains and hazelnuts, ground in the rotary stone mills, symbolized the female principle as food giver and as creatrix. The concave stone gave nutrition and wisdom, while the pestle or grinding stone represented the male principle, symbolizing will or force.

To the earliest tribes of the Atlantic the food grinding ritual was the transformation of the soul, while the red ochre symbolized travail and sacrifice before and after the transformation. In this simple rite we see the beginning of sacrifice and vestiges of the quest for transcendence common to almost every religion in the world.

I must tell thee that all of these
miracles grow out of a certain earth,
a soft red clay,
which is to be found everywhere.

Fama et Confessio
Frater R: C:

BLOOD OF THE EARTH

One of the earliest forms of the Grail was probably a grinding stone or perhaps a cup fashioned from bone used to reduce red ochre clumps, a common element in shamanic magic, to a fine paste. This pigment, according to numerous authorities, represented the placental blood of the regenerated earth child, emerging from the womb of the Earth Mother.[45]

Parallels can be drawn between Christian symbolism and the artifacts collected from Star Temple and henge sites. To the shaman the red ochre pigment is the "Blood of the Earth." To the Christian mystic it represents the blood flowing from the wounds of Christ, to the alchemist it is the philosopher's stone. To the ordinary Christian the contents of the mystic chalice was symbolized by wine as a substitute for blood, a form of magical blood which can transform the supplicant spiritually when he or she partakes of Holy Communion. The Neolithic magician and the Druid seer as well as the initiate or epoptae (εποπταε) of the Dionysian cult achieved a similar transformation through long periods of sensory deprivation, fasting and the taking of a psychedelic drink. But each of these traditions are based on transforming the human spirit and each is interwoven with

---

[45] Shuttle, Penelope. *The Wise Wound*. London: Gollancz, 1977.

legends about a sacred cup used to collect, create or consume the sacred substance. [46] (Plate xi)

To certain early Christian converts, those who remained somewhat pagan at heart, the son of the Goddess was transformed into a God who sacrificed himself so that the world could become pure and harmonious. Likewise, to the shaman, the entire cosmos is transformed at dawn on Spring or Winter Solstice. The time of year matters little because, in either case, the transubstantiation has the same purpose: to purify consciousness. Just how this process was achieved in both Christian and megalithic surroundings can be reconstructed from the stations of the cross, a labyrinthine quest performed by Christ as he labored towards Calvary and by reconstruction of the cross-like chambers and spirals incorporated into the circular architecture of the Star Temples.

At Newgrange sunlight is directed through the Grail Stone to the rear of the mound where a number of rituals are conducted by a shaman or sibyl. In one of these rituals the purifying power of the lightbeam falls upon one or more of the Grail Stones to consecrate the symbolic bread, or host in Christian terms. This is known as "the flesh of the invisible God." The grain was then mixed with ergot or a mushroom extract.

Symbols of Power

In both Christian and shamanic rituals, magical power is derived from the sacrifice of the god in the sacred cauldron, which is then reanimated by the lightbeam, but in

[46]Allegro, John. *The Sacred Mushroom and the Cross.* New York: Doubleday, 1970. p. 154. The Christian metamorphosis of the child into a God was preordained at the child's birth at Winter Solstice (Christmas) and fulfilled at his corporeal death on Spring Equinox (Easter). In both cases sacred mushrooms may have played a role.

each case the symbolic blood, be it lamb's blood, red ochre or the blood of a mother giving birth, was diluted or washed with holy water. (Plate xii)

In the cathedrals and abbeys the sacred water is percolated into the baptismal fonts by a fantastic series of sprues and capillaries, the new born child is then washed with the water in a symbolic ceremony echoing the ceremonies conducted in the Star Temples. At Newgrange, prior to reconstruction and the collapse of the mound, rain water was filtered down through interstitial layers of peat and gravel. This special water was held in a stone cachement basin in the east recess which, when full, reflected the markings of the celestial bodies and their orbits carved on the white limestone roof slab just above it. The child was baptized here under the symbols of power carved in the stone.

Numerous clay cups have been found at Star Temple sites, indicating that smaller cups were used to decant portions from a larger cauldron, in typical Dionysian fashion. As in the psychedelic experience the consumption of the liquid and Eucharist would release the lightbeam energy, held fast in the soul of each supplicant. A state of grace, both social and spiritual, would be achieved causing, in turn, an infusion of psychic ecstasy accompanied by a sense of regeneration. [47]

In the past six thousand years Western Europe has gone through hundreds of cultural upheavals, but oral traditions about a triple initiation or Trinity remain intact. In every proto-Grail story, the ineffable cup and cauldron are

---

[47] The elements in this solstice ritual are purely magical as was Paleolithic shamanism. It is probable that a mushroom and/or ergot mixture was at work here. Judging from the precision of the Star Temples, it is also probable that the use of psychotropic compounds in ancient cultures was highly regulated and ritualized.

central to the quest for grace. This is usually achieved in three stages: by treading a labyrinth or questing, by synchronizing the soul with the Earth's motions against the backdrop of stars, and by meditation.

The mystic spiral, triple in nature, is the dance of the Earth as it spins on its orbital cycle through the void. In this ritual, the questor or *myste* performs a similar dance on Earth, synchronizing his or her mind with nature. This kind of magic derives from Shamanism and can be found in the Cabala, Tarot, the mysteries of Eleusis, bardic ceremonies and Sufism to name only a few manifestations of the archetype. (Plate xiii)

Oral tradition has also connected the cup mark on the stones and the carved spirals with the grinding motion of the Earth's sidereal dance. Irish legend tells us that a female spirit named Dectine performs the dance in front of the megaliths at *Brug na Boinne* (Newgrange) as part of the annual solstice ritual. At Newgrange, the grinding is symbolized by the basin stone and grain mill or 'quern.' This is based on the Paleolithic idea that the spinning Earth is a grain mill or a rotary quern supported by a celestial pole. [48]

The similarities between the architectural features of the Star Temples and the Grail stories are too numerous to ignore. Both the Star Temple ritual and the quest for the Grail by the Knights of the Round Table were enacted in the same locales five thousand years apart. The Star Temples, the oldest stone buildings on Earth, are tributes to a thriving and brilliant culture reflected in Star Temples such as Knowth, in Ireland, and Kercado, in France. Both structures were begun around 4200 BC, which makes them at least seventeen hundred years older than the famous step

---

[48] Santillana, Giorgio, and Hertha von Dechend. *Hamlet's Mill*. Cambridge: MIT Press, 1968.

29

pyramid at Saqqara. By comparison, the writings of Chretien de Troyes and Wolfram von Eschenbach were made public at the beginning of the thirteenth century AD, so, a span of six-thousand years separates the mounds from the manuscripts that document their rituals. Some human agency must be at work beneath the surface here. Did certain secret societies transfer data from generation to generation over six millennia?

In the 1960s, scientists began to look at the Star Temple builders with new eyes. Speculation that the megaliths were older than the oldest pyramids stimulated further speculation that they might have been part of a heliocentric "lost" society. Ceremonial cairns, almost identical to Irish, French and Swedish structures, incorporating small trilithon arches, large amounts of red ochre, totems of the killer whale and the now extinct great auk, have been excavated in Labrador and along Penobscot Bay in Maine. [49]

When we look at the Star Temples and the mysterious people who built them, we may actually be looking at an archipelago of cultural centers or gathering places built on similar cosmic assumptions. Perhaps the tribes were unified during the interglacial periods and became more autonomous as the ice sheets withdrew. But because most of the sites display a lightbeam structure, and seem to have been used for astronomy, we can assume, with a moderate degree of reliability, that each family practiced some kind of ritual astronomy central to the life of the clan at that location. This is easy to explain. The enigmatic microcultures that dotted the Atlantic coast at the dawn of humanity were made up of fishers and sea mammal hunters, very

---

[49]Tuck, James. *Ancient People of Port au Choix.* (Memorial University Institute of Social and Economic Studies) #17. Memorial University of Newfoundland, 1976.

similar in level of technology and religion to the much earlier Magdalenian cultures of Southwestern France which were responsible, for example, for the magnificent cave art at Lascaux. Their form of writing and communication was probably symbolic and based on the hypertext of geometric star and planet observations, but their Shamanism transmitted the ceremonial aspects from clan to clan. [50]

Geometric markings on small fishing weights, formed in the abstracted shape of the Great Goddess, and stone gouges used for carving wood panels were unearthed in Bosulan, Sweden as early as 1957. But the Swedish artifacts are identical to weights and chisels found at the Turner Farm site in Maine along Penobscot Bay. Where these tools artifacts from a panatlantic culture which fanned out from North America at the end of the Ice Ages? And is it a coincidence that the zig zag markings on the fishing weights are almost identical to hypertext markings carved on the larger stones at Newgrange in Ireland and at Gavrinis in Brittany? These questions can only be answered with further research, but Alexander Marschak points to evidence that hand held devices, carved from reindeer bone, which he interprets as lunar "pocket calculators," appear throughout the Atlantic zone. Is there a continuity here or are these artifacts simple and spontaneous inventions isolated to specific cultures? We may not be able to answer this question easily but judging from these artifacts, and the similarity in stone cairn design, there must have been a strong continuity of culture or at least trade between cultures over a long period of time — perhaps from 20,000 to 5,000 BC — a continuity which featured the ceremony of the concave

---

[50]Ellegaard, Alvar. "Stone Age Science in Britain." *Current Anthropology* Vol. 22 #2: April, 1981. 99-125. See also Cole, Sonia. *The Neolithic Revolution*. London: British Museum/ Natural History Series, p viii. 1970.

stone and a belief in a divine creatrix. If this continuity can be established it would mean that certain basic rituals changed only slightly from Cro-Magnon to the megalithic era. [51]

Recent evidence points to the possibility that the megalith builders were actually settled at a much earlier period and that they owned domesticated animals such as the horse, the common house cat, the dog and the pig for many thousands of years. Is it possible that the cave painters evolved in relative isolation for more than fifteen thousand years? Are they our direct ancestors or is there a missing link? Even more provocatively, is it possible that cultures, like the people of the final Paleolithic of Europe or Clovis in North America, could have lasted twenty thousand years, traveling the Atlantic rim in dugout boats or complex rafts, navigating by the beam dial and other chronographic devices? Could small groups or adventurous families have transmitted the rituals of red ochre, the skull cup or basin stone and various healing prayers back and forth across the seas as part of their ancestor worship?

Throughout this entire twenty-thousand year period, even when the glaciers were still very much a part of life, the so-called "lost cultures" seem to have managed to live in some degree of comfort, especially at places where rivers entered the sea. As the glaciers receded it would be natural for a wandering population of hunter-gatherers to inhabit the raised beaches and to perceive the huge stones as building blocks for a more permanent architecture.

The Maritime Archaic people of Labrador inhabited the post-glacial raised beaches and lived in wooden communal long houses built upon a base of stones. The English, Irish,

---

[51]Marschak, Alexander. "The Art and Symbols of Ice Age Man," *Human Nature,* #9, September, 1978.

Scandinavian and French groups did the same. They made use of the small square arch (trilithon) in cairn building and they oriented their mounds toward the solstices and equinoxes. Certain Labrador cairns, dating to about 5500 BC, have been shown to be astronomically aligned. They are similar to the cairns of Sligo in Ireland and date from the same period — plus or minus two hundred years. This leads to the most astounding question yet presented, a question that cannot be answered by our present state of knowledge: Were the original Irish cairns, viewable today from Clare to Galway and from Sligo to Mayo, built by early Americans? We have always believed that migrants to the Atlantic sea coast would be from Europe, but could there have been migrants to Europe from North America? Perhaps they followed the Northern edge of the Atlantic rim around in both directions? [52]

No one has medically typed the raised beach bones from Ireland to see just which groups are represented, but it is possible that the two groups were related by traversing the polar circle at some point, meaning that the earliest Irish, rather than being Indo-Europeans, may have been archaic North Americans or even trans-polar Amerindians, like the Freedom people of Greenland who existed by hunting whales and musk ox.

A new and refreshing picture of a people lost to time and history, is finally emerging in learned journals. They were deep-sea fishers, cairn builders and explorers, mariners who left traces of their prowess at navigation around the North Atlantic rim. Many tools found in Maine and Labrador are almost identical to those found in Sweden. It appears that certain raised beaches in Labrador,

---

[52]Modern DNA typing tests of the kind used in forensic investigations may prove beneficial in this situation.

supported these explorers as did the raised beaches of County Galway in Ireland and the Bay of Biscay in France. They may not have migrated around the entire Atlantic rim — perhaps the cairns and tools were traded over vast differences — but there is a connection. [53]

Additionally, the raised beaches of Sweden, Denmark, France and Holland may have been occupied and visited on fishing expeditions for thousands of years with no permanent habitation before the cairns and megaliths were constructed. Herodotus could not have known just how long Ireland or the other megalith-rich areas were inhabited. Their perception, from a vantage point in the Aegean, was simply that a very old culture did exist outside of the Gates of Hercules. [54]

In Maine, the Red Paint People were the legendary inhabitants of a treasure land known locally as Noorembega.

[53]Willoughby, Charles C. *Prehistoric Burial Places in Maine.* Boston: Peabody Museum of American Archaeology and Ethnology, 1898. Kraus Reprint Co., New York, 1971. For the Irish view see: Charlesworth J.K. "The Palaeolithic Implements of Sligo." *Proceedings of the Royal Irish Academy*, 39c 1929. For a far more recent North American survey see: Fitzhugh, William. "Residence Pattern Development in the Labrador Maritime Archaic." In *Archaeology of Newfoundland and Labrador 1983*, pp. 6-47. (Annual Report # 4, Historic Resources Division.) ed. Jane Sproull-Thomson and Callum Thomson. Government of Newfoundland and Labrador, 1984.

[54]Mitchell, G.F. and Sieveking, G. "Flintflake, Probably of Palaeolithic Age from Mell Townland, Near Drogheda, Co. Louth." *Journal of the Royal Society of Antiquaries of Ireland,* #102. 1972. Mell Townland is four miles from Newgrange and is part of the ancient Boyne complex. If there was late Ice Age activity in the Boyne Valley or on the raised beaches nearby, we might argue that Drogheda is one of the oldest continuously inhabited sites in the world. The same might be said of Vannes in Brittany and Glastonbury in England. Bear in mind that a land bridge between France and England existed until 7000 BC but Ireland has been isolated by water since the interglacial Ice Ages, so if anyone reached Ireland in sufficient numbers to sustain a building colony, it must have been by raft or boat.

Ptolemy called the Irish of the raised beaches the Hyperboreans, meaning the people above the wind. This is, incidentally, a word similar to "Hibernian," which has long been a tribal designation for the Irish, while "Hibernia" is another name for the Emerald Isle.

The perception of the length of occupancy of the transatlantic megalith territories has only recently been made accurate. As recently as World War II, National Socialist (Nazi) propagandists in Germany thought of the ancient people of Western Europe as Indo-Europeans which they called "Aryans." The Germanic dream world, in the North Atlantic was called *Ultima Thule.* We now know the Northern Indian Aryans were a Bronze Age arrival and that most of them were possessed of dark features and smokey brown skin much like modern Dravidians or Pakistanis. However, we should bear in mind that the Nazis were not the first racists. Many Greeks of the so called, "Golden Age," including Aristotle, held similar "nutty" ideas about slavery and about the people living beyond the Gates of Hercules. The French of the Court of Louis XIV believed immortality was possible if one could but find Atlantis. Droves of starry-eyed mystics continue to think of the earliest inhabitants of Wales and Ireland as fair skinned Aryans. None of which is any more true than the idea that human beings and dinosaurs inhabited the Earth at the same time or that all Pit Bulls are inherently vicious. [55]

Actually, the legends of ancient Ireland refer to the first inhabitants of that island as Fomori, Fir Bolg, Milesian and Tuatha de Danann. These four groups, excepting a short-lived Iron Age Greek enclave called the Parthelonians, turn

---

[55]Gimbutas, Marija. *The Goddesses and Gods of Old Europe, 6500-3500 BC.* Abridged. London: Thames & Hudson, 1986. Professor Gimbutas has suggested that a Neolithic group, the Vinca culture aboriginal to Yugoslavia, was responsible for much that has been attributed to the Indo-Europeans.

out to correlate roughly with the Mesolithic Maritime Archaic or raised beach people; the early Neolithic Larne Tree Clearance Culture, a later Neolithic or copper age group of Iberians possibly from the Quadlaquiver region or Los Milares, and the Bell Beaker Picts from Scotland who arose from the Danubian culture in the Bronze Age. Some of these identities have some basis, while others are pure racist speculation. So maybe these groups, when seen as a whole, would comprise a lost civilization thought of by the Greeks as Atlanteans. But however they were perceived by the ancient Greeks we now know that their genes still run in the Basque country, in the Gaelic areas of Ireland, along the shores of Brittany, in the mountains of Wales and the Highlands of Scotland and in the Cantons of Switzerland and Tuscany and that many of these gene pools have migrated to North America over the past two centuries.

[handwritten margin note: Where + I Shaun would have been married]

The New Astronomers

The tribes that evolved into the Celts appear to have enjoyed a lifestyle so advanced, even elegant, that, until recently, science could not explain their existence. Now, however, with the help of new disciplines like ethnoastronomy and astroarchaeology, the people of the dawn are emerging.

As it happens, every new branch of science must work its way through a period of acceptance. Modern astrophysics brought on an understanding of energy markedly different from the views of Sir Isaac Newton. In the once new science of psychology, C.G. Jung introduced a refreshing change from the tedium of "psychoanalysis" and, as we begin the twenty-first century, archaeology is undergoing the same kind of make-over, it is splintering into cross-disciplines and multiple research arenas; ethnoastronomy is just one of these areas. It is only one of the many objective disciplines that are replacing the staid and biased subjectivity of archaeology. [56]

Most early antiquarians believed ancient Europeans, such as the inhabitants of the caves of Lascaux, or the builders of Stonehenge, were far too primitive to develop a sophisticated understanding of astronomy, but the newest evidence from astronomic observations of their temples supports the opposite conclusion. [57]

Not all Victorians were narrow minded. In the late nineteenth century, Sir Norman Lockyer read a key paper to the Royal Society claiming the megaliths align with planet motions. He was scoffed at, but since he was a respected member of the society with not a few high rank-ing predecessors, and supporters such as John Aubrey at Stonehenge, Abbey Breuil in France and Charles Vallancey in Ireland, his ideas found a few open minds. Following Lockyer, many scientists successfully used astronomy to validate theories about the megaliths, not only at Stonehenge, Newgrange or the Pyramids, but around the globe. Lockyer died in 1920, but even before the funeral was over, his ideas about correlating star positions to the megaliths were ridiculed in the daily news. Oddly, many modern news media researchers continue to display the same Victorian inelasticity. Many policy-makers continue to think of ancient societies as barbaric or, more recently, as "satanic." This goes hand-in-hand with the assumption that barbarians could never have developed a sophisticated religion, astronomy or navigation system, let alone large

---

[56]Langley, Samuel P. *The New Astronomy.* Smithsonian Institute, Washington, D.C., 1889. For a modern assessment of the role of astronomy and astrophysics. See also: Krupp, E.C. *In Search of Ancient Astronomies.* London: Charlotte and Windas, 1979.

[57]Baity, Elizabeth Chesley. "Archaeoastronomy and Ethnoastronomy So Far." *Current Anthropology,* #14. 1973.

scale stone architecture. People, like those who scoffed at Lockyer, will have to change their minds about their own ancestors because, in many cases, classical astronomy can be used to explain the megaliths, especially since astronomy was the purpose for the megaliths in the first place. [58, 59]

Some seven thousand years ago numerous Atlantic rim tribes, such as the Tardenosians on the Iberian Peninsula — the suspected ancestors of the Basques, emerged as identifiable groups with housing and kitchen middens. Their environment was no longer ruled by ice and snow and yet they retained many elements from the cave dwellers. They held to the worship of the spirits of their ancestors, including rituals of transformation and the sacred totem dances. They continued to worship the animal and plant life around them. The Mesolithic shaman still used the bull roarer of the cave dwellers, a sound making device made from a weighted thong, to call down the sky spirits. The carved masks that transformed the eagle into a man and the skin that transformed the dancer into an elk or a bear were still used. As they continued to totemize their ancestors, and as the ice sheets melted away, the migrating hunter-gatherers began to inhabit raised beaches. They carved canoes from tree trunks with stone chisels and fashioned weights in the shape of the Goddess to lower their fishing lines. [60]

---

[58]Lockyer, Sir J. Norman. *Stonehenge and Other British Stone Monuments Astronomically Considered.* 2d ed. London: Macmillan, 1909. For Stonehenge and Avebury see: Aubrey, John. *Monumenta Britannica—Survey of Stonehenge,1663.* mss. British Museum. London: Kings Library, 1698.

[59]Thom, Alexander "A New Study of All Lunar Sight Lines." *Archaeoastronomy.* Supplement 2, 1980. S78-S89.

[60]Fitzhugh, William ed. *Prehistoric Maritime Adaptations of the Circumpolar Zone.* Mouton Publishers, Toronto, 1975. Michelle, John. *A Little History of Astroarchaeology,* London: Thames and Hudson, 1977. Most of the research conducted by Lockyer in England and Vallancey in Ireland, was widely published and purposefully ignored.

The Radiocarbon Controversy

Radiocarbon dating has been used to fix the relative dates of artifacts since 1952 when professor Willard F. Libby presented his historic laboratory techniques to the scientific community. Unfortunately, the first forms of the technique were imperfect. The original dates were not calibrated against tree rings or other standards of comparison. Dates derived from this method were accurate for artifacts taken from dry climates, but very inaccurate for damp Western European areas.[61]

The first fast electronic computers were coming into play in the early 1950s. These wonder machines were used to perform tests on architectural measurements and generally carry out previously impossible empirical surveys. In 1963, Gerald Hawkins an English-born American astronomer, postulated the first verifiable Summer Solstice alignments for Stonehenge using an electronic computer to prove his proposition. In 1965, a film featuring Hawkins was produced by the Columbia Broadcast System (CBS). In this spectacular film the sun appears to rise above the heel stone on Summer Solstice. Winter Solstice, lunar, and Venus alignments were also discussed. [62]

The radiocarbon breakthroughs were used for a decade with no radical impact. But coincidental research into tree ring correlations, conducted in the late 1960s, ushered in a

---

[61]Suess, H.E. "Bristlecone Pine calibration of the radiocarbon time-scale 5200 BC to the present, in radiocarbon variations and absolute chronology," *Proceedings of the 12th Nobel Symposium,* 303 12. New York: Wiley, 1970.

[62]Hawkins, Gerald. *Stonehenge Decoded.* New York: Doubleday, 1963. and *Beyond Stonehenge.* New York: Doubleday, 1969. Hawkins entertained the idea that astronomical alignments existed at Stonehenge before he began his research because the astronomer Norman Lockyer pointed them out sixty years earlier. Hawkins also knew of Aubrey's work with the lunar post holes at Stonehenge.

subtle academic war. Younger, more objective anthropologists in North America, Russia and France, wrested control of antiquarian studies from the old guard. British supremacy in world affairs was now open to healthy doubt.

In 1965, H.E. Suess, an American professor of chemistry, announced yet another major breakthrough when he published a paper comparing the tree rings of the California Bristle Cone Pine, the oldest living thing on Earth, with uncalibrated dates from prior samples. Suess' revolutionary findings allowed previous dating to be recalibrated against a fixed, standardized scale for the first time. The traditional time and dating curve for Atlantic Europe was no longer valid. Some of the Star Temple dates were too young by a thousand years. [63]

Carbon-14 dates of 2650 BC taken at Newgrange were recalibrated to 3250 ± 200 BC. Calibrated French dates of 4200 BC for Kercado, in the Gulf of Morbihan, confirmed the older time scale. The passage tumuli of Western Europe could now be seen as the oldest stone buildings on Earth. [64]

This abrupt change in dating, with its far reaching implications, was not the last news to shock the old archaeological world. In the late 1960s Star Temple sites, far older and more significant than the Pyramids, began cropping up over a wide area along the Atlantic rim, as well as North America and Sweden. By 1970, journalists writing in newspapers as diverse as *The Washington Post* and *Pravda* were demanding answers. [65]

---

[63] Suess, H.E. and Mackie, E. "Thoughts on Radiocarbon Dating." *Antiquity*, XLV 1970, 197-204.

[64] The megalithic alignments at Carnac in Brittany have been recalibrated to about 3200 BC. The Temples of Karnak in Egypt date to about 2040 BC.

[65] Renfrew, Colin. *The Explanation of Cultural Change*. London: Duckworth, 1973. p. 14

As Lockyer predicted, the megaliths held astronomical significance. It is doubtful any virgins or male consorts of the Goddess were sacrificed by the Neolithic builders, although goats and pigs were cooked and eaten at most of the sites as part of the original ritual. The archaeological record further tells us that the practice of cremation and inhumation burials came in during the Indo-European incursions in the Bronze Age, (at least two thousand years after the Star Temples were built,) and was continued by the Iron Age Druids. Human sacrifice was rare even to the Druids but the horrific vision of blood thirsty savages cavorting around a fire to orgiastic rites, a practice invented by Roman Catholics, Calvinists and Victorians for propaganda purposes has, sadly, never faded.

New evidence, based on the non-racist and non-diffusionist model developed by Colin Renfrew, indicates that monumental architecture and small scale planting and farming were well-established in Western Europe around 4000 BC. There is even the possibility that a stone plough was under development at that early period along the coasts of the Bay of Biscay, in France. [66]

The old theories, based on a supposed Indo-European "invasion," began to crumble under the scrutiny of Carbon-14 technology. Pottery dating and new artifact collections establish conclusively that Western Civilization as we know it did not begin strictly in the Tigris and Euphrates. Instead it began in dozens, or even hundreds, of places in Europe, Africa and around the globe. This may be hard to accept, but the evidence is now pouring in. It may take the public a century to adjust, but the new approach has one distinct advantage: it shows humans to be equal and generally

---

[66]ibid.p.127

41

proves that no ancient culture was superior simply because they possessed a form of writing on parchment. [67]

An earlier population, referred to hereafter as The Dawn People, were navigators of the Western seas. Their artifacts appear in Labrador, Maine and Sweden as well as England, France and Ireland. Outstanding among these artifacts are numerous stone monuments built to venerate the Vernal and Autumnal Equinoxes and the Winter Solstice. These permanent structures are distributed around the north Atlantic Rim and seem to derive from cultural roots traceable to the cave rituals of the Final Paleolithic. [68]

The racist idea that a written language, metallurgy, or agriculture drifted from east to west without local spontaneous contributions came under serious challenge as soon as

---

[67]Wheeler, Mortimer *Still Digging*. London: RKP, 1955 and Hawkes, Jaquetta. *Mortimer Wheeler, Adventurer in Archaeology*. London: Weidenfeld and Nicolson, 1982. Wheeler was the dean of British archaeology for many years, appearing on television on many occasions. He was not above outright pontification when the feeling moved him. His digs in Pakistan were notoriously inept and his dating chronology and interpretations off by millennia. Yet the British public continued to hang on his every word. Jaquetta Hawkes, herself an archaeologist, attempts to paint Wheeler as a hero. Instead, she inadvertently exposes him as an immoral cad, exploitive of women, a male nymphomaniac by reputation, and unscrupulous. Wheeler bent his interpretations to please the ruling class of which he was a benighted member. To Wheeler — a Celtophobe and blatant anti-catholic, anti-semitic and racist — the Welsh and Irish were rustic, simple-minded peasants incapable of evolving from architecturally sophisticated ancestors. Likewise, the Atlantic Star Temples were part of an invasion by superior Indo-Europeans. When asked about the contradictions posed by tree ring and radiocarbon breakthroughs, he said: "...a whole lot of our thinking will have to be rethought." In spite of this admission he spent the rest of his life suppressing new information, especially data that might reverse his own interpretations.

[68]Harrison, R. J. "Origins of the Bell Beaker Cultures." *Antiquities*, 48 1974, pp 99-109, 1974. Also: Case, H.J. "Beaker People, The First Metallurgists", *Paleohistorica*, #12 pp 141-177, 1966. And: Ap Simmon, A.M. "Food Vessels." *University of London Institute of Archaeology Bulletin*, # 1, pp. 24-36, 1958.

the megaliths were seen to contain an architectural language. The obvious question was being asked by many scholars. This question cannot be answered simply, but the Star Temple builders may hold a partial answer. They seem to have developed a number of ideas quite on their own. If there was a Bronze Age drift from Northern India, Turkey, Egypt and Persia, why did it not appear in Western Europe until the third millennium, long after the Star Temples were built? The answer is that isolated groups around the Atlantic rim made spontaneous local discoveries and that the only significant cultural drift was a global swapping of ideas from many points in many directions over many centuries? In other words, the people of Atlantic Europe and Labrador in the fifth millennium, were fully aware of their ancestral links to the Paleolithic. Not only did they worship totems in a manner identical to their ancestors, they passed their beliefs on by casting structures in permanent stone. [69]

Limestone was plentiful in the meadows as the glaciers receded, and it would be natural to use this material to build shelters and temples. At first stones were simply piled up, but as time went on purposeful structures were built. In the Orkney Islands and elsewhere, a number of groups developed a post and lintel structure, perhaps at first as a doorway to a sod house then as part of a wooden house, but later as a gateway to a place of meditation, tomb or temple. This "three stoned structure, often called a trilith, (tri: three, lith: stone) consisting of two upright orthostatic stones to bear weight and a cap stone to distribute the weight from above, represents the basic motif for other architecture in the Western World, including the Gothic arch. The Mound

---

[69]Shee-Twoig, Elizabeth. *The Megalithic Art Of Western Europe*. London: Oxford University Press, 1981. Shee-Twoig's book is the single most important work on megalithic art ever produced.

Builders were the first to build these arches and the Star Temples around them, but why? One explanation comes to mind. It is possible that the earliest inhabitants of Ireland, for example, carried with them a creation legend which put the development of the human race in a cave which was, presumably, the belly or womb of the Great Mother. Although speculative, it seems that these Atlantic Maritime people were attempting to recreate the womb of the creatrix so that each trilithic structure in each cairn, house or Star Temple would remind them of the walls, floors and ceilings of the caves of their ancestors. By 5000 BC the trilith came in many sizes. In its fundamental role it was incorporated into a simple three-stoned dolmen or quoit with no accompanying mound or cairn, which acted as a permanent boundary marker. Often these dolmen were used to expose a corpse to the elements thus, in the beliefs of the builders, recirculating the soul of the deceased back to nature. [70]

At most structures where a trilith is in evidence, we also find at least one zigzag or oval carved into the side stones and the outside kerb. These figures, in complex combinations, are the basal elements of an early Atlantic hyperlanguage, a written language that predates written languages in the Middle East by two thousand years. Further, the ikons are usually positioned to intersect with a lightbeam, or its shadow, as it passes into and out of the temple. Examples of this hypertext can be seen on many megalithic temples in England, Portugal and France, especially Gavrinis on a small island near Carnac.

---

[70]The straight sided post and lintel structure was augmented by a slant sided variation which formed a triangular aperture. In some sites in Ireland, both the triangular and straight sided versions are seen together, most notably at Knowth.

Eventually, mounds were built wherein more than one arch played a role. Here the cult of the dead and rebirth merge. The beam passing between the trilithon represents life, the inner chamber of the Goddess represents death and the emerging rainbow of light, which is created when the beam passes through the archway on its way out of the cavern — after touching the quartz crystals and the sacred writing — represents rebirth.

Eventually, the trilithon, and the number three which is its numeric equivalent, became the ikon for the entire process of death, rebirth and fertility. In a more animistic fashion the trilith represents the beam, the Goddess and the issue of their union: the divine child. Anyone can visit these monuments, the zigzags and spirals are on clear display, but without question the finest carvings reside at Newgrange, and its companion mounds, in the Boyne Valley. [71]

The Newgrange Mystery

The early academic literature on the megaliths is full of mistakes and omissions. In the early 1960s, the late Michael O'Kelly, a distinguished professor of archaeology at University College Cork, was charged with the awesome responsibility of rebuilding Newgrange and deciphering the mysteries of the markings on the stones. Although the Solstice lightbeam was well known locally, O'Kelly was the first to report on it in learned journals. Unfortunately, he failed to mention a few salient aspects of the phenomenon. He noted, for example, that the sunbeam came into the inner chamber through a roof box and not through the main entrance. He failed to mention that the beam struck the

---

[71]The idea of a large chamber with a corbelled vault fed by a long tunnel comprised of trilithons, may have been developed at Knowth, in the Boyne complex, for the first time anywhere. See Appendix B.

basin stones and the triple spiral on its travels through the inner chamber.[72, 73]

O'Kelly knew the stones encircling Newgrange were similar to the stones at Avebury in England and Carnac in France, but the idea that a building technique might be passed on across vast distances in the Neolithic period went against conventional wisdom. He knew Stonehenge was built in at least three phases by different cultures, but he did not make the connection that Newgrange may have also been built by and for many clans. Unfortunately, the real key lies at a closed excavation mound and temple complex known as Knowth one mile to the west of Newgrange. [74, 75]

Politics At Knowth

Knowth is a huge six thousand year old temple mound which was built as part of the Boyne Valley astronomical computer system and observatory complex.

This controversial temple is located about one mile to the west of Newgrange, and about two miles from Dowth. It is situated on a strategic bluff overlooking the Boyne River and, before it was torn down by archaeologists, it was

---

[72]O'Kelly, M.J. *Newgrange. London:* Thames and Hudson, 1982. O'Kelly failed to report his suspicions that the so called "pit burials" found near the outer ring of stones were actually cooking pits — for sacrificial goats and pigs. He also failed to mention that few human remains were found. Although the mound was finished around 3600 BC, it was still being used for rituals by tribes other than the builders in 1800 BC.

[73]*Proceedings of the Irish Academy and Report of the Board of Works to the Irish Senead Funding Agency.* Irish Government Printing Office, 1985.

[74]As the years of excavation wore on, Professor O'Kelly confided that megalithic mounds in general might well be gathering places, designed with the same technology that developed the corbelled vault which can be reasonably dated to 4000 BC± 200 at Loughcrew, Kercado and Knowth.

[75]Martin, Cecil. *Prehistoric Man in Ireland.* New York: Macmillan, 1935. Martin postulated that a Paleolithic culture did exist in Ireland, but his theory was ignored until recently.

similar in shape and height to both Newgrange and Dowth. The three mounds are further united by a very narrow serpentine road which some scholars think was used for processions in pagan times.

There are also noticeable differences between the three mounds, mainly that Knowth was actually the site of a medieval village and Christian settlement and is at least five times as difficult to excavate than the other two. We thankfully know little of Dowth since it has only be superficially excavated. Currently, most authorities feel that Dowth and Knowth are older, larger and at least three times as complex as Newgrange but, ironically, Newgrange is the big tourist attraction. It should also be pointed out that these three mounds are surrounded by dozens of smaller mounds, each with astronomical significance. Thus, in an area three miles long, and less than one mile wide, we find more than fifty of the most precious archaeological treasures in the world. [76]

Unfortunately, the monuments of the Boyne have not been well maintained. Professor George Eogan, the chief excavator at Knowth, has long exhibited a cavalier disregard for these sacred treasures because he thought of the entire valley as a mortuary complex. This he assumed from his boyhood, as he grew up in the area and was told by priests that the mounds were "Pagan Tombs." Ethically, any good archaeologist should respect any dig site regardless of its pagan nature or its functionality, but in Ireland you do what the clergy tells you to do.

In terms of survival the Boyne Valley mounds have three strikes against them. First, they exist in Ireland,

---

[76]A similar problem exists in England where Stonehenge gets most of the attention, when in fact Avebury and Silbury Hill are far more archaeological significant and older. Both Silbury Hill and Glastonbury Tor, although bigger than the Boyne mounds, have similar angles and astronomical uses.

where economic priorities are aimed at the future and at erasing poverty through agrarian production and the tourist trade, not at the pre-Christian past. Secondly, all antiquarian digs fall under the aegis of the highly politicized Board of Public Works; no private digs are possible. The third strike comes from the ignorance of the populace itself. Since the mounds are thought of as tombs, locals and tourists alike continue to deface them.

The first digs at Knowth took place in the late 1960s. No tombs were discovered so the mound was almost completely and haphazardly dissected and by the late 1970s the mound was virtually leveled. True, grid lines were used, elevations were taken, and catalogs were kept, but the lack of funds caused the project to move forward hurriedly or stall altogether. The church made donations, but only if the dig concentrated on a first century Christian foundation. Funding from any church body is the archaeological equivalent of strip mining or gill netting. Still, the work went on. Amazing carvings were discovered, the place was clearly a pagan temple.

For Eogan, the first frustration must have been that he did not locate the big tomb full of the gold that legends, and old-fashioned reputations, are made of. He found no human remains that were uncontroversially dateable to the original construction layer. He did not accept Martin Brennan's lightbeam ideas, or O'Kelly's careful reconstructions, even though O'Kelly frequently demonstrated the lightbeam at Newgrange to Eogan and many credentialed visitors, including Arthur C. Clark, international film crews, church officials and an ever-watchful fleet of Irish politicians. In spite of reports that Knowth was built with astronomy in mind, reports published in learned journals by skilled and legitimate scientists, Eogan refused to consider Knowth as an astronomical site. To the empty-handed

Eogan, the mounds of the Boyne Valley would always be single purpose tombs. (Plate xiv)

Predictably, his book on Knowth, in which he mentions the word "tomb" more than three hundred times, contains a number of alarming contradictions and omissions. First, the few human remains Eogan did find in the inner chambers at Knowth were Bronze Age or even Viking. This means the mound was at least two thousand years old when the cremated remains were placed in the chamber. By contrast, the Star Temple people buried their dead at sea or allowed the bodies to return to the elements by placing them on wooden or stone platforms, as mentioned earlier, in the style of certain Native American Indians. [77]

In frustration, and to pacify his betters in the church and the government, Eogan turned to what can only be termed "sabotage." Although he would never admit it publicly, he knew the lightbeam entered Knowth from the east at Spring Equinox sunrise — on or about Saint Patrick's day or Beltaine, in the pagan calendar; the day infrared, and its resultant life forces, returns to Earth. He also knew that a lightbeam was formed in the west passage at Autumnal Equinox sunset. Clearly, most of the passages in the Boyne complex were connected to lightbeams. Eogan's workmen, students, photographers and artists, some of whom defected from the official camp, report having seen the lightbeam in both chambers and swear they mentioned it to him. Eogan not only refused to listen, he intensified security around the place and used much of his budget to build a massive barbed wire enclosure.

---

[77]It was believed that totem animals, such as the Raven or Jackdaw, would take the body, and its' spiritual energy, to the sky. This practice explains why so few skeletal remains have been found. It also hints at an extremely archaic origin for the earliest Irish and North American people.

The Cauldron and The Grail

To further make certain no one could test the lightbeam theory, he directed his workmen to dump rubble on a direct east-west axis blocking the east passage. He could have spread the stones into sorting areas or erected the pile slightly to the north or south, instead the debris heap stood eleven feet high blocking any direct light to the passage.

In another act of misplaced hostility Eogan unearthed a central chamber in the East passage and immediately declared it a burial chamber, even though no skeletal remains datable to the origin of the mound were located. This chamber does, however, hold one of the most mysterious treasures on Earth. At the center, Eogan located an elaborately carved basin stone, weighing more than three hundred pounds. This basin was set in place more than five hundred years before Newgrange was built and is more elaborately carved than the basins at Newgrange or Dowth.

This curious stone clearly shows a symbol, similar to an Egyptian ankh, in a sunburst carved into its convex face. This alone would be enough to arouse curiosity, but this particular Grail-like stone also displays an ikon of the Great Mother in the act of uniting the universe. The Goddess ikon is intersected by two deeply carved grooves which trace the bowl's circumference, implying a sense of eternity. To Eogan this meant the eternal sleep of death, implying the cauldron stone is a funerary object, but no bones, ashes, or human remains were found in it. Like the plain Grail Stone at Newgrange, the Knowth basin probably intercepted the beam of light. This might be borne out by further research, the cauldron does lie directly in the hypothetical path of the Spring Equinox lightbeam, as if it were an altar. [78]

---

[78]Eogan, George. *Knowth*. London: Thames and Hudson, 1986. p. 46. Unfortunately, no further research can be done since the passage remains occluded by Eogan's debris pile. Still, some features can be compared to other sites. The reflecting pool at Knowth is similar to the moon pool at the

Blood of the Earth

No discussion of Knowth would be complete without the inclusion of yet another, far more serious, caper again with professor Eogan at its center. In the Spring of 1981, two workers at Knowth unearthed a broken pillar made from rare green chert. This smooth column, 22 centimeters thick at its widest point, once stood 1.6 meters tall and, judging from it's location, could have only been used as a gnomon or foresight for the Saint Patrick's Day (Vernal Equinox) beam dial. [79]

More than five impartial witnesses saw the workers excavate the stone and a number of people actually photographed it, but within days it was gone and no one seemed to know anything about it. However, an unofficial photo survey taken in the rain during one of the worker's frequent tea breaks, revealed a sinister facet to the disappearance. Apparently Professor Eogan ordered the precious stone buried beneath a cement wall, never again to see the light of the Spring Equinox or publication. It would not be completely contentious to assume some early lightbeam and cauldron rite took place here and that the adjacent pool would reflect events in the sky. Eogan knew that anyone with a basic skill in astronomy could prove the lightbeam entered the east passage if they knew the exact original position of this obelisk. [80]

Jefferson Memorial in Washington D.C. It is also functionally identical to portable cauldrons used by the Celts to observe the heavens. For a discussion of the Great Mother ikon as engraved on the cauldron stone at Knowth see: Dames, Michael *The Silbury Treasure*. London: Thames & Hudson, 1976.

[79]Local legend has it that Saint Patrick stopped the worship of fire at Knowth by observing the mound from one mile away on Slane Hill. This could be true because Slane Hill looks down on Knowth, and there is no question that fires, lit at Knowth, could have been seen from that hill.

[80]This beautifully shaped and finished stone was found lying in two parts at the mouth of the east passage near a reflecting pool, less than five feet from its original location.

The Dawn People Speak

In 1974, the brilliant British archaeologist Colin Renfrew paved the way for the refreshing idea that the Star Temple builders of 4000 BC may have invented their own navigational and astronomic technology in relative isolation. Renfrew, being no armchair archaeologist, conducted extensive digs in the remote reaches of the Orkney Islands off Northern Scotland and is the leading excavator of Maes Howe, which admits a sunbeam at midwinter sunset. He also excavated the Quanterness Cairn, dated to the mid-third millennium; and the Ring of Brogar, a huge stone circle, sometimes called the "Stonehenge of the north." Renfrew's open-minded ideas have a wide influence. [81]

The architecture of the Star Temples and the maritime abilities of the builders suggests that various clans exchanged ideas and tools in a wide area around the sea rims and river mouths of Western Europe, possibly even North America, while remaining isolated from non-seafaring old European cultures such as the Vinca from the Danube.[82]

---

[81]Renfrew C. *Investigation in the Orkneys.* London: Thames and Hudson, 1982. p. 66-67. For a similar North American view See: Tuck, James "Port au Choix Assemblage." *Canadian Journal of Ethnography,* 1968. A red paint cairn in L'Anse Amour, Labrador has been precisely dated to 5500 BC.

[82]Gimbutas, Marija *The Goddesses and Gods of old Europe.* 3rd ed. London: Thames and Hudson, 1986. According to professor Gimbutas, the Atlantic Goddess is a buxom and endomorphic creatrix. The Neolithic Danubian Goddess is wasp waisted and ectomorphic with feline eyes, so significant differences in aesthetics must have existed by the fourth millennium. Although Gimbutas was essentially correct in most of her speculations she was not aware of the latest Radiocarbon dating technology and has difficulty explaining how the Atlantic Goddess religion was in place a full twenty thousand years before the Danubian. Although an important scholar, many of her followers have turned her into a posthumous cult figure by using her theories as a rationale for entrenched feminism, much to the detriment of her research.

Blood of the Earth

The Dawn People were particularly fond of shellfish. They exploited the scallop for its protein, but they also used the shells as jewelry, and as containers for oils, balms, unguents, paints, herbs, spices and drugs. Rich purple dye from certain mollusks was a rare item, as was amber. They used berry juice and blue woad, a wild plant that produces a fine azure dye, to tint wool and hides and to create tattoos. The tattoos were probably identical to the markings on the megaliths. In the Atlantic rim cultures, small and localized domestication and exploitation of sea mammals was common for at least ten thousand years prior to the construction of Stonehenge III. Evidence from the hilltop at Loughcrew in Ireland, circa 3800 BC, reveals a lifestyle very similar to that of the Maine and Labrador people of the same era. Settlers on both sides of the Atlantic relied on shellfish, hunting and fishing. Most inhabitants from the late phase of the Paleolithic to the Celts used red ochre in an astronomical ritual centering on a concave vessel. [83]

The Star Temple builders, on both sides of the Atlantic, may have navigated on high seas in rafts or leather long-boats tied together. They used offshore sighting of the megaliths for ports of call. They took their bearings with plumb weights and used nets to seine fish. They also farmed in local areas and used domesticated animals. [84]

Stone circles and megaliths were used for ritual and sidereal navigation as well as for the timing of the cycles of migratory animals. Some of the clans continued to follow wild herds, using the stones to standardize their hunting,

---

[83]Shee-Twoig, Elizabeth *Megalithic Art in Western Europe*. Oxford, 1981. Shee-Twoig detected stain, dye and paint fragments in many locales off the beaten path, especially in Portugal's somewhat drier climate. In some cases she found fully preserved painted stones.
[84]Bourque, Bruce J. "The Turner Farm Site: A Preliminary Report." *Man in the Northeast*, vol. II (1976): 21-30.

while others settled in to produce hand goods and tools for barter. Honey from wild and domesticated bees and milk from reindeer, goats or domesticated cows provided dietary advances. The intelligence of these people, based on their diet, could hardly have been retarded. Still other tribal groups followed the sea-lanes, trading in jet, ivory, scallops, fish and pelts as well as amber. These commodities were bartered at ports of call and around the Star Temples on feast days, so a rich inter-cultural trade must have existed. [85]

In the fifth millennium, an enriched culture spread around the entire Atlantic rim from Portugal to the Orkneys and from Galway, Ireland, to L'Anse Amour in the Canadian Maritime provinces. The availability of a balanced diet, including minerals, glucose and protein, provided an exponential leap in health, art and computational skills. By the time Newgrange was finished, circa 3200 BC, settlements, like the Boyne and Kercado were well integrated. The descendants of these early Star Temple builders survived using only stone and bone tools, until the arrival of metal-using Indo-European migrants. Eventually the combined tribes evolved into what Julius Caesar knew as the Celts. [86]

---

[85]Certain notched finger stones used for navigation along the sea coast in Maine and Labrador are identical to those found along the raised beaches in West Cork. The native Eskimo population calls the standing stones "Anoukshooks," meaning the stones are not of Eskimo origin. Many artifacts supporting a transatlantic connection are located in the Maine State Museum in Bangor. See: Sanger, David. *Discovering Maine's Archaeological Heritage*. Maine Historic Preservation Commission, 1979.

[86]Howell, John M. "Early Farming in Northwestern Europe." *Scientific American*. November, 1987. p. 118-126. ed. *Arctic Anthropology*, Vol. 12, # 2, 1975. (Papers from a Symposium on Moorehead and Maritime Archaic Problems in Northeastern North America, held at the Smithsonian Institution, February 27-March 2, 1974.) Fitshugh (see above) has found a trilithon and cairn connection as well as evidence for large stone Neolithic

Blood of the Earth

The similarities in architecture of the Star Temples in Atlantic Europe and the cairns of North America indicate that fundamental ideas about trade, art styles, farming, writing, and navigation (the standard definitions of civilization) might have been shared as early as the fifth century BC. Fishing expeditions from places like Gavrinis, either purposefully directed or blown off course, could have drifted to North America. Likewise, North American adventurers, following the glacial perimeter close to the polar arc in search of the Killer Whale, may have been thrown off course and drifted south to Ireland or continental Europe.

The Dawn People must have also used seal pelts for clothing and sails, yet they were not Eskimos or Amerindians in a strict sense. New evidence suggests that thousands of small hunting expeditions may have been mounted beginning twenty thousand years ago. Many of these could have become protracted affairs in any number of directions with numerous origins and dozens of final destinations. [87]

Obviously the mounds were constructed to stand the test of time. The weight of one of the kerb stones surpasses twenty tons. One visit to Newgrange will tell you that someone was keenly interested in building a permanent and stable platform here, an observation chamber capable of capturing moonlight, starlight, sunlight and firelight, a chamber wherein a trained observer could watch and

---

shoreline navigation in Labrador. See Also Rouse, Irving. *Migrations in Prehistory: Inferring Population Movement from Cultural Remains. New York:* Yale University Press, 1986. Current evidence suggests geese and whales, of the genus Orca, navigate by the stars, especially during their migrations.

[87]Gardner, Joseph ed. *Mysteries of Ancient America.* New York: Readers Digest, 1986.p. 84-91.

record planetary motion, lunar phases, star configurations and even solar events with accuracy. [88, 89]

Because they are built of stone, the Star Temples will endure. There can be no doubt that Kercado, in the French Gulf of Morbihan, with its date of 4200 BC, will remain one of the most significant, structures anywhere on Earth, regardless of what is discovered when it is excavated, and Newgrange will always be one of the most beautiful stone buildings in the world. [90]

Legends based on Shamanism, were amplified at the Star Temples and each tale remained in folk memory for thousands of years, probably because they are written on the stones in code. (Eventually the stories of an heroic Atlantic race drifted into the Greco-Egyptian world, not the least of which is the mysterious legend of Atlantis.)

In each society, the dominant architectural model is a mirror of tribal ideals, cosmology, nostalgia, fears, likes and dislikes. In Washington D.C., the American love of democracy is displayed in the Jefferson Memorial as it

---

[88]Fell, Barry. *Bronze Age America.* New York: Little-Brown, 1982.

[89]Tuck, James. "An Archaic Indian Cemetery in Newfoundland." 1970. In *New World Archaeology: Readings from Scientific American.* New York: W. H. Freeman & Co., 1974.

[90]No corrected dates have been published for Dowth, but there is every possibility that Dowth is older than Knowth or Kercado as it does have a December twenty-first chamber—for a Winter Solstice dusk beam. Based on the type and depth of carving and the functionality at Dowth it is roughly contemporary with the Loughcrew monuments and the court cairn culture of the late fourth millennium. As stated elsewhere, Dowth may also have a Winter Solstice dawn beam opening at the southeast side. Unfortunately, the top of the west side and center section of Dowth, were torn down for road-stone by the British in the nineteenth century as were many of the Loughcrew cairns. Still, Dowth has three basin stones. A speculative reconstruction would indicate that the Loughcrew sites held at least ten basin stones and that some of the cairns may have been used as parabolic reflecting telescopes.

overlooks the moon pool toward the city's tallest structure, a gnomon or obelisk called the Washington Monument. This in turn points the way to the Lincoln Memorial. In other cities our cultural neurosis is revealed in architecture: the glass curtain wall expresses vanity, the thrust of the skyscraper ever higher expresses a phallic identity crisis.

In the Gothic era, the cathedral became a way of reorganizing the local economy wherever they were built, while at the same time reminding each citizen that a spiritual force is present in all things. The church in Rome administered the cathedrals, but the spectacular setting and the massive architecture strikes awe and inspiration into the hearts of the onlooker.Likewise, the settings upon which the Star Temples and henge monuments are built, the proximity to sea or river, the surrounding hills, the perspective from each of the temples, are almost always spectacular — not just scenic, but breathtaking. The builders seemed to be proud of their choice of location. It's almost as if they wanted a future generation to reconstruct their mysteries. So whatever else they prove to be, the Star Temples are time capsules and nature computers, designed to preserve the Neolithic legends and track the exact cycles of nature in every aspect.

The Compass and the Celtic Cross

In spite of their isolation, or perhaps because of it, the astronomer hunters of the Atlantic dawn managed to develop an agricultural calculation system of their own, a system of ritual dance and prayer linked with the overhead passage of various celestial orbs. They did not inherit this almanac system from Indo-Europeans or spacemen, they inherited it from their ancestors.

Both the decorated ice cave and the Star Temple were used as small working copies of the cosmic theater — each acted as a well-oiled horolog, a stone timepiece driven by light and shadow. Since they were employed as almanacs and horologs, the Star Temples can be thought of as early computers driven by a stellar operating system. The Star Temple populations, like their cave dwelling ancestors, linked their daily life to celestial events. The carved megaliths are simply components of hunting and farming computers. The carved stones served the same ritual and meditative purpose as the cave paintings. [91]

A partial picture of the Dawn People and their children's children can now be pieced together. There were no gossamer clad Atlanteans, no Egyptian colonists in the early Atlantic. The Star Temple builders were simply hard-working astronomer hunter-gatherers who kept records of their observations and inscribed their records in stone.

The children of the Dawn People, the Star Temple builders, were not flying saucer travelers. They were rational human beings forced to live under celestial laws. They followed rules of social behavior based on nature and astronomy. They were frightened by storms and earthquakes, just as we are. To insulate themselves against the chaos of nature they calculated the rhythms of their world and tracked the planets and stars. They apparently enjoyed a wide lens stretching from the entire east coast of North America, from Florida to the Polar Circle to the shorelines of Western Europe. They were mobile and adapted to their biome, so adapted that their astronomy and architecture have survived for at least seven millennia.

Overland arrivals to Brittany and Scotland from Eastern Europe must have marveled at the already old Star Temples and must have wondered about their geometric

---

[91]Pilcher, J. R. et al: ""Land Clearance in the Irish Neolithic: New Evidence." *Science.* #172, 1971, p. 560-562.

markings. From Irish artifact collections it seems plain that the Star Temples and their decorations continued to impact political movements within their sphere, long before the time of Christ and long after. [92]

The Atlantic astronomers were the first to make extensive use of geometric markings in large stone structures anywhere on Earth. They were also the first to use a written symbolic logic, based on celestial events. The walls of Jericho and the oldest pyramid were not yet built when the spirals and zigzags were placed on the megaliths in Portugal or Ireland. This was a true language. Hundreds of combinations of markings can be made from the megalith carvings. The cup symbolizes eternity and oblivion, the spiral symbolizes quest and initiation, but beyond these lie thousands of vocal combinations and ikons, even songs or drumbeats, relating to celestial events and the human role in the cosmic conception.

Throughout the centuries, Gaelic speakers have held the legends, temples and art products of the ancient magicians in awe and many paintings and manuscripts, as well as oral stories, reveal that the Star Temples were still venerated in the twelfth century. The megalithic language was a hypertext made up of ovals, wheels, wavy lines, and half moons. Since it is commonly carved in stone, this text is a shorthand for astronomic events and worship styles, and although it is not yet completely reconstructed, it is a major factor in the Grail mysteries. Clearly, the goal of the Star Temple enclosure was to harmonize life on Earth with heavenly events. The temple mounds and henges remain easily accessible to anyone. This argues against elitism in the ancient sphere

---

[92]The blending of bronze with flint technology took two thousand years in itself, so this is not far-fetched. Early bronze tools were metallic clones of the stone tools. The finer developments in bronze and gold casting did not appear until the early second millennium.

and suggests that a nascent form of democracy was in progress when the temples were built. The rituals, held at the mounds, seem to have been conducted in public and, although a body of priests or priestesses may have conducted the ceremonies, political power seems to have been distributed more or less evenly across the entire populace.

From the positions of the stones and carvings we know that the Star Temples count and keep track of the cycles of nature. They balance and equalize human behavior against the effects of the *primum mobilis,* or first cause, yet they are made of immovable stone. A visit to Newgrange will support this view. Most of the carved stones found adjacent to the Star Temples, or in them, were, and still are, open to public view. Many of them can seen from miles away. So it is probable that a system of checks and balances, a system of distributed knowledge, wealth and labor, was operating within those precincts.

The political balance of the Star Temples can further be demonstrated in the four directions of the circular Celtic cross. rudiments of which can be found carved on the stone of the seven suns at Dowth and in many other locations. This well known Celtic Christian symbol reflects an ancient origin, and some of the Dark Age crosses found in the Boyne Valley were actually carved from huge stones dragged away from the Star Temples. This would indicate that even the Christian monks and nuns of the fifth century, the men and women who sculpted the great crosses of Kells and Monasterboice, knew of the continuity between the old and new religions. [93]

The cross, in its megalithic and pre-Christian form, represents the balance of the seasons, the four directions

---

[93]This idea is the essence of the Pelagian heresy. See Ferguson, John. *Pelagius, An Historical and Theological Study.* New York: Dutton, 1957.

combined with the four elements. It represents Winter, Spring, Summer, Fall as measured by the solstice and equinox cycles, but it also represents Imbolc, Beltaine, Lugnasad and Samhain, the four ancient feast days. The Celtic cross represents the eight festivals as an eight rayed ikon. Wherever it appears in the ancient world some form of ritual astronomy can usually be observed.

Hapgood:
they want a remedy
the old remedy.
The old God.
But it's more,
it's Light: more Light...
We want a new revelation.
The longer it's withheld
the lower we'll sink.
Light! Light!

A.S.M. Hutchinson:
If Winter Comes

GENESIS ATLANTICA

The final decade of the twentieth century saw the ritual astronomy of the Star Temple builders grow beyond pseudo-science. No longer would the Star Temples be associated with flying saucer sightings. While old school archaeologists were debating their shopworn and blatantly sexist theories, a new wave of scientists were uncovering an ancient cosmology within the megalith network, an explanation of creation which influenced the troubadours and the authors of the legends of the Grail, as well as the mysterious architects who designed the Gothic cathedrals.

The knights who quested for the Grail in the medieval literature conducted their quests five thousand years after the shaman, daubed with red ochre, performed his spiral ceremony in Ireland or Labrador, and yet the similarities in the two archetypes are uncanny. Both were symbols of the divine children born from the Atlantic Genesis legends. Both knight and shaman acted as heroic identity figures, inspiring their clans to greater spiritual heights. The shaman quested for perfection and balance promised by the voices of his cave ancestors. The knights quested for the perfection and balance promised in the inexhaustible cauldron of Cerridwyn.

In a deeper analysis we see that the quest is really a struggle for the cauldron of memory, or what Jung called the "Collective Unconscious." Every land has many legends steeped in memory lore. The magician, looking out on the Celtic Sea, needed to memorize a great many magical formulae, stories, and legends before practicing a single ritual operation. These magical practices were based on the stone circles and the sky, and as such were never forgotten. Over time, the magician became the bard, the troubadour and the knight errant. So the basin stone was as crucial to the operation of the temples as the grinding mill, and the art of memory was the human interface. [94]

One of the great legends of memory, now translated and well documented, is that of Ossian, pronounced *O-sheen*, one of the most celebrated of the Irish heros. Ossian's story is one of wonder and magic. He migrates to the land of Tir na Og, the land of Og, the land of the spiral light God. Once there he acquires magical powers, not the least of which is his ability to rebirth or transform himself into various deities and animals. He also has the ability to fly. But the Ossian fable is not the only source for the story of the questing knight. The legend of Setanta is probably closer to that of Gawain.

Setanta is an Irish, prehistoric, folk messiah mentioned in *The Tain bo Cullainge* or *The Cattle Raid on Coolley,* an

---

[94]Santillana, Giorgio, and Hertha von Dechend. *Hamlet's Mill.* Cambridge: M I T Press, 1968. Preface. This book is important reading for anyone attempting to understand the cosmologies of Atlantic peoples.

eighth century apocryphal text. The cattle raid may have been an actual Iron Age event, but the Setanta story embedded within it is at least two thousand years older. This can be adduced because the birth of Setanta is keyed to the Winter Solstice rituals in the Star Temples. We known this because the narrative tells us snow was on the ground and the trek began on the Monday after Halloween (Samhain). Setanta's mysterious birth, like Arthur's, is part of the Celtic warrior theme. Both are born in mystery and both stories involve a Winter Solstice birth in a grotto. In other words, Setanta is an Occidental precursor of both Christ and King Arthur. [95,96]

In an astonishing prehistoric parallel, Setanta, according to *The Tain,* is born when snow is on the ground (Winter Solstice or Christmas) in the inner chamber of a mound (grotto) used for grain storage in the Boyne Valley.[97]

Like the Virgin Mary, Dectine is visited by an angel who arrives on a lightbeam or rainbow. The angel tells her, also like the Virgin of Christian allegory, that she will bear

---

[95] Kinsella, Thomas, trans. *The Tain.* Dublin: Dolmen Press, 1981.
Setanta's story finds uncanny parallels in Christ's immaculate conception. Most significantly, both large and small containers are represented in the Setanta legend. The sacrifice of the megalithic magician is remembered here.

[96] The three side chambers and the passage at Newgrange form a cross when illuminated by the lightbeam. The mound, in addition to all else, was the embodiment of the ancient Earth-Moon Goddess, the same Goddess worshipped in the caves of France and Spain during the late Ice Ages. So, at Christmas (Winter Solstice) we find a dynamic illuminated cross within the interior of the Goddess.

[97] The Setanta story is older than the Christian saga by at least three millennia. It takes place in the Boyne Valley at a time when the Star Temples were still in use as granaries and birthing hospices circa 3200-2200 BC, long prior to their collapse. In the aboriginal Setanta legend, Dectine mates with a sunbeam or rainbow spirit within the Star Temple. She then dances around the megaliths tracing the triple spiral, the motion of the Earth against the background of the stars. She is a sibyl. Her tourney is a feminine version of the quest for purification.

a special son. Soon after this visitation, she selects an earthly husband, like Joseph in the Christian variation, a surrogate named Conchobar. Both impregnations are miraculous. Mary's is prophesied by an angel, Dectine's by the ingestion of a draught from a small cup after a visitation from an angel. [98]

Unlike Joseph, who is traditionally painted as an elderly carpenter, Conchobar is a tribal chief who acts as mentor to the sacred child, but he is not the lightbeam husband. That honor is reserved for an invisible visitor. The legend parallels Christ's immaculate conception and birth in many respects. Because his actual father is of the lightbeam, Setanta is born and reborn simultaneously and, also like Christ, he has both a lightbeam father and a foster father.

The time frame of the Setanta story is wide sweeping. He is an Iron Age Celtic warrior in a Neolithic milieu, clearly the original bards wanted the two ages to be connected. That Setanta is the hero of the bards cannot be denied, as he learns eloquence and hunting skills as well as prince craft from them.

Setanta is the son of the Great Mother Dectine — equivalent to the later Greek Hecate, Diana, or the Roman Cybele — by her supernatural marriage to Lugh — Zeus. As such, Setanta is similar to both Perseus and Perceival. The similarities between *The Tain,* the Setanta story, and the later medieval quest legends are almost beyond coincidence. In the Setanta saga the divine child becomes a Celtic Warrior. In the medieval version, Arthur, as a raw youth becomes the sanctified Grail Knight. In *The Perlesvaus,* Gawain defends the honor of his mother and must endure

---

[98]Dectine's cup is clearly a Grail prototype.*Siochanta,* in ancient Irish, means "peaceful," while the similar word *siocan* means "frosty weather," another reference to Winter Solstice. Folcloir, *Irish-English Dictionary.* p 94 See also Kinsella, Thomas *Ibid p-23.*

numerous quests and hardships before beholding the secrets of the Grail. Likewise, Setanta, born as the result of a quest for a sacred bull defends the honor of his mother, Dectine, by becoming a warrior. [99] (Plate xv)

Fosterage is also a factor in the development of the Grail warrior-king. In *The Tain*, Setanta is fostered to the warrior chieftain Conchobar. Conchobar, in turn, places him in the hands of the druids and bards for training in the metaphysical and martial arts. He will, in the final analysis, turn out to be a Renaissance man, schooled in poetry, music, warfare, and statecraft. Likewise, in *Le morte d'Arthur*, Arthur, the son of a warrior king, is fostered to Merlin by his father Uther Pendragon. Merlin, a druid, or a hermetic scholar, or both, then directs the young king to pull Excalibur from the megalith. [100]

Almanacs in Stone

One of the problems in approaching the Atlantic Genesis from an archaeological direction lies in the confusion surrounding the dating of the Star Temples. Traditional archaeologists place the "passage graves" well within the Bronze Age and attribute them to the Indo-Europeans, thereby erasing any strictly Atlantic contribution. If there is no Atlantic contribution there can be no Atlantic Genesis legend. But we know the legends have more than Indo-European elements in them. The myths can be dated by internal evidence. Setanta, for example, was born when the mounds of Brug na Boinne were still being used. We know,

---

[99]Lumiansky, R.M., ed. *Morte d'Arthur*. Princeton: Princeton University Press, 1983.

[100]Chant, Joy *The High Kings: Arthur's Celtic Ancestors*. New York: Bantam, 1983. There are similarities in the maternal side of the story as well. Both Arthur and Setanta are born to women of the fairy faith (Igraine and Dectine) through fertility magic and deception.

by the carbon dating of debris found beneath the collapsed walls, that most of the mounds were fully collapsed by the end of the Bronze Age, so either the Setanta myth is Neolithic and survived all incursions, or the outsiders were converted to a style of worship reflected in the Star Temples. Perhaps a little of both explanations took place.

It is now generally accepted that the average calibrated date range for mounds of the passage temple type is between 4000 and 3600 BC, not 2200 BC as stated by the British archaeologist Glyn Daniel. Professor Daniel must have been indulging in wishful thinking when he wrote:

"Already, new surveys are showing the inaccuracy of some of the earlier observations and undermining the hopes of those who believe the builders were slaves of an astronomical cult." 101

Daniel's pontification was an indirect attack on the diligent research of Professors Alexander and Archibald Thom and other qualified scholars who offer proof that virtually every megalithic site is astronomically aligned and linked to other sites over vast distances, even across large bodies of water. The builders of Newgrange probably knew about the existence of Kercado in France, just as Gothic architects at Chartres must have known about the work of the builders at Notre Dame in Paris. 102

The facts are not in Professor Daniel's favor. The surveys he alludes to, especially those conducted in Ireland, proved him wrong. In the twenty years since Daniel's

---

101Daniel, Glynn "Megaliths." *Scientific American.* July, 1980. p.76.

102Thom, Alexander and A. S. Thom *Megalithic Remains in Britain and Brittany*. Oxford: Oxford Press, 1978. The sites differ in shape and alignment as well as in measurement probably because they are set upon an ancient grid which would require them to be unique to their particular latitude and longitude. This would be especially true if they were built using a large central structure, like Newgrange, Carnac, or Stonehenge, as a start point.

proclamations, he made other similar pontifications, hundreds of astronomical connections have been established for the mounds and henges and stone rings. When the dates were adjusted — according to tree ring techniques, stable radioactive studies, photoluminescence and other hi-tech methods — it became apparent that most explanations of the development of civilization in Western Europe were built on quicksand. [103]

Despite strong resistance to non-academics entering the field of academics with less specific training, a picture of an Atlantic Genesis continues to develop. Each new piece of objective research is shedding fresh light on the controversy. There are many fragments still to find, but great store is being placed in the accuracy of oral traditions.

In France, as the Christian era progressed, many abbeys were either built on mounds or adjacent to stone rings. Some chapels were even constructed from the ring stones because they were convenient or to preserve cultural continuity. For this reason, and because France possesses a vast array of dolmen, cairns and Star Temples, including the largest single standing stone alignment on Earth (Carnac) and possibly the oldest passage temple (Kercado), the French archaeological community has long been interested in tracking down the true nature of the megalithic civilization. Likewise, in Ireland, the fabulous abbeys of Melifont, Monasterboice and Kells are situated within a ten-mile radius of Newgrange and each was built on an ancient foundation. Some observers think the crosses of the old abbeys were carved from large megaliths sledged away from the Star Temples by ox cart. Tara, one of the famed capitals of the Irish high kings, lies about twelve miles to the west of

---

[103]Brennan, Martin. *The Stars and the Stones*. London: Thames and Hudson, 1983.

Newgrange. The mounds there date across the Neolithic bandwidth and continue into the Bronze Age, indicating that Tara was used by compatible tribes for many centuries. Nowhere is there evidence of a full scale land or naval "invasion" until the Vikings invaded in the Dark Ages. Tara's mounds were also active in Christian times and play a central role in Saint Patrick's attempts to convert the kings of Ireland. [104]

The same sequence holds for Portugal, the Basque and Catalonian area of Spain, Cornwall, Brittany and much of France. Although tribal and clan boundaries were strong, much peaceful trade was carried out and the practice of building upon old foundations was common throughout territories once dominated by the megalith builders and eventually the Celts.

There are hundreds of potential Star Temples sites around the Celtic Sea and the Bay of Biscay. Still more uncharted sites can be found in Portugal and along the northern rim of Spain from Santiago, near the Atlantic, to Gerona, near the Mediterranean. But wherever they are found the megaliths are the remnants of a lost civilization, a true civilization that enjoyed life half way between the late Ice Age and the first farming experiments. The unique Atlantic hypertext and the cosmology carved on the megaliths, held a relatively large population together. But what exactly was the Atlantic Genesis? How much did the builders "know" about the universe? [105]

---

[104]MacAllister, R.A.S. "Teamhair Breg: A Study of the Remains and traditions of Tara." *Proceedings of the Royal Irish Academy*, Vol. XXXIV, 1919, p.231.

[105]Charpentier, Louis. *Le Jacques et le Mysteries de la Compestella.* Paris: Laffont, 1972.The road between Santiago and Gerona neatly correlates with the famed pilgrim's route called "The Road of Saint James of Compestelle."

In the fourth millennium BC, mounds, standing stones, cairns and other permanent structures began to appear on raised beaches in Western Europe. The people who built these monuments possessed an extensive knowledge of deep sea fishing as well as whale, dolphin, and seal migrations. This knowledge could not have been maintained without an extensive almanac of tide tables and a method of transmission of this knowledge from generation to generation. Anthropologists have long believed that this data was transmitted through oral methods alone, but recent discoveries at the "L" shaped passage cairn on the small island of Gavrinis on the French Atlantic coast, reveals that the Dawn People were actually "printing" the tide tables on massive stones. Today these stones continue to track the tides and moon phases around the island with precision. The undulating carved lines, similar to those at Knowth, indicate that a mystery school or rite of passage, a kind of Grail quest based on tidal information, was held here. [106]

However, Star Temples were not simple tidal observatories or almanacs — they were also designed to attract the populace to seasonal festivals. The best correct archaeological evidence now available indicates there was no widespread or all-powerful priestly elite at work behind their construction. The site plans point to the assumption that rites were open to virtually anyone who could make the pilgrimage and that they were operated by a well-integrated group of tenders and operators who acted as ritual guides and maintenance personnel, not a priest class, drawn from many walks of life and from male and female populations.

This road also intersects at least a dozen highly decorated Paleolithic cave dwellings including Altamira and Lascaux, probably the first cathedrals.

[106] Hibbs, James "The Neolithic of Briitany and Normandy." In: Scarre, C. *Ancient France*, Edinburgh University Press. 1985 P 271-319. Gavrinis was built coeval with the average date for the three Boyne Valley Temples.

Genesis Atlantica

The statistical tracking modes of the Star Temples, like the paintings and carvings on the cave walls of late Ice Age, were based on fertility magic. But is fertility magic necessarily primitive? Is it not rather a blend of raw human emotion and an innocent faith in nature? The idea of the creation of the universe held by the Star Temple builders derives from their ability to observe and track the activities of celestial bodies. The precise, almost obsessive, tracking of day and night sky events is scientific in method and yet the goal of the exercise is wish fulfillment, something from the dream world. The goal of astral rituals, put into play by the first agriculturalists, was to magically influence events so as to improve survival and fertility.

The Star Temple people built their civilization (with a flexible definition we can surely call it a civilization) on innocence. To them the divine child (innocence) was created by the penetration of a rainbow or beam of light into the dark womb of the void mother. Geometric markings hammered into the megaliths which surround many of the Star Temples, express this theme clearly. The markings are not doodles, on the contrary they are expressions of a primordial and intuitive insight into the functions and creation of the universe. In this sense the Star Temples can be thought of as computerized almanacs, each stone a page in a massive stone manuscript, and from them we can begin to reconstruct the lifestyle of a lost society, a society steeped in the process of ritual astronomy — a society with enough leisure time to observe and record the minute details of plant and animal cycles, and yet a society under stress from growth and the weight of its own knowledge. [107]

---

[107]MacAllister R.A.S. *The Archaeology of Ireland.* London: Benjamin Blom, 1928. Reprint: New York: Arno, 1977.

By the time the Star Temples began to collapse, a wide diversity of tribal lifestyles were being practiced within an isolated social framework, especially in Ireland. Some groups chose to remain hunter-gatherers and probably also shamanic. Others were agriculturalists and mineralogists. Some buried their dead in group tombs, others cremated their dead, and still others practiced excarnation. Between these extremes stood hundreds of pocket cultures with eclectic burial practices, art and tools. [108]

In this mixed population the shaman's intuitive animal calendars — based on the return of the salmon, reindeer and geese migration, the meanders of the whale — were translated into widely circulated legends. The stone circles became bare and even more abstract but, converted into stories, the carvings were made manifest in portable art such as clay bowls, jade pendants, silver and bronze torques and, later, gold ornaments. The spiral and the analemma, the two symbols which formed the later Celtic cross, became the symbolic common denominators linking most of the Star Temple societies. The spiral appears on almost every major art object traceable to the Bronze Age. (Plate xvi)

Winter Light

The most serious astronomical festival in the Atlantic Neolithic year took place close to what we now think of as Christmas. The Atlantic tribal soul was tied to the waxing and waning of the moon and to the apparent rising and setting of the sun through the Grail Stone and the Star Temples. But it was tied more intimately to Winter Solstice, being the longest night of the year and the longest night of the soul, than any other festival.

---

[108]Deubner, L. *Attische Feste*. Berlin 1932. Also: Gleadow, R. *The Origins of the Zodiac*. London: Jonathan Cape, 1968. p. 76.

December twenty-first is the date upon which the sun appears to balance on the southeastern horizon above Newgrange, and the date upon which the sun appears to begin its march back along the horizon to its summer extension. It is also a time when many people become inexplicably sad. Modern research has established that this Winter sadness can be reversed by the application of light to stimulate the pineal gland, so perhaps the lightbeam ritual was a healing procedure, a way of assuring a reenergizing of the light power.

On December twenty-first, the sunbeam can be observed entering various Winter Solstice mounds and crossing various stone rings. At Newgrange, this activity is marked by the triple spiral situated less than three feet from one of the stone basins, but each temple has its unique signature.

The Star Temple builders were fascinated by darkness and shadow. The exact rituals of these diurnal light and dark worshippers may have lapsed from direct memory, but not from the unconscious mind. For centuries they were modified and stylized. The intellectual aspect of the rites was flexible. The shaman became a druid or hermit. The sibyl became a maiden, but ultimately the old religion survived. The human beings who built the stone observatories and earthworks six thousand years ago were building monuments to their idea of creation, and their great-great grand-children continued the tradition.

The Atlantic Genesis was based on an eternal principle, an almost heliocentric cosmic view, symbolized by the triple spiral, and by carvings depicting the rising of Sirius as a rayed circle or the passage of Venus as a double circle, the sun as a single circle with a dot in the center or the moon as a circle of undulating lines. We might also locate the apparent rise and set of the sun in the repetitive diamond pattern and the rise and set of the moon in a linear undulating pattern. Each festival day was marked by symbols cut into stone. These patterns were also used for decorations on hides and as tattoos on human skin.

This entire scriptural language, which encompasses a huge and dynamic body of scientific observations retained in the memory of the stones, can be thought of as the proto-Grail religion, a scientific body of data inherited by subsequent tribes and clans until it was handed down to the Celts and to the Hermetic sages who translated the old religion into a written and intellectual form attributed to Hermes Trismegistus.

Hermes

Occidental religions share a basis of initiation in the cauldron rite. The central cauldron ikon became so common over so many centuries that the essential ceremony (ritual astronomy) did not die when interdicted by the Inquisition in 1210. Although the crusade against the Albigensians tortured the believers to death in hideous public displays and put many good people to the merciful flames, it did not eclipse the desire to worship nature on specific dates determined by the sun, moon and stars. Instead the process of initiation, especially the sense of communal democracy intrinsic to these mysteries, went underground only to surface as Alchemy.[109]

Bards, gradually Christianizing, rhymed to declare the rebirth of the old God in a new form. Again Christianity was forced to combine with Celtic traditions to gain favor. As the Breton culture flourished, many poets and orators traveled freely to Athens and Alexandria, down the

---

[109]Robertson, J.M. *Pagan Christs.* New Hyde Park, N.Y.: University Books, 1967.

Garonne, through the Languedoc and into the Mediterranean at Narbonne — a well-fortified seaport — thence to Africa. The writers, architects and musicians who traveled these byways enjoyed access to the writings of Hermes Trismegistus, Plotinus, Origen, Philo and Enoch and were well aware of the Mithraic traditions held by the founding fathers in the first wave. They were becoming Christians, but they remained Hermetic in outlook.

In The *Asclepius,* attributed to Hermes, we find the admonition:

> *"Knowest thou not Asclepius that our land is the image of heaven, the representation on Earth of every celestial ordinance? Our land is the temple of the world."* [110]

This passage echoes the *templum mundi* conception of Philo which is, according to Hermetic scholars, traceable to Imhotep the original architect of the pyramids, but it cannot be entirely original with Imhotep since the astromagical and architectural basis for the Pyramids was known on a wide scale at least two thousand years before the pyramid of Zoser. The Hermetics of Alexandria were also praising the megalithic Star Temple architects and the Dawn People. [111]

Coins used in Western France, minted both before the arrival of the Romans and after AD 450, depict a chalice prominently displayed beneath an arch, indicating a continuity in chalice worship and the importance of the arch for both pagan and Christian epochs. The tricephalic hero, the

---

[110]Scott, W. *Hermetica.* (Vol I) in 4 vols. (Aesclepius) London: Oxford Press, 1924.

[111]When the soldiers of Maximus scattered to Armorica and settled near Mt. Saint Michelle, they savored a book of ancient stories called *The Grael.* This manuscript contained metaphorical explanations of the rituals of the Mithra cult, which included the castration of priests (the wound of Arthur), the worship of the Goddess, and elements of the Tarot, known as the Major arcana.

Dagda — Arthur in embryonic form — can also be found on coins and many art objects. One may speculate that through these artifacts, and a general commitment to the old religion, the citizens of New Britain were attempting to rebuild a celestial temple on Earth in the tradition of their ancestors. [112]

The Persistence of Mithra

As the Roman Empire receded from power in the west, some socio-political structure was needed to fill the gaps. Hidebound Christianity worked well in Rome, but did not take hold quickly in the extreme Occident, at least as it was presented to the peasants of the Atlantic rim.

The remix of the Roman Mediterranean system with Christian symbols and the already ancient Atlantic system, mastered and managed by the Celtic tribes, became a melting pot in which the *ars naturae and ars magia*, which beat at the heart of the Hermetic mysteries, could take hold. So Mithraism, the religion implanted in Celtic countries by the Roman armies, enjoyed a sustained appeal in the west because its ceremonies could be adapted to each clan's ikonography. Furthermore, similarities between the celestial Shamanism of the Atlantic Star Temple and Mithraism suggest that Mithra was linked to the sun and the lightbeam at a very early period. The most common image of Mithra was that of a lion-headed (leocephalic) angel (the lightbeam god). A sword entwined with snakes (a classical Excalibur prototype) was held in the angel's right hand while the left hand often held a bowl (Grail-cauldron) or wreath of stars,

---

[112]Cunliffe, Barry. *The Celts,* McGraw-Hill, New York, 1979. p.253. Although the migrants were Welsh and Irish and the locals were Gauls and all three still spoke some form of Gaelic, Greek became the written language in educated circles. Scholars and monks also knew Latin. English wasn't developed for at least eight hundred years.

implying that the bowl reflected the stars. This image is not dissimilar to that of Saint Michael, the Dark Age winged angel, who holds a sword, stands on a snake or dragon and wears a crown of stars. Plainly we see in Lugh, Mithra and Michael, at least some of the basic ikons practiced in Atlantic Shamanism.

In Southern England, Mithra was a compilation of the twelve zodiac signs, and in a frieze near Glastonbury he is seen fighting a heavenly bull, just as Theseus encountered the Minotaur and Saint Michael encountered the celestial dragon. In yet another frieze, this one located near Albi in Southern France, Mithra is seen holding the keys to the Hermetic heaven and Earth — an image often associated with Saint Peter in Christian doctrine and Melchizedek in *The Pentatuch*; and various apocrypha. At Chartres we are treated to a depiction of Melchizedek holding these keys. The transformation of Melchizedek into Mithra and again into Saint Michael is further supported by wide variety of frescoes and sculptures depicting the winged Michael with the same two keys, a sword and a balance for the measuring of souls. [113]

That Mithra was a product of the New Stone Age can be adduced from the idea that he was supposedly born from a stone which broke open at his birth in a subterranean grotto; this not only seems parallel to the supernal and occult birth of Christ — who was born in a grotto (manger) — it also echoes the events surrounding the birth of the Irish Setanta and the Welsh Arthur. Are we looking at many variations of the same mysterious hero? Christ, who is thought of as the lamb of God, was sacrificed during the vernal equinox. Mithra performs a bull sacrifice on the

---

[113]Robertson, J.M. *Pagan Christs*. New Hyde Park, New York. University Books, 1967. p.18. In many examples Saint Michael is carrying a chalice.

same day. Arthur holds his highest ceremonies and the Knight's quests begin at Pentacost.

If a cross can be a transformation of a sword we find another interesting parallel. In a restored Mithraic temple in Glouchester the god is seen sacrificing a cult bull with a sword. Could this be the sword which eventually became Excalibur, the Emerald Sword in the Arthurian cycle? Suffice it to say that the hallows of the crucifixion are remarkably similar to the magical implements of Celtic magic and the Tarot. [114]

A parallel to the Grail initiation can also be found in the Mithra cult. Like modern Freemasons, the priests of Mithra taught their followers to transcend the mundane world through three degrees or grades (Latin: *grada* o r *gradatim.*) In Mithraism, the first degree was based on a sword and crown; the second, a book and the third, a cape or cloak of invisibility used with a cauldron and chalice. Each temple of the Mithra sect was divided further into competitive cadres with animistic names such as The Lions Men or The Eagle Workers. Bulls, bears and dragons were also commonly-used epithets. Here we see the basis for many later secret societies, including the Freemasons, and a parallel to the medieval Grail initiations. The very word "Grail" comes from the Provençal French word Graal which extends from Latin *gradal, Gradual* and *gradatim,* meaning initiation by stages or degrees, the same context and phrasing used in the Mithra cult. [115]

---

[114]The emerald sword appears as the sword used to behead John the Baptist and is mentioned in *The High History* as the cult object quested for by Sir Gawain. It also progresses from a Spring Equinox sword to a Summer Solstice sword, as Saint John's day falls on June twenty-first. Much of this has to do with the Tarot and is covered in volume two of the present trilogy.

[115]It is not known which of these grades were superior. It is well known that the priests of Mithra called themselves "Lions," but there may have been

We may never unravel the true nature of Mithraism because we are forced to rely on texts taken from the reports of the Inquisition after 1200. These depict Mithraism as a superficial and evil religion, a heresy in every way. Deeper research shows a compassionate side to Mithraism as practiced in the Celtic world. Mycenaean and pan-Celtic bull sacrifice can be seen in the central ritual of the sect, but there was much more to it than simple bull sacrifice. For example, we know it was an action oriented religion. Planting and harvesting were regulated by the rites. The emphasis was on education, ethics, charity, fasting, the struggle between good and evil, and sexual continence.

We also know that Mithraism was open to men only, but members often selected wives from the women who followed the Goddess Cybele, the overseer of the harvest. Both orders celebrated the feast of *agape* or friendship, complete with chalice and the belief in immortality. Not only was this feast echoed in the Christian gospels as The Marriage Feast at Canna, it was continued by the troubadours and became part of the "courts of love" instituted by Eleanor of Aquitaine. One might even find parallels between Mithra and Cybele in the marriage of Arthur and Guenevere.

Contrary to popular belief, Mithraism and Cybelism did not die out. They managed to survive in pocket cultures incrementally removed from Rome, especially in old Celtic strongholds like Narbonne, Vannes — near the great stone

---

higher grades. All of the animals are circumpolar or zodiacal. The most interesting aspect in the British variations of the cult is the Bear as it pertains to Arthur's name in Gaelic. In keeping with the military origins of the sect, each cadre may have been assigned specific functions. Lions=the priest sect, Bulls=farmers, Bears=warriors, Wolves=hunters, Fish (salmon)=wisdom, Eagles=navigators, almost like merit badges earned in modern scouting.

alignment of Carnac — and Glastonbury watched over by Saint Michael's Tor. These cities were ideally suited to maintain both pagan and Christian values simultaneously because they were located at the crossroads of civilization. Trade was conducted in the old languages and the old stories were learned by each generation. (Plate xvii)

Christian Rome could not count on automatic conversions in the west because many Welsh, Breton, Irish and Scottish chiefs were not despotic and could not order their people to blindly adopt anything as important as a new religion by simple fiat. Tribal lords and tribal heros, tribal queens and tribal finances were still as important as any religion in these areas, at least until the seventh century. The missionary doctrine of sin and redemption, offered by the first wave of Christian zealots was anathema to the post-Roman Celts who believed, as did their ancestors, that their souls were immortal and would go to a paradisiacal underworld — the Cauldron of Aanwyn or the Dagda — regardless of how they lead their lives. As time went on, and as the papal zealots continued harassing the Westerners, threats of damnation in the afterworld would tear many away from their aboriginal roots, but for many centuries Christianity, without Shamanism, did not appeal to the clans and in a few areas Christianity never really caught on. Because of its compatibility with Celtic beliefs, especially the Atlantic Genesis myth, Mithraism was instrumental in stimulating ancient values in Brittany, Southern England, and in the southern capitals of Albi and Toulouse. Mithraism grew, or remained, in these areas because the priests of Mithra practiced religious tolerance. Jews were attracted to Mithraic areas, as were Greeks and Egyptian

Gnostics, because they could trade openly and discourse without fear.[116]

Albigensians and Cathars

From the first century on, Manichaeanism based on the teachings of the Persian prophet Mannes, grew up, especially in the Dordogne and the Languedoc. It too offered freedom for those who would worship the old gods. From Manichaeanism a religion called Catharism sprang up in the same regions of Southern France with it's center at Albi, thus the name Albigensianism. [117]

Albigensianism was held in such high esteem by both the peasants and royalty of Southern France that by 1200, it was actually rivaling Rome for converts. For this reason it was labeled a heresy by the Inquisition. Like the Grail rites, Shamanism and Mithraism, the Cathars practiced purification rituals based on the teachings of the Persian prophet Mannes. But since these doctrines were liberating they created much work for the Inquisition. As far as the papacy was concerned, there was very little difference between the fourth century rites of Mithra or Cybele and those of the twelfth century Albigensians and, although Jews and other Easterners were welcome in Carcassone and Albi, the main cities in the Albigensian domain, all were tarred with the same brush in the Vatican. [118]

---

[116]Cumont, Franz. *The Mysteries of Mithra*. Reprint. 1902. New York: Dover, 1956.

[117]For this reason historians have called it Albigensianism, but it was far more widespread than this central capital.

[118]Marx, Jean. "Le Cortege du Chateau des Merveilles." *Etudes celtiques*, IX (1960). Also: *The Legend Arthurienne et le Graal*. Paris: Dupont, 1952. The leaders of the Mithra cult are castrated to assure purity of purpose. The Bogomils and Cathars practiced a similar ritual. Ironically, the Crusade against the Albigensians circa 1210, marked the downfall of the Crusades in general. By 1280 the fortified outposts in the Levant were abandoned

Probably the most directly threatening aspect of these so-called heresies from the perspective of the church, was their overlapping intelligence-gathering or spy networks. The various secret societies were pressed against a common foe so, for example, the Albigensian would send envoys to the pagan Irish, the Bogomiles in Eurasia and to Glastonbury and Fecamp in order to test the strength of their allies in the west. The Knights Templars, Hospitaliers and other orders of the crusades, would do the same with a vested interest in educating the masses. [119] (Plate xviii)

The Templars were active in the network — acting as police authorities in matters of dispute and arbitration — as were all manner of intellectuals seeking new and lost knowledge, such as the works of Aristotle, long since suppressed by the church. [120]

---

[119] I am personally convinced that the doctrine of democracy was the common denominator running through all of these sects and that only fascists would wish to destroy the ideal of freedom for each individual.

[120] It is probable that the Grail cultus at Glastonbury Abbey looked upon by the Benedictines as a treasure house in the year 1150, was a Mithraic-Albigensian, Celtic and Christian sect all at once. During the crusades it encompassed the doctrines of the Knights Templars, The Knights Hospitaliers, the troubadours, and numerous other cults.

I married Isis on the fifth day of May,
but I could not hold on to her very long.
So, I cut off my hair and I rode straight away
to that wild and old country
where I could not go wrong.

Bob Dylan

GUENEVERE AND ARTHUR

The apotheosis of the Atlantic Genesis appears in the characters of King Arthur and Queen Guenevere. Although they have literary roots in the legends of the Welsh poets of the Dark Ages, their essence was still very much alive in the politics of the Middle Ages because they were the perfect example of the alchemical marriage, so inspirational to the troubadour poets. To the medieval poet, Guenevere and Arthur represented the survival of the ancient dyad and acted to support the ideal of courtly love. In so doing they represented the survival of Neolithic egality.

Through their writings, the new bards of the crusades revealed an entire court of mythic knights (including Gawain, Perceival and Lancelot) ruled by a powerful Neoplatonic philosopher (Arthur) and an independent Celtic queen (Guenevere) who represented the Goddess ideal. The entire pageant, including a nascent sense of democracy and the vision of The Holy Grail, revolved around a circular table, a table which symbolized democracy, the Earth's revolutions, the celestial orb, the labyrinth of Theseus, Stonehenge, the Star Temples, the Zodiac and dozens of other metaphors.

In the earliest Grail dramas Arthur is a messianic chief who leads the Celts onward against the oppressor. But his quest for purity is conducted in the name of the Goddess, and ultimately his leadership extends to all peoples and classes who wish to be free under her banner. Here the Goddess quest is political, but the same dyad can be seen at work behind Theseus and Ariadne or Saint George and the damsel. It should be obvious to anyone who reads even the most commercialized versions of the Grail quest legends, that Arthur and Guenevere were metamorphosed versions of the lightbeam father and the void mother of the Star Temples. [121]

We are told much about the politics of secret groups such as the troubadours or the Knights Templars, we have their trial transcripts and their manifestos, but there is scant little cast in writing that gives us insight into their rituals and their intramural communications, except the legends of the Grail. Medieval storytellers may have adapted the Grail and Round Table motifs as a convenient tactic designed to teach megalithic science and the old values without offending church authorities. Constant redactions and changes were being made to the old legends in various secret societies throughout the Dark Ages and the early Medieval era.

Although seldom used for ritual purposes after the decline of the Roman Empire and the advance of Christianity in the Dark Ages, Star Temples like Stonehenge and Avebury remained focal points, especially vital to the revival of Celtic magic and literature. To fit the emerging medieval standards of a spectacular court held within a strange castle, the Star Temples, presided over by a magnificent Earth Mother Queen and an even more mysterious Sun King grew to be symbolized, in literature, as the Round Table of Arthur and Guenevere, while the

---

[121] Theseus is also endowed with a magical sword hidden beneath the megaliths by his father Aegus.

remembrance of the megalithic theaters of ages past was manifest in the activities, quests and rituals of the legendary denizens of their court. [122]

The Grail Castle, with the Round Table at its center, was transfigured from a rude stone cairn or painted cave to the main hall of a Norman keep. Guenevere evolved from the Great Mother and the Indo-European White Goddess. Likewise, Arthur was transformed from the Paleolithic lightbeam God and the bear clan shaman to a Hermetic-Christian king. Merlin, who takes on the identity of the hermetic Fisher King, is nothing more than the druid and shaman transformed into a Celtic wizard. The chalice was transformed from a skull cup — or an even earlier ring mark carved in stone — into the golden chalice of Gothic literature, a remarkable twenty thousand year evolutionary cycle. [123]

The castle of the Grail or the Fisher King, as described in *The High History of the Holy Grail,* represents the outer, mundane, world. The Round Table at the castle's center represents a convened court or tribunal, almost like a tiled meeting in Freemasonry. The Grail chalice, which is the master ikon or *monas hieroglyphica,* the one symbol which contains and can describe all of the others, resides at the center of the table and at the center of the castle, just as the Grail Stone resides at the center of the Star Temple. Due to its location between the walls of the castle and the chalice

---

[122]Richmond, I.A. and O. Crawford,*The British Section of the Ravenna Cosmography.* London: Oxford University Press, 1949. The Celtic word for the Goddess as a bear translated to the Greek was Artio. Her son would be Artios. So if Arthur sprang from this Greco-Celtic root he would have been the son of the mother bear or the small bear. As it happens a small bear does exist as a circumpolar constellation Ursa Minor.

[123]Jarman A.O. *The Legend of Merlin.* Cardiff: University of Wales Press, 1960. See also: Parry J.J. "Vita Merlini." *Studies in Language and Literature,* #3, August, 1925, University of Illinois.

ikon, the Round Table represents a spiritual transition from the mundane to metaphysical. It also implies that when human beings perceive this initiation tableaux, they will make similar internal psychological transitions. [124]

The Fairy Faith

The transition of the Grail rite from Shamanism and Celtic lore to medieval literary masterpiece could not have been performed without a unifying theme. The written stories of Arthur and Guenevere, the Grail and the knights of the Round Table could not have emerged from popular folk tales without the pre-existence of a belief in something magical just beneath the surface. Many scholars believe this "something" was a deep and abiding faith in the fairy people, a folk wisdom that taught that the wee people were the original and perpetual inhabitants of the mounds and megaliths.

A widespread belief in the fairies continued long after Christianity took hold. Even in the twenty-first century, legends of Leprechauns and Kelpies are respected in Celtic countries. The bards of the Dark Ages may have known how to twist a tale, but folk tales of fairies and Banshees were also conveyed by the audiences just as pop songs are sung today. But songs and poems were not the only ancient element to survive; the megaliths survived because curses and direct warnings against the destruction of the megaliths are common in the Gaelic tradition. In Ireland, at least until the end of the twentieth century, the penalty for desecrating a fairy fort (cairn) was crop failure and infertility, both animal and human. The witches called this "hexing" and "crop blasting," and a sufficient body of evidence exists to

---

[124]Yates, Frances—*The Occult In The Elizabethan Age*. London: RKP, 1981. p83-85. Yates traces the *monas* to John Dee and Christian Cabala.

conclude that certain cults maintain the curse of protection over the Star Temples to the present day. Many of those who suffered the famed "Potato Famine" were convinced the blight was a fulfillment of a curse for desecrating the fairy forts. [125]

In The *Elucidation*, written by an anonymous master, we discover a major facet of the fairy or pixie influence on the medieval intellectual. When Guenevere is estranged the king falls ill by the poison of the moon making the land infertile.*The Perlesvaus* further portrays the destruction of the land of L'ogres (Og's land or Lugh's land) by the suppressive arm of the church. [126]

The Golden Bowl

At the time the Arthur and Guenevere stories were transported to Brittany from Wales and back again, circa AD 580, the legends of the heros and the rituals of the megaliths were well mixed. In one example, the fairy forts (*puis* — Breton) were said to be inhabited by beautiful maidens who offered food and drink from a golden bowl to all who passed. This hospitality ended abruptly when a deranged, Christian chieftain named Amangons ravished one of the maidens and purloined the bowl, showing no respect whatever for the old ways. Amangons' brutal act caused the trees to lose their foliage and the rivers to dry up. [127]

Here again we see the infertility theme. Most importantly, the court of the rich Fisher King could not be found anywhere and the state of grace provided by that

[125]Evans-Wentz, W. *The Fairy Faith in Celtic Countries*. New York: Universe Books, 1966. p. 77-82.

[126]Potvin M. Mss, *Perceval le Gallois ou le conte du Graal*. 6 vo. Mons Belgium, 1866-1871.

[127]Stone, Merlin. *When God Was a Woman*. New York: Harcourt-Brace-Javonovich, 1976. p.4 (Cerridwen.)

powerful monarch simply disappeared. These infamies caused the queen of the fairies (a Guenevere prototype) to cast her most powerful spell upon anyone who would desecrate a mound. Only the recovery of the famed bowl could rebuild the old life. [128]

In the earliest versions of the herogenic myth the future savior of the Grail rite is nowhere to be found. The king is mentioned, but is not a direct participant in the drama. His legend is told separately from the legend of the bowl entrusted to the feminine faction, but the missing cauldron eventually serves as the basis for the quest at Arthur's court. So the Grail eventually reunites the old God and Goddess as two separate hermetic themes. Any attempts to recover the golden bowl — by quest or Tain — are attempts to reestablish the balance of nature intrinsic in the fairy faith and the Star Temples. Here then, Arthur and his court united with Guenevere and her maidens are rebuilding a lost megalithic utopia with strong hints of Mithra and Cybele. In almost every sub-plot, the cauldron is linked to primal psychology and magic. [129, 130]

---

[128]Guest, C.*The Mabinogion*. Note that Amangon, the Christian, is cast as the evil doer. The story reveals the continual friction between pagans and Christians in the Dark Ages.

[129]Perceival meets the Green Knight (Hermes) at a megalithic mound (castle Green) where a ritual beheading takes place. This is a harkening to the cult of the severed head practiced by the Bronze Age Celts. In Mallory's version Arthur must pull a sword from a megalith. The Celtic warrior tradition of raiding or Tain, often on horse back, is probably the basis for the Grail quest in folklore.

[130]Wentz, W. E. *The Fairy Faith in Celtic Countries*. p. 399 fn. On April 7, 1909, Evans-Wentz found a Roman coin, dated to the reign of Marcus Aurelius and dedicated to Mithra thrown up as a votive offering to the stones at Kercado, a Star Temple in Brittany. These stones had been worshipped continuously for almost four thousand years when the coin was offered.

Monks and Troubadours

The Grail stories took on a special acceleration between 1150 and 1180, especially at the court of Eleanor of Aquitaine and at Glastonbury Abbey in Southwestern England, about thirty miles on a straight line from Stonehenge. This date range coincides neatly with the tenure of the Norman abbot, Henri Blois, whose brother, Thibault, happened to be the brother-in-law of King Louis of France, Eleanor of Aquitaine's first husband. As abbot of Glastonbury and a bishop, Blois was a consanguineous witness to political events in Paris, Toulouse, London and Champagne. Because his family were troubadours he was either a troubadour or a troubadour sympathizer, leaving no doubt that the highest possible level of intelligence passed through Blois as abbot of Glastonbury, especially when the alliance of Paris and Champagne (Capet and Blois) would directly affect Western Civilization for all time.

Under the apt guidance of Blois, the monks worked feverishly to rekindle the Grail quest as an initiation into the mysteries of Hermes and Mithra. Hermetic books of many kinds and in many languages were copied and sold. This was a lucrative trade. Pilgrims from many lands paid well for bound volumes of esoteric books, and a constant stream of pilgrims came from the Holy Land and Europe to pay homage to Glastonbury, the place where Christ may have trod and, according to thousands of testimonials, a place of miraculous cures due to the legend that Glastonbury was the final resting place of Joseph of Arimathea and the chalice used by Christ at the last supper, or, if you prefer, the chalice used by Joseph to collect the blood and tears of the saviour. [131]

---

[131]Smithitt-Lewis, Lionel. *Saint Joseph of Arimathea at Glastonbury.* Reprint 1922. London: James Clark, 1978.

To accommodate the tourist trade, prayer books were mass produced by neophytes, but the more esoteric books were copied by specialists who were sent to other abbeys to study illumination technique. Glastonbury's library was transformed into a clearing house which experienced a level of production equivalent to a small modern printing plant.

This happy pace continued until the death of Abbot Blois. Shortly thereafter the abbey fell on bad times. It was razed to the ground by arsonists sent from the Bishop of Bath, who, to quote an observer of the times, "...made it his mission to burn out wycthes and many forms of pagan idolatry." So, although it was a heinous act, we do learn from the Bishop of Bath that he thought pagan idolatry was taking place at Glastonbury.

Interestingly, there remains extant an account of monks sacrificing their lives in the fire to save a sacred book secreted within the high alter. This book may have been the secret book of the initiations of the Templars at Glastonbury. Written in Provençal French, the preferred language of the Norman patrons, it was called, in its English translation,*The High History of the Holy Grail* and is closely linked to a book titled *The Perlesvaus* which is available to us in various editions. [132]

---

[132]Scott, John *William of Malmsbury, the Early History of Glastonbury*. London: Boydell, 1981. William hints that the Knights Templars worshipped a cat's head (Lion's head) at nocturnal rites in Glastonbury's grounds. This would not be inconsistent with the fact that the Blois family enjoyed financial links to the Templars of Champagne and elsewhere on the continent. For an inventory of the books in the library at Glastonbury see: Bale, J. *Illustrium maioris Britanniae scriptorium summarium*. Being a summary of the major British illustrated scriptoria as of the Tudor period. Ipswich: 1548. In mss: Le Roux de Lincy,*Sur le Abbay de Fecamp*. Vol. 1 p. 292f. Bodliean Library, Oxford.

Guenevere and Arthur

In addition to shifting the center of clerical power from Glastonbury to Wells, where a new cathedral was underway, the fire deprived the monks of the use of the world-renowned scriptorium, mainly because it was completely gutted, and secondly it stopped the flow of pilgrims, and their tithes, to the shrine. Stories about secret rites conducted at the abbey continued long after the fire and the death of Abbot Blois. But the pilgrim's path to Glastonbury fell into disrepair and revenues to rebuild the church were not forthcoming from the crown. The only way to generate more money was to invent a spectacular drawing card, a Celtic miracle or vision with far-reaching impact. Unfortunately, the pilgrims of the era were growing wise to the simony and the dozens of fake miracles practiced by various ecclesiastics. So the monks of Glastonbury, probably in league with the King — with his own political agenda — conveniently discovered the bones of King Arthur and Guenevere in the center of the Abbey ruins.

Perhaps the announcement of the discovery of King Arthur's resting place was not a hoax. Perhaps the monks knew of the graves from a very early period. Perhaps there really was a King Arthur and he is really buried at Glastonbury, but hoax or revelation it generated many beneficial side effects for the abbey and the crown. The abbey was rebuilt in a short time by the generous donations of pilgrims, accelerated by the glimpse of King Arthur and his bride as they lay disinterred. But the discovery of the grave of Arthur also satisfied King Henry's fears that the mythical Arthur would be far more dangerous to his hold on the throne than Arthur the corpse. In Henry's seemingly paranoid imagination, King Arthur, and all that he stood for, could not easily come back to molest future Plantagenets once he was reduced to mortal status. In any case, the abbey at Glastonbury grew far larger and more

91

splendid than many of its counterparts by the turn of the thirteenth century and King Henry regained public confidence, at least for the short term. Although probably a subterfuge designed to prop up Henry's power in England, digging up Arthur and Guenevere was not far-fetched at the time. Many pilgrims actually believed Arthur was a real king and lots of folks still do. Perhaps the monks, beset by tradition, believed the bones were authentic and seized a propitious moment to reveal their treasure to the public. [133]

It is now plausible to see Glastonbury, even after it was rebuilt, as a fountainhead for the Grail literature as we know it. In the skillful hands of Glastonbury's famed scribes the lightbeam of the Star Temples became both Jesus and Phanes, the shining one or "first created" of the Greek Orphic sect. Phanes in turn was merged with Mithra and Christ as well as characters of the fairy faith such as Ossian the Irish fairy warrior from Tir na Og, or Setanta the warrior hero born of Winter Solstice. Ultimately, Arthur, commanding his many knights, each represented by a Knight of the Temple and a seat around the fairy throne, became all of these characters. Through the wondrous scribes of the abbey network, Arthur and Guenevere were well on their way to permanent installation as co-arches of the most profound source of Occidental mythology ever devised.

Because Abbot Blois was educated in the troubadour stream, and because the Angevins and Plantagenets supported alternative expressions of religion in their free thinking courts, the minstrels and poets living in and around the abbey system became the news broadcasters of

---

[133]For a general analysis of Anglo-Saxon survivals see: Bonser, Wilfrid. *Survivals of Paganism in Anglo-Saxon England.* monograph. London: John Johnson Press, 1934.

their day, and in that capacity made certain that the Round Table legends were spread across Europe. By the end of the twelfth century, the quest for the Grail and the Round Table legends were so well known to anyone who could read, that Chretien de Troyes' book of the Grail, *Le conte du Graal*. written between 1180 and 1185, became the world's first best seller. But there is another book of the Grail, an initiatory book. This "High" book was so important to the troubadours that we must concentrate on it in the final volume of this series.[134]

In the troubadour milieu Guenevere and Arthur, representing an aboriginal Atlantic Adam and Eve, and the Atlantic Genesis model, the idea that creation emerged from the union of the void and the lightbeam, were eventually spread to all strata of Western European society, even though the literature was commonly written on two levels. The courtly and educated classes could understand the story almost as non-fiction and without metaphor, but the Grail story was also a fiction, a romance, an apocryphal legend disguised as a fable for the mass market. When the books were read aloud the uninitiated would hear a *fabliaux* of magical wonders while the more advanced listeners could identify a hidden hyper-text by secret words or gestures learned only through initiation. [135]

The official church would have us believe that alternative religions were a disorganized mish-mash of confusing rites and orgiastic practices, but this was never demonstrated, except on the strength of forced confessions and spurious evidence. In reality, the ancient rites of the Grail

---

[134]Nitze, W.A. ed. *Le haut livre du Graal, Perlesvaus*. Chicago: University of Chicago Press, 1932.

[135]In Celtic poetry we encounter literary and mnemonic forms known as the "triads" which are still practiced in public festivals called *Gorshedds* in Wales and *Ard Feis* in Ireland

were at work just beneath the surface of many well-organized secret societies. The cabalistic and Neoplatonic cults consolidated their power through the knighthood during the first crusade, and continued wielding subtle influences into the Renaissance. This was made possible by the publication of a number of secret books and initiatory guides which were passed from family to family. One of these was the original manuscript of the Grail rite, known as *The High History of the Holy Grail*. Once the mysteries of the Grail were released to a wide, albeit secretive, audience the symbols were made permanent and are still with us. Christian and Judaic cabalists, from Raymon Lull, in the Spain of the crusades to Ficino,Pico della Mirandola and Bruno in the Italian Renaissance, were inspired to include elements of the Grail rite in most of their writings as they attached themselves to popular social movements in each generation. [136]

The quest stories were not aimed exclusively at an elite caste. Ideas of aesthetics and love, liberation and freedom were also attractive to farmers, small land holders and the upwardly mobile mercantile classes. To the rural populations, fired up by monks, hermits and minstrels the survival of the old gods provided a much needed source of self-esteem. To initiates and peasants alike, Arthur and Guenevere, whether they be bones on display at Glastonbury or a folk story passed down through secret societies and guilds, represented the persistence of Occidental ancestor worship and Shamanism.

Most of these secret societies were sincere, well-organized and humanistically motivated, but no matter how they differed outwardly, the sects seem to have shared

---

[136]Jung C.G. *Symbols of Transformation*. Bollingen Vol. 5, New York: Princeton University Press, 1956. p. 137-138

fundamental elements. Each of the alternative religious groups, active between the decline of the Roman Empire and the end of the Crusades, were formed for a specific social and spiritual function. They did not stand against Christianity as much as they wished to fill in for its deficiencies. The core ritual, common to many of these societies, focused on a life-giving cauldron, chalice or baptismal font, and a desire to elevate the human spirit through the understanding of the Goddess and her consort, the lightbeam god. In Gnosticism and Cabala as well as esoteric Christianity, inspiration and guidance were provided by rules of chivalry and courtly behavior — translated through Neoplatonism and Mithraism — to form a glorious literary puzzle. To the troubadours the very names of the king and queen were keys to the mysteries.

Who Doth The Grail Serve

The name Guenevere, meaning White Goddess, shares a Celtic root with "quern" a grain grinder, and the word "Queen." In Arthurian terms, referring to Queen Guenevere, the name derives in part from "Grannia", one of the Gaelic names for the Grain Goddess (Greek: Demeter; Roman: Ceres). So, in this case, we have an animistic totem evolved into a literary queen who weaves the Celtic, Roman and Greek versions of the Neolithic Goddess into one tapestry.[137]

There are many spellings of the great queen's name. The usual spelling is "Guenevere," with Welsh "Gvenour and Breton "Gwenivere" as fundamentals. The Irish spelling is "Guanhamara", pronounced like the Irish place name Connemara, where the Goddess (Bronze Age Epona) rules over

---

[137]In Mallory's version Arthur's mother is Igraine. This is phonetically close to Grannia.

herds of white ponies. In Welsh, the prefix "Gwen" means *white* and *smiling* or as an adjective *sacred*. Thus, in Wales "Gwenhwyfars" is the sacred smiling White Goddess, while in Cornwall, where another Gaelic dialect is spoken, she is all of these and also the emanation of the planet Venus under the name Gvenor. So at least in the Gaelic mind, Guenevere is the old Earth Goddess with magical attributions from the Moon and Venus. [138]

The secret and shamanic message of the troubadours, that in fact the supernatural life of man is based on animism and the worship of the cycles of nature, was picked up and echoed in architecture by the Knights Templars and the builders of the cathedrals. It must have been exciting for poets like Chretien de Troyes, who was writing actively around 1190, to stroll through a cathedral building site, knowing that many of the themes being built into the walls and stained glass windows were inspired by esoteric teachings in the troubadour and Templar underground. [139]

In the folklore of the Grail quest, as known to Chretien, Guenevere, the white Goddess, balances the world against the chaos. To the shaman, Guenevere would be recognizable as the tidal aspect of the great Mother Goddess. She wields her power through her control of cyclic, predominantly lunar, events. She is, for example, the prime force behind every eclipse. Like any strong tide she can cause havoc unless tide tables are kept, thus the need for the Star Temples as stone computers. When benevolent, she can

---

[138]Arthur, the luminous one, (the lightbeam god) would naturally be her consort. The supernatural birth of the infant Arthur, like that of Christ, was heralded by the presence of a number of stellar events. He may represent more than one of the circumpolar constellations (Bear, Plough, and Cepheus) and the sun simultaneously. Perhaps the constellations tell an evolving legend about Arthurs life and transcendence.

[139]Fulcanelli. *Le Mystere de la Cathedral*. London: Neville Spearman, 1975.

guide the questing knight (shaman) through the labyrinth, as does Ariadne in the Theseus story. But as Venus, the Eastern Star, she has more emotional appeal. In the guise of the five pointed star she can charm the shaman knight into a hopeless state of "puppy love," which she does in the Lancelot parable. [140]

As already seen, Guenevere's dance can be discerned in the *Tain bo Cullainge* as Dectine's dance around the stones of Newgrange. This stylized ritual dancing was very much a part of the troubadour tradition and is traceable to shamanic cave ceremonies. Recent research suggests that the cave painters of Lascaux were possessed of dance rituals based on heartbeat rhythms approaching seven cycles (systolic and diastolic) per second, the critical threshold at which humans enter twilight sleep. To the shaman, each animal possessed a different metabolic rhythm. The distinctive flub-dub sounds of the human heart were probably signaled separately from the rapid complex heartbeats of a deer or a dog, and each totem animal seems to have been assigned a cosmic rhythm which formed the acoustic background for an ecstatic or "hallucinatory" dance. The macrorhythms of the animals, the annual and migratory or monthly or even diurnal rhythms, were also accounted for in the dance.[141]

---

[140]Some authorities insist that Morgana and Guenevere are really two aspects of the same Goddess and that the Paleolithic Goddess was worshipped as having many attributes that were later divided amongst the tribes.

[141]Cunliffe, Barry *The Celts.* New York: McGraw-Hill, 1979. p. 48-49. The Atlantic cow woman was Bo, Boianne, Bahnba and other derivatives of the milkmaid name. She was also the river Goddess, implying a night sky river. Since the only night sky river associated with milk is the Milky Way we can assume Boinne was the Milky Way Goddess. The only Goddess situated in the Milky Way is Virgo, the harvest queen. The copper-using Bell-Beaker People, who are possibly the ancestors of the Picts, were probably the authors of the patrilineal system. The opposite bilateral or matrilineal prac-

In Atlantic Shamanism the cosmic cycle inspired the dance pattern while physiological rhythms, derived from observation of animals and humans, formulated the tempo of the dance. This rite still exists in Native American tribes, the Hopi Katchina for example, but the survival of Shamanism is not restricted to aboriginal peoples. Traces of Shamanism can also be found in isolated contemporary Celtic populations. The lifting up of snakes, something that was supposedly done in Ireland before Saint Patrick "cast out the snakes," is still performed in small sects in the Appalachians and the speaking in tongues or "glossolalia" is still performed in congregations as august as the Anglican church.

We can also see vestiges of ritual astronomy in the folk dances performed on stage at the Grand Ole Opry' in Nashville, dances performed in stars, circles and squares modified even as they were imported from Europe, but derived from everyday life on the American prairie during the Westward expansion. In England, Mexico and Sweden, and in dozens of other countries, variations on the maypole and hobby horse festivities are still seen on holidays. The conservative city of Philadelphia is proud of its annual mummers parade and little need be said about the pagan nature of Mardi Gras in New Orleans, or Carnival in Brazil. These festivities are carry-overs from ancient

---

tice seems to be associated with the more aboriginal flint-using people who were never wholly suppressed by the Indo-European caste system. If we can say the Celts were volatile partially because their lifestyle was disturbed by internal pressures from these conflicting kinship systems, we can pin-point at least one reason for the Arthur-Guenevere merger. The marriage, especially as a recreated fable, would contain extremely important sociological cues. The couple could be married in legend to set an example for the warring tribal families dotted around the countryside. Arthur was a unifier and it was probably hoped that when Arthur and Guenevere were married, the antagonisms between tribes would be put to rest.

Solstice and Equinox celebrations and are shamanic in nature. Even urban street dances with modern names like The Hammer and The Bop, The Pony, The Frug, The Chicken and The Vogue can be traced to Paleolithic mask ceremonies and retain obvious ritualistic labels. [142, 143]

Almost everything regarding the Holy Grail, Arthur, Guenevere and the Round Table can be understood as an allegory for certain pagan mysteries or what we now call ritual astronomy. From their celestial thrones, Arthur and Guenevere preside over the rites of Pentecost, May Day, Summer Solstice, Lugnasad, Halloween, and Winter Solstice. [144]

Earlier, a number of pagan festivals were mentioned, but the sheer quantity of pagan elements to be found in our modern culture is most fascinating. Mummeries with Neolithic overtones were popular enough to survive through many sources, not the least of which was Asian Buddhism arriving via the Pacific Rim. But in North America the European versions remain predominate.The spooky night of All Soul's Eve, Samhain or Halloween, usually involves a procession of masked children ceding a day each year to the goblins. In modern day England, the "Robin Goodfellow" who plays the role of The King in the mummeries, may have been an actor like those in the late medieval mystery plays. He, or a bear representing him, along with The Fool, The Queen of Night, Jack Straw, Jack-in-the-green, Schwart Peet (in Holland), Jack-O-Lantern,

---

[142]Pfeiffer, John. *The Creative Explosion*. New York: Harper, 1982 pp. 107, 210.

[143]Haddingham, Evan: *Secrets of the Ice Age*. New York: Walker, 1979.

[144]The selection of a surrogate as president of a lodge of illuminated masters is a very old concept and was surely at work within the social fabric of the monasteries which supported the Grail legends in the Dark Ages. It appears also in Mithraism.

Cupid and the Hobby Horse, still appear in greeting cards and films and remain thinly disguised versions of Atlantic totems and Aegean sky spirits. [145]

Elizabethan plays — containing many White Goddess ikons and metaphors, such as Spenser's *Fairy Queene*, Shakespeare's *A Midsummer Night's Dream* and Ben Jonson's *The Alchemist,* continue to be performed. These plays emerged from the initiation ceremonies of secret societies like "The School of Night" and the "Family of Love," two well-documented pagan sects who held private stagings for dignitaries, including the Queen.*The Fairy Queene*, being a play within a play, may have been a depiction of a mystery initiation in which the Queen actually played a role. And surely, the transformation of Falstaff into a stag in *The Merry Wives of Windsor* is shamanic.

Although the inner workings of these cliques were intense and sober, the outward appearance was often bawdy. Participants in these revels — especially wild at equinoxes and full moons — sometimes overran entire estates and villages, provoking the ire of Puritan and Calvinist writers who heaped invective upon them, calling the entire pagan revival at court "heretic in the extreme." The Calvinists were particularly aggravated with what they called "The False Trinity." To them the triple spiral, so common in early Celtic Christianity, the spiral seen illustrated in*The Book of Kells* and at Newgrange, was a pagan symbol which stood in direct competition with the

---

[145]Bord, Colin and Janet Bord. *The Secret Country*. London: Paladin, 1978. See also: *Earth Rites In Pre-Industrial England*. London: Paladin, 1977. In the traditional mummeries the herdsman or shepherd is identified with Bootes, the hobby horse or soul taker, with Epona and the Greek star deity Pegasus. The Queen of Heaven can be the Moon, Venus, Virgo or even Cassiopeia. Clearly Guenevere is all of these celestial bodies at different times.

traditional Trinity consisting of the father, son and holy ghost.

These suppressive factions spread and persisted in their hatred of the old religion, especially as it manifested itself in literature and art. John Knox, the nemesis of Mary Queen of Scots, rose to power in Scotland during the later years of Elizabeth's reign partially by equating Ovid, Aristotle and all forms of classical learning with idolatry and papism. Nevertheless, preachers like Knox could never dampen the political power of the mummeries and fairs held on festival days in the old calendar.Even more serious and radiant, the twin ikons of Guenevere and Arthur stood head and shoulders above John Knox in many parishes. Mainly because the ineffable pair were "of" the people and could not be severed from the body politik by anything as simple as fire and brimstone rhetoric.[146]

In his highest literary manifestations Arthur, the pagan King — only Christian in a cosmetic sense — is thrice crowned, identically to Hermes Trismegistus. In *The Perlesvaus,* we see the Christian Trinity, the bardic triad, and the triple-faced deity of the Celts superimposed in the three knights. By extension we can envision Arthur as a unified ikon of these three faces. Gawain is the white knight or knight of white magic. Lancelot is the knight of love, while Perceival holds the honor of omniscience.

As Arthur's fame spread through the crusades he presented many masks. In a wider and much later sense, especially in Mallory, Arthur is painted as the embodiment of his twelve knights, whom he has divided into three groups of four represented by three classic paladins,

---

[146]Rogers, John. *The Displaying of an Horrible secte of grosse and wicked Heretiques naming themselves the Familie of Love.* London: 1578. mss. Warburg Institute.

Perceival, Gawain Lancelot and Galahad. He is no longer a simple Celtic warlord. To the crusaders he was a virtual deity. To astronomers and navigators he was the star king, Cepheus or the old sun king Og illuminating the planets and warming the Earth, in a pastoral sense he was the Bear God and the lord of the lightbeam. Finally, to the alchemists, Arthur was the hermetic Fisher King, the guardian of the highest Grail secrets. To many there was never any question that his symbolic power would prevail over, or at least remain alive within, Christianity. But in spite of his exalted status Arthur was subordinate to Guenevere in the old religion. [147]

Queen of Heaven

To the crusaders, gallants and damsels at the courts of Eleanor of Aquitaine, Arthur and Guenevere were the Atlantic Adam and Eve. To the troubadour poets Guenevere was the Queen of Heaven, and Arthur was an idealized Apollo. Most other characters in the quest prose are manifestations of these two in myriad variations. As zietgiests of their people they represent a second, more sublime sphere above the mundane. But there is a third, super-celestial sphere which transcends the sun, moon and planets. In this third sphere Arthur and Guenevere become dynamic heavenly bodies, the zodiac beasts, the stars in them, the planets that interact with the suns ecliptic, the stars at the pole and the sun and moon themselves. Not only is this dyadic cosmic theater animated, it is both the source

---

[147]Scott, W. *Hermetica.* Mithra goes through three phases. There is also ample evidence that a triple figure, not directly linked to Arthur but certainly related in a mythological sense, was at the root of the rituals of the Knights Templars during the crusades, well known for worshiping a brazen head or other disembodied head referred to as Baphomet.

of animation or *primum mobilis* and the source of light or *primum lux*.

In the long run, the Calvinists were unsuccessful in eradicating the worship of Arthur because folk traditions and oral history were far too strong. The same etiology applies to Guenevere. Her ikon was the five pointed star or pentagram, the geometric mark etched by the planet Venus. Her power was felt in the tides where she was the manifestation of the moon. She was the Roman Cybele, the Irish Indo-European Tara identical to the Tara of Tibet) and Virgo of the zodiac, but she was also a star cluster. In the final resolution of the Grail mysteries she is found in the night sky, seated on a throne as Cassiopeia. In this multiple aspect, she could preside over the Grail secrets with a force equal or exceeding Arthur's and, in the eyes of the peasants of the seventeenth century she was unsuppressable. The *High History* makes no attempt to elevate Guenevere; she is already on high. If she is removed from the throne, the entire Round Table collapses. If she is disgraced, the land goes dry and a "slothful will" (involutional melancholia) drowns the king in sorrow. (Plate xix)

At the penultimate levels of the mystery, the King and Queen are cast in the stars even beyond the suns ecliptic. They are manifestations of the cosmos itself, the center of the grand scheme of galaxies and stars. Once we see Guenevere and Arthur and their courtly manifestations as constellations, we are no longer looking at simple planets in orbit or even to anything as mysterious as the Indo-European Sun Goddess or the Celtic warrior hero. Once we arrive at the constellatory theater we are looking directly into the cauldron of aboriginal "Western" cosmology, Arthur and Guenevere are the Adam and Eve of the Atlantic Genesis.

In the stellar sphere — which could be called a preview of the void — Arthur, Guenevere, the Grail, the Round Table and the tricephalic knight become the guardians of creation beyond which is unknowable emptiness. They are gods beyond which is the unnameable, unmentionable god, the pre-Celtic Tetragrammaton. This is the core of the religion of the Celts and their Atlantic ancestors, the megalith builders. It is also the final realization in the Grail initiation, an initiation so atavistic one could suspect their was an older, almost forgotten, religion at work here; perhaps something we have inherited from the Ice Ages. [148]

The Round Table in the Stars

The legends of the star king and the queen of heaven will seem like disconnected motifs if we cannot trace at least one direct link to the Grail mysteries, and the ikon of the Round Table may provide us with that link. The Grail appears to Perceival as it hovers above the Round Table. Most missions and quests begin and end at the Round Table, and it too has a celestial equivalent. In its astronomical form the Round Table is the zodiac, the ancient shaman's circle of animals illuminated by the major stars which touch the sun's ecliptic. Esoteric tradition hints that Guenevere and Arthur — Cassiopeia and Cepheus as elders of the Atlantic Genesis — moderate a court which meets at the Round Table in the stars. On Earth it is the mundane table, the heroic spiral and quest, but it can also be a storyboard in the night sky in which we see the adventures of the knights errant reflected in the stars. Except for the Grail itself, the

---

[148]Chretien may have modeled his descriptions of Guenevere on Eleanor of Aquitaine or her daughter Marie of France. See Kelly, Amy *Eleanore of Aquitaine and the Four Kings*. Cambridge: Harvard University Press, 1978 pp.100-103.

Round Table is the single most hermetic element in this family of mysterious ikons. It is the celestial realm mirrored on Earth, the ultimate hermetic metaphor:

"Heaven above, Earth below, everything over under shall show." [149]

All knights, hermits, giants, warriors, pages, and masculine spirits sitting around the table are transformed faces of the solar Arthur as he appears to progress through the night sky and various heavenly constellations. For example, the knight Gawain, who eventually sees the vision of the sword used to behead John the Baptist (the Summer Solstice lightbeam), may also be thought of as the constellation Perseus with its bright star, Marfak. In a later literary transformation, Lancelot becomes Perseus by nature of his guardianship of Guenevere come Cassiopeia.

Similar attributions can be made for each knight and hermit and whole books could be written on each. By the same rule, all queens, widows, damsels, serving girls, and witches mentioned in the Arthurian manuscripts are aspects of Guenevere. The maintenance of the Queen and Arthur in their heavenly thrones must have been one of the major daily exercises in Celtic-Christian mysticism. When translations from oral Gaelic folklore to written prose were made, probably beginning in the eighth century, the Round Table metaphor became the perfect literary device. [150]

---

[149]Festugiere, R.P. (O.P.) *La revelation of Hermes Trismegiste*. Paris, 1944. Reprint, Laffont, 1974. Prologue.
[150]This is one of the core secrets of Arthurian hermitism. Jung, C.G. *Symbols of Transformation*. Bollingin, Princeton, 1964 pp. 340-341.

The Cauldron of Greek and Celtic Myth

The mysteries of Eleusis, a temple complex near Athens, originated with the aboriginal people who populated Greece before the arrival of the Indo-Europeans. These pastoral people were aboriginal, practicing an atavistic religion probably similar to the mysteries of Eleusis and Delphi and were therefore similar to the Atlantic types who built the Star Temples to observe similar rituals. [151]

The mysteries of Persephone at Eleusis, which reached a peak around 500 BC, were similar to the rites now being reconstructed for Star Temples and henge monuments such as Newgrange, Kercado, and Stonehenge. We might therefore ask if there is not some pan-European aboriginal source for the Persephone drama, a source which may take us back to Neanderthal or Cro-Magnon rituals. In the well-documented Greek version, the Goddess Demeter and her consort Dionysus (later Zeus) are baffled by the disappearance of their daughter Persephone, abducted while in the act of gathering poppies, a simile for opium and a drugged or "swoon" state, by Pluto the lord of the underworld. [152]

In this case, Pluto is the magician of transformation (the Jungian shadow). In the mysteries, and these do connect directly to the medieval Grail mysteries, Pluto is not only a god of the dead, he — sharing with Zeus and Poseidon — is master of one third of the universe and of masculine fertility. The Greek and Celtic mysteries come into play here because the Gallo-Romans based their god Orcus, known in Roman Gaul as Dis Pater, on figures like Pluto and

---

[151]Hoffman, A. and Wasson, G. *The Road to Eleusis*. New York: Harper and Row, 1978.
[152]The use of Opium is well-documented from the Bronze Age Hallstatt culture and suspected as far back as the Paleolithic Age in Western Europe. Guenevere and Arthur echo the relationship between Demeter and Dionysus, especially when Guenevere is seen as the most powerful force.

106

Orpheus, lords of the subconscious underworld. These remained in place when the Grail and troubadour cultus began to form in Brittany in the sixth century and were widely published during the crusades. (Plate xx)

In the rituals of Eleusis, as enacted at the height of Athenian power in the Greek Golden Age, it was crucial that Pluto entice Persephone in her human form into a state of expanded consciousness. She must see more in order to understand the mystery. To do this Pluto has her drink a psychotropic substance from a special goblet, the Kykion — κψκιον — another proto-Grail. Pluto then transforms himself into *Iakchos* — Ιακχηοσ — an anthropomorphic man-fish who performs a passion play, based on ritual astronomy. This is not a strictly Atlantic ritual, clearly the man fish can be traced to Vishnu and the Vedic scriptures, but the Atlantic contribution is also apparent, especially in the transformation process and in the fact that the audience becomes an intrinsic part of the mystery. At Eleusis the spectators sing hymns to the man-fish, a figure who shows up fifteen hundred years later in the Grail literature as the Fisher King. Only Iakchos can return the maiden Persephone (essentially the vessel of the Grail) to the world of light and only the Fisher King can reveal the Grail secrets to Perceival. In pure shamanic terms Pluto, as the dark magician, carries the Goddess away, probably into a cave or mound. But ironically it is he who must undergo the transformation. In the classical scenario, Pluto is transformed into a magician of light and only he can bring Persephone back. Thus the Grail initiation is a test of transformative survival. Can the knight survive the test? Can the shaman elevate himself from atavism to humanism? Will Persephone return?

While in the central sanctuary the pilgrims to Eleusis, and presumably the Star Temples saw, and participated in, a theatrical presentation for both the greater and lesser mysteries. These experiences were almost surely enhanced by mushrooms and/or detartrated rye-ergot, (an LSD-like substance) which would produce an indelible vision in any pilgrim. They saw what Persephone saw. They saw the newborn child of the great mother held aloft by the priest or priestess, and they saw the grand symbol of the mysteries, an ear of corn emerging from its husks, allowing them to finally understand the relationship between celestial fertility and the fertility of the Earth. With this initiation they became known as epoptae — εποπται — those who have seen. [153]

Another Greek import, which bears directly on the Atlantic Genesis and the Round Table motif, shows Andromeda, the daughter of Cepheus and Cassiopeia, in the process of becoming a constellation. At first she was betrothed to Agenor — a complex hero, slain by Perseus but related to almost every known sky deity. So in Perseus, Andromeda, Cepheus and Cassiopeia we have four circumpolar constellations, equally divided as to gender, and either pair could be Guenevere and Arthur prototypes to different cultures at different times. These constellations are visible above Europe and North America and, although it is doubtful they were called by these names at the dawn of myth making, it is probable that they were used as navigational and ritual guardians at a very early period and played a massive role in formulating the Grail quest legends.

The legend of Attis and Cybele can be used to trace the Arthur-Guenevere archetype to Roman influence. This marriage stands at the core of Mithraism and is probably a

---

[153]The female child, Persephone, is Igrain-Guenevere in Wales but, she is also Demeter or Kore in the Greek and *Gore* in Gaelic. Her mound at Tara, pronounced *Terra* in Irish, via Latin influence, the Earth Goddess, has supplied archaeologists with the oldest recorded dates from that site.

ceremony performed within the cult. Like Arthur and Christ and the Phoenician Tammuz, Attis is wounded and dies, but is resurrected in the spring due to the ministrations of Cybele. Like Guenevere to Arthur, Cybele attends to Attis as part of her function as the mother of mothers, the guardian of wild things, cities and towns, nations and nature. She was also responsible for the welfare and responsible behavior of the populations of the towns and nations. During a festival held each Spring to witness the resurrection of Attis, Cybele was attended by Dactyls and Corybantes, carrying snakes and baskets of fruit, each group in competition to honor the Goddess with dancing and music.

The Grail writers, especially Chretien with his direct connections to the highest echelons of the "Courts of Love," were influenced from many directions. They documented the rituals of Asian and Roman cults and merged them with the aboriginal Atlantic legends. The Grail legends closely follow the Spring Equinox festivities which remain decidedly consistent and pagan in tone throughout Western Europe, the Aegean and the Americas. [154]

The similarities between the proto-Dionysian and proto-Celtic versions of the mysteries are obvious. Many of these festive rituals merged as if stirred in the great cauldron of Celtic myth, the cauldron which is supposed to lead to the afterlife and rebirth. Did the Medieval quest writers see the similarities spontaneously or were they shown the similarities as part of an initiation ?

Similarities between the Grail quest and the Hermetic quest for enlightenment are hinted at in both the Hermetic literature and dozens of proto-Celtic legends. Did the

---

[154]The Dionysian transformation is often confused with the transformation of Christ at Easter and may be an actual precursor.

anonymous master of *The Perlesvaus* have knowledge of Attis and Cybele, Boinne and Lugh, Cepheus and Cassiopeia as well as Mithra and the megaliths?

A Once and Never King

In spite of protestations by romantics, no convincing artifact or historical record has ever been presented and no argument has ever been constructed that would firmly establish any given "war chief" as the one and only biological Arthur. If such a *rara avis* did exist, he was, more than likely, a symbol for the territories subscribing to the religious observation of the bear totem, or a hero of the tribes that used the bear (lesser or greater) as a pole constellation.

The possibility that a Dark Age hero chief named Arthur or Ambrosius led the Celts in throwing off the Saxon yoke in AD 460, is of small importance to the Grail mysteries, since the West Saxons were dominant in the long run. No, instead of a flesh and blood Arthur we are really looking for an ancient spirit leader who returns again and again to liberate his people. Arthur, the leader of the guild hall or lodge, is in the service of his lady and his circular court, who in turn serve the people from a basin or cauldron. The queen, damsels and seneschals of the processional are the Grail bearers. The knights are the Grail seekers and each is in disguise, none less than Arthur. This is a virtual point for point recasting of the shaman's dance ritual wherein the dancers take on the attributes of totem animals.

The name Arthur is a complex pun. In shamanic terms he is the bear king, a remnant of the Ice Ages. Generally the name is derived from *arth,* the Welsh word for bear, pronounced eir-*th*. This is sufficiently similar phonetically to our Anglo-Saxon word "Earth," derived from the Frisian word *ard.* Unfortunately, the subtle and dynamic interplay between the languages as they changed one another isn't fully understood.

Could it be possible that these facets of the Arthurian logos represent a complex cycle of alpha-numerics and puns used by the bards and later troubadours to convey multiple messages in Greek, Latin, Gaelic, Breton and Provençal French? There is compelling evidence for such an assumption. The term for the high king in ancient Ireland was *Ard Ri*. In Irish the words: *athair, athar* and *aithreacha* denote father, implying both heavenly father and father of the family. As we have already seen, the name Arthur takes on the Earth Mother form in Wales when pronounced *aurthes*, spelled "arthes," meaning "she-bear." It is thus entirely possible that Arthur was the son of the she bear, the son of the cosmic star mother, at least to a clan or tribe that settled in certain regions of England and Wales. The bear totem, worshipped for two hundred thousand years on both sides of the Atlantic, could hardly be forgotten. Arthur, as the son of the bear mother, is the final manifestation of the magician-liberator in Celtic-Christian guise. [155, 156]

The Round Table legends, as lightly veiled sky myths, stood at the center of the Dark Age Gaelic revival, especially in Wales and Brittany. Arthur, as the bear hero,

---

[155]Focloir *Irish-English Dictionary*. Dublin: Talbot, 1979. p. 13. Lewis, Henry ed. *Collins-Spurrell Welsh Dictionary*. London: 1969. p. 27 *aruthr* can be expressed as an adjective meaning marvelous or strange. In other words the Welsh word "mabinogi," meaning frightening story, is a partial synonym for the word "aruthr." By combining the two meanings it may be possible to conclude that an"Arthur" was a story about the quest of the bear queen's son whose name was Arthur.

[156]This does not explain the relationship between Igrain, Arthur's mother in Malory, and the king. If Igrain is the she bear in the sky, Arthur would be a liberator king, born from the bear mother. Arthur can thus be explained, almost entirely, without recourse to Persian or Indo-European sources.

symbolized strength and a kind of compassionate natural democracy. During the strictly oral period Arthur was pagan in tone, but gradually, as the various generations refined the myth, especially in writing in the Greek influenced Breton language under the direct influence of Neoplatonism, he became a Christian, Hermetic and Dionysian hero.[157]

That the pseudo-historical Arthur was a pure fiction also comes to light in a hilarious literary pun. The Welsh word "arthur," as an adjective, is not a reference to a king or a bear, but to a marvelous and strange saga told in the old style and language. When the Welsh noun *aruther* (bear father) is expanded to the adverb *aruthredd,* meaning "violent and frightening tale," we see the complexity of the pun. It's almost like slang. Arthur is both the name of the literary form and its hero. A similar pun is relevant for the mysterious Welsh collection of stories called *The Mabinogion.* In Wales a *mabinogi* is a story, but the root word *mab* means young man or man child. The Welsh word *og* as a verb refers to cutting the wheat, but when extended as *ogof* a noun, it takes on a rather odd meaning, "ogof" means cave or cavern. If we simply put these elements together we see

---

[157]Oral traditions about the bear constellations as pole stars and migratory or navigational aids, were probably revealed at fireside story sessions in the Ice Age. The tradition of fireside storytelling extends to traditional Welsh poetry festivals, the Gorshedds. These gatherings persisted through the early Christian periods and remain part of Gaelic life into modern times. In Scotland the head man is called Bard and is elected as the poet storyteller of the year at a festival called the (Scottish) Gaelic Mod. The word Bard is also evocative of the *ard* root word, but in this case it means high ranking poet. The Arthur referred to in much of the Grail text, notably Wolfram, is the bear constellation. For a partial discussion of astrology in Wolfram and Arthur's constellatory origins in Atlantic folk myth see: Denert, Wilhelm: *Astrology in Wolfram von Eschenbach,* London: Trans. 1960.

basically what the tales were designed for and where they came from.

The famed collection of stories that make up *The Mabinogion* is derived from orally transmitted shamanic sagas of the hunt told to and about young men, possibly those entering a secret knighthood, young Celtic warriors going through a quest or rite of passage. If we were to dissect the rebus further we would see that the "ogof" or cavern is a Paleolithic cave as well as a reference to the cavernous Star Temples and megaliths which, it was believed, were the holds of the fairies which preserved all legends.

So a *mabinogi* is a tale about youths seeking the meaning of the hunt and the cave temples. Although the stories harken back to times when pure monarchs or emperors did not exist and when the Celtic world was ruled by chieftains and queens, they have clearly been adapted to fit the needs of the crusades. In other words, the stories of King Arthur, Guenevere and the Knights, and especially the quest for the mysteries of the round Star Temples, grew from these old, almost primordial legends with only cosmetic variations.

Actually, Arthur was already famous in oral tradition before *The Mabinogion* was compiled. This is brought out by the tone of the stories themselves. When Arthur is introduced he is almost passive, perhaps an omniscient narrator. The tale begins with a strange lack of fanfare. As the curtain rises the king is already on stage. He is an eternal figure, a hero who was once a god and will again become a god. The compilers of the early Breton and Welsh literature assumed their audience possessed prior knowledge of Arthur's stature as an old chieftain hero or as one of the old gods, another indication that he arrived, virtually intact, from the pre-Christian era. [158]

Since he has no established existence outside of oral tradition and since the few bones dug up by a band of desperate monks at Glastonbury remain unaccredited, and since the literature grown from Celtic tradition is fable in the first place, we must see Arthur as almost entirely totemic. Like Robin Hood, Arthur took on a meta-literary life in the public eye and, to some writers, any rationale that proves him to be real is justifiable. The fact remains that Arthur is really another name for "cosmic force." Scholars, who attempt to create an actual life for him, miss the point entirely. Arthur was, is now, and always will be an inspirational ikon and a metaphor for the lightbeam God —be he Christ, Apollo, Attis or the nameless one. [159]

The Bear Goddess

Transformations of man into hero, hero into God or God into hero; gender transformations from the proto-Celtic sun Goddess Grannia to Apollo, for example, were common in the sixth century Greco-Celtic world. In Brittany, where the Grail legends were translated from oral Welsh to written Provençal French, transformations in mask and gender were common. The Celts and Greeks who merged in Brittany in the Dark Ages, shared a social bond and could trace their roots to similar Neolithic ancestors. Both were politically subjugated by the Romans and both evolved from a bilateral kinship system, a democratic structure resurrected in Brittany in the wake of the Roman flood.

---

[158]Jones, Gwyn and L. Thomas.*The Mabinogion*. New York: Dutton, 1950.
[159]Nutt, Alfred. *The Mabinogion*. London: Dent and Sons, 1927. Nutt also uses *The Mabinogion* to contrast elements in the Grail literature. See also Nutt, A. *Studies on the Legend of the Holy Grail*. New York: Cooper Square, 1965.

In a bilateral society, both male and female naming systems are used. A child is thus known by his mother's family names as well as his father's. As we have just seen, Arthur and Guenevere can be traced, through analysis of this bilateral naming convention, to Mithra and Cybele, but more importantly they can be traced to the Paleolithic bear cult and the Great Goddess of the mounds. In creating *The Mabinogion* and the basal Grail works, the writers of the Breton Lays, like writers in every generation, simply reported on what they could see, hear and feel. In each case the literary trail wends close to a real painted cave, a henge monument, or a Star Temple. Arthur's magical sword, "Excalibur," used for the *calibration* of the old stone measurements, is pulled from a stone, while Guenevere's castle (the megalithic Star Temple) is constantly under siege. The earliest Atlantic peoples (the most likely originators of the Fairy Faith) seem to have envisioned the male force, which eventually grew into the Arthur legend, as a sunbeam, named Oc or Og. This became Och, Oak, Loc, Luk, Lugh, Lud and eventually Lucifer (Latin, light bearing). In Isaiah 14:12, Og was born from Venus, or Sirius, the Dog Star, but he is always a lightbeam deity. Oc or Og was not the sun itself but an Orphic Phanes, the condensed essence of light and the all-seeing eye which takes in that light. [160]

The deity's influence must have been immense because from this name we derive our name for the entire western world — the Occident, the world of Oc. Originally Ogmios was an eight-rayed fertilizing God, a supernatural entity governing intellect. It was he who gave the Western world Ogham, pronounced OM, the ancient Atlantic written language which was still in use when the Grail texts were trans-

---

[160]Oc also stands at the root of the Latin *octo*—eight. Connecting the old God with Ogmios the year of eight seasons.

lated from Welsh and Breton to Norman French. Ogmios, as known to the post-Roman Gauls of Brittany, was more sensate than intellectual. But as the Atlantic world ebbed eastward to the Greeks and the Aegean, OG began to blend with Mithra, the polymorph, and the Zoroastrian Ahura Mazda.[161]

In his original Neolithic form — as The Dagda or cauldron bearer — Arthur watched the human world and gave divine guidance from the blackness of the firmament. When he was translated into Arthur *rex bellorum* and immortalized in writing in the eighth century, his dreamworld provided the backdrop for dozens of mystery plays. He is, however, a capricious God and is, like The Dagda, prone to melancholia and very unreliable. He thus forces his followers to self-reliance. His only physical obligation is to impregnate the Goddess in the Star Temples. When he fails, or when the child dies or disappears, the land dies.

To rejuvenate the land he must appeal to the Goddess of the harvest and wild things. Only Guenevere, as a nature mother can save him. In order for the magic to work she must be held on high while Arthur remains earthbound and helpless. It is important to stress that the cultural balance achieved by this bizarre system is an early form of democracy, a kind of megalithic Hermetism, expressed in legend and architecture and finally manifested as the quest prose, The Round Table and the Gothic cathedral. [162]

---

[161]The highest concern of most mythologies, and resultant architectures, in the Atlantic Rim culture seems to have been liberation not suppression. Most evidence supports the idea that the Indo-European settlers were benevolent and compassionate.

[162]Towns like Narbonne, on the Mediterranean, were always Celtic in nature and most people of Albi and Toulouse were Celts. The Inquisition earmarked them for genocide because they preached against Rome and worshipped a

Guenevere and Arthur

Gradually, from the seventh century to the fourteenth, Arthur was transformed in folk tale and literature from the bear shaman to the thrice-crowned king seated on the stellar throne, much like the constellation Cepheus. By this same process, Guenevere was transformed from the Paleolithic Mother of the Void, to the harvest Goddess Grannia, or the Spring Goddess Cybele and finally to the stars of the constellation Virgo or to Cassiopeia, seated in her W shaped throne at the center of the night sky, a pole star in the same circle as Cepheus. She is obviously also akin to Andromeda the lover of Perseus. Perhaps she has more than one lover. Could this be the root for her tryst with Lancelot?

There are many natural places where we can observe the union of the God and Goddess. We find it in a rainbow, we sense their power as we timidly peer over the lip of the Grand Canyon, we see their fertility in Tibet when the peaks of the Himalayas penetrate the snow-filled clouds bringing purifying water to the Ganges and we see the union as we watch the growth of a flower or a stalk of corn. Regardless of their stellar configuration, and which myth you select to study, the two figures are linked in Occidental mythology for all time in a dyadic marriage, an ideal state of spiritual love, a state completely isolated from daily existence. But, with the exception of the Star Temples, there is only one form of architecture in Western Europe that can exactly capture this state of ecstatic union, that being the exterior and interior of a Gothic cathedral. The marriage of Arthur and Guenevere, and the spiritual fervor attached to that marriage, comes into focus best in a place

---

solar divinity, probably a Solar Goddess. Their rites were similar to Christian ceremonies, but featured a shamanic battle with chaos. The papal ligations called it a dualist heresy, but its higher secrets resolved in a profound monotheistic realization; the ultimate realization of the Albigensians was of the one God. This was probably as threatening as any heresy could be.

117

where literary themes, music, astronomy, legend and architecture are combined. Only the Gothic cathedrals allow us to observe the entire polyphony of themes so crucial to the higher learning of the Middle Ages. The cathedrals represent a knowledge network strung, like a diamond necklace, across Western Europe, and only they can reveal the final mysteries of the Grail.

Before the fall
when they wrote it
on the wall
When there wasn't even
any Hollywood,
they heard the call
and they wrote it
on the wall
for you and me,
we understood.

Steely Dan
The Caves of Altamira

THE SPIRAL IN THE STONE

In a daring paper given to the British Archaeological Society in Moscow, Vladimir Ivinski, a respected Soviet geologist, broke down multiple political barriers by demonstrating the existence of the spiral, the pentagram and other geometry at Stonehenge. Ivinski realized Stonehenge and the other monuments were built as working models of the actual solar system. [163]

According to Ivinski, Stonehenge and the earlier Star Temples, as well as numerous recumbent stone rings, were built to track geometric figures in the sky. True, each temple was a locus for tribal ceremonies — weddings, births and even funerals — but each gathering seems to have been ritualized to celebrate a kind of *sacred geometry*, the sky touching the Earth at each locus. That the sky and the Earth need to touch in order to promote harmony may seem obvious to those who follow the Celts and the Hermetic

---

[163]*London Times,* July 3, 1979. p.1f.

argument, but for newspaper readers in London, New York or Moscow, it was remarkable.

Ivinski's work was not unprecedented. In 1965, Gerald Hawkins, aided by a computer, showed how the sun would appear to be balanced on the heel stone at Stonehenge at dawn on midsummer. Most Americans hadn't heard of Stonehenge, let alone Newgrange, prior to Hawkins' research,while the British public thought the stones were druid altars. [164]

Hawkins suggested Stonehenge and the other Star Temples might have been constructed to serve as agrarian computers, but Ivinski went further. The Soviet scientist agrees the megaliths compose an ancient stone computer network, but he thinks the computers were used to plot celestial graphics, geometric shapes which could be traced out by human motion on Earth, perhaps for processionals or for other magical ceremonies. To prove this, Ivinski used a large computer to correlate the motions of the planets with the locations of the henge monuments and he claims the ancient temples remain capable of tracing geometric patterns to the present day.

Ivinski found true celestial geometry in every site he studied. The numerous mounds and rings he investigated spun out pentagrams, octagons, and conical sections in consistent geometric signatures. Not only did Ivinski support Hawkins' research, he claimed the computer language underlying the Star Temples was founded on the size and shapes of the orbits using a heliocentric model, five thousand years before Copernicus. Ivinski's six-year survey found hidden geometric figures in the stone arrangements, geometry which correlates with the actual planetary orbits within a one percent margin of error. He felt that various

---

[164]Hawkins, Gerald. *Stonehenge Decoded.* New York: Doubleday, 1965.

megalithic sites were dedicated to a given planet, star or constellation. In Ivinski's scheme, Stonehenge is dedicated to Venus as well as the sun and the moon. Hawkins also found Venus correlations at Stonehenge. Alexander Thom has tracked the moon in almost every phase at dozens of sites and Newgrange displays many different geometries. Each monument displays a spiral in some form so, based on this preliminary data, it seems the spiral or triple spiral, probably as a form of labyrinth, is a basal form, perhaps even a common denominator. [165]

The Spiral Path

The original version of Stonehenge and its surrounding monuments was probably built in response to a population explosion. As the Bronze Age began, as metal tools came into play and as trade with a wider variety of cultures grew common, the need for magnificent structures, incorporating the technology of the Irish and French temples with the architecture of the central continental groups became paramount. The tribes needed a larger, more secure and inland place to entertain envoys from the Greeks and

---

[165]Thom, Alexander. Megaliths and Mathematics. *Antiquity*, 40, 1966 121f
—*Megalithic Lunar Observatories*. London: Oxford, 1971.
—and Thom A. S. *Megalithic Remains in Britain and Brittany*. Oxford: Oxford Press, 1978.
—"The Standing Stones in Argyllshire," *Glasgow Archaeological Journal* 6 1979: 5-10.
—"A New Study of All Lunar Sightlines," *Archaeoastronomy* JHA Supplement 2, 1980: S78-S89. Extensive research in Spain has not been conducted due to suppression by the Franco regime and church politics, but studies sponsored by the EEC and the monarchy are now underway. Preliminary studies indicate that Iberian megalithic measurements differ insignificantly from Irish and Breton sites. Las Millares in southeastern Spain and the temples at Tarxien, Malta (Goddess temples with centrally placed basin stones intact) seem to be part of this network extended into the Mediterranean.

Phoenicians, and to stage gala markets and festivals. The Star Temple would no longer be a small, seaside meeting hall. It was now a cathedral.[166]

In the early twentieth century the public of Western Europe and North American believed the stone circles were Druid sacrifice pits. It was difficult for "proper" people to accept the idea that a pre-Celtic peasant, who wore skins and lived in a crude thatch, could possibly develop an astronomic sense or a standard measurement, but the first builders of Stonehenge and Avebury did just that.

Research has come a long way at Stonehenge. We know it was built in at least three stages by many generations. It was dormant for a time between the Neolithic and the early Bronze Age and then rebuilt and inhabited by a new tribal group. We know it tracks the planets and stars. We know it has solar and lunar systems built into it and we know it was a place of ritual. Although Stonehenge is now open, it might have been thatched in its original form and the lightbeam would have been admitted through slits in the roof. We also know that many megalithic sites are connected to Stonehenge by lay lines and straight tracks, almost as if the old roads were set up in a radial navigational grid.

The idea of straight tracks was brought to light just after World War I by a diligent lay-scientist named Alfred Watkins, an engineer who owned a meter company in Herefordshire. Watkins' research into the nature of ancient

---

[166]Castleden, Rodney *The Stonehenge People*. London: RKP, 1987. p. 259. It is a simple deduction that tribes of all kinds came to Stonehenge for feasts and trade. Castleden finds it difficult to accept his own conclusion that at least one million people inhabited Britain at the end of the Neolithic. Some observers believe his figure is conservative.

nature of ancient trackways would have gone unnoticed if he had not published a number of books. [167]

Watkins and his supporters felt the Straight Tracks were important because, if they did actually exist they would prove, beyond a shadow of a doubt, that the megalith builders were skilled land and sea navigators, possibly even heliocentric in outlook, and that most megalithic sites were lesser or greater nodes in a vast communications network.

Although his views were not acceptable to academia, a number of his readers formed pen-pal groups, called "Postal Clubs," especially in Southwestern England, to keep an eye out for any irregular aspect of the landscape. Post-cards were sent back and forth between members to communicate their finds, and thousands were sent directly to Watkins who cataloged them for future study. Of the hundreds of *official* archaeological projects mounted in the later half of the twentieth century — many of them rescue missions moving in slim advance of the cement and tarmac spreaders — not one has dealt directly with Watkins' hypothesis. [168]

An Eternal Quest

As stated in the introductory chapter, one key to the Grail mysteries lies in the basin stones in the Star Temples. These strange objects may be the prototypes for the baptismal fonts in the great cathedrals. They can take the form of an actual cauldron or a simple indentation called a cup and

---

[167]Watkins, Alfred. *The Old Straight Track*. Reprint, 1921. London: Garnstone, 1973. and *The Ley Hunters Field Guide. Hereford:* Watkins Meter Company, 1927. out of print, in British Museum.
[168]If Ley Lines are real they are quantifiable by their width, length, and frequency of important sites. For French Straight Track based on Neolithic salt routes see: Guichard, Xavier. *Eleusis Alesia*. Paris-Abbeville: Francois Paillart, 1936.

ring mark. Stonehenge displays two small examples in the recumbent "altar stone" and a number running along the top of the cap stones.

The preliminary ritual at Newgrange and Avebury, Stonehenge and Carnac seems to be based on a spiral peregrination between temples, in an almost reptilian fashion. The processionals at Eleusis near Athens and those reconstructed at Chartres echo this megalithic parade. Each participant moved with the planets against the background stars as well as the Earth and moon as they circled the sun. Each of these events was also marked in a reflecting pool or well adjacent to the temple. [169]

The quest for perfection, symbolized by the spirals carved on the megaliths, usually practiced at spas or holy wells, combined with divinatory magic, has existed around the world for a very long time. Shinto priests, Zen Buddhists and Arabic Sufis seek the same state of consciousness. Christ's ordeal at the stations of the cross is just such a quest, predicted by prophecy and symbolically played out. [170]

The Water Witch

In the 1940s, a retired civil engineer and dowser named Guy Underwood made a number of important discoveries in the decipherment of Star Temple locations. His only

---

[169]Meautis, George. *The Mystery of Eleusis*. Benares: Theosophy Press, 1932. Jung, C.G. *Aion, researches into the phenomenology of the self.* Princeton: Bollingen, 1959.

[170]Nasr, S.H. "Sufism and the Perenniality of the Mystical Quest," *Studies in Comparative Religion*, Autumn, (1970). The Sufi's and Cathars dressed alike. For a description of Albigensian dress at the time of the crusade, especially the similarity in the dervish costume see: Nelli, Rene *Le Phenomene Cathare*. Toulouse: Privat, 1964. See also Colin, R. *A Theory of Celestial Influence*. New York: Sam Weiser, 1987. and Niel, F. *Montsegur, The Mountain of Inspiration*. Paris: Atlier Grenoble, 1967.

major work, entitled *Patterns of The Past,* is nothing short of astonishing. Underwood confirms the megaliths were laid out by water wand techniques even before the solar and lunar coordinates were considered. This could mean that the builders believed, as did the shaman of the Paleolithic Age, that heaven and earth were connected at certain perfect locations marked by underground water systems which acted in a spiral fashion. Building a Star Temple on one of these locations would thus bring life to both heaven and the underworld and would naturally produce magical environmental "feelings" and a balanced spirit of place. This is fundamental to the oriental art of "Feng Shui", or tracking the dragon energy, and the ancient Occidental art of "Geomancy", or landscape reading, and bringing the earth spirit into harmony with the celestial spirit. Underwood pointed out that the Star Temples brought the heaven and earth elements into harmony by uniting astronomy with the energy of the artesian watercourse.[171]

As expected, the pattern often described in Underwood's survey was a complex spiral, or a spider-like shape with radials sent out from a central focus. Underwood did not travel to Ireland or France, but surveys have been conducted by world-renowned dowsers from many nations and all confirm Underwood's thesis. So we can arrive at the tentative conclusion that some form of dowsing or water witching was probably used to survey most true Star Temple sites before major building commenced. In some cases the dowsing would be unnecessary since the sites were often used as temples long before permanent buildings were erected. The triple spiral at

---

[171] Hood, Thomas. *The Use of Both Globes, Celestial and Terrestrial.* Oxford: Ashmolean Mss. 1592. Graves, Tom. *Needles of Stone.* London: Garnstone, 1981. Underwood, Guy. *The Pattern of the Past.* London: Abacus 1989.

125

Newgrange may be a paradigm of the cosmic forces exerted on the water ways beneath the temple. [172]

The language of the spiral, the symbolism of the rotary cycles of nature and the Grail in stone, suggests the Boyne Valley and the Severn-Cotswold people knew the Earth's energy was intimately concentrated in the course of inland waterways and that this energy arose from subsurface aquifers, referred to by Underwood as "aquastats" and blind springs. He also discovered that Stonehenge and Salisbury Cathedral were built above complex spiral underground water channels.

Copies of the spirals Underwood discovered were often etched into stones found around the Star Temples, the triple spiral at Newgrange for example. At Chartres, the labyrinth betrays a similar water pattern. Oddly, the well beneath is exactly as deep as the roof is high, or stated obversely the labyrinth floats equidistant from the bottom of the well and the peak of the roof. (Plate xxi)

So these various architectural phenomenon from widely separated eras portray the hermetic riddle in stone. When viewed separately they remain curiosities, but when viewed as a whole they reveal a connecting link between the subterranean and super-celestial worlds and a third link between the first two worlds and man's ability to decipher them and communicate the results in a non-verbal hypertext. In other words, to the Gothic architect and his predecessor, the Star temple builder, the action of the spiral and the telluric earth forces beneath and above it, was evident in everything and to him this was the godly paradigm that needed preserving, not the crucifixion, although that ikon might reveal the same thing. In the builder's mind every observation could be reduced to this simple pattern. Thus the spiral, and

[172]Roberts, Jack. *Exploring West Cork.* Skibbereen: Key Books, 1989.

especially the triple spiral, grew to represent the ultimate symbol of dynamic celestial motion. (Plate xxii)

This same hermetic spiral — in its position equidistant between heaven and the underworld — can also be found in the Atlantic Genesis. It can be seen in the Indo-European story of Gilgamesh, in the myth of Theseus, and within the Holy Grail legends. It is also the way the universe appears to behave when observed from a fixed point on Earth. The spiral then is the key to ritual astronomy and the quest myth, the central ikon which unlocks the mysterious symbolic language of the Grail, a language which has been transmitted through ceremony and dance for at least six millennia. [173]

Maypole and the Hobby Horse

The ceremony of the spiral labyrinth, the quest for water and food, to say nothing of the need for reassurances about fertility, are linked to the phallic Maypole. [174]

The populations of Western Europe and North America still tune in to the spiral action of the Earth's spin while dancing around a Maypole. Each year the women of the prestigious Bryn Mawr College (founded by the Quakers in 1885 near Philadelphia) to this very day erect and dance

---

[173]Neugebauer, O. *The Exact Sciences in Antiquity*. 2d ed. New York: Praeger, 1969.

[174]Bord, Colin and Janet Bord. *The Secret Country*. London: Paladin, 1978
—*Earth Rites In Pre-Industrial England*. London: Paladin, 1977. p. 182. The Puritans were successful in having the maypole festivities curtailed in 1644. This restriction lasted until 1660 when the Maypole was reinstated by the monarchy (Charles II) and by an act of Parliament. The Maypole traditions continue today. The author saw a Jack-In-The-Green parade in London in 1973 and a massive maypole celebration in Stern Grove, San Francisco, in 1979. For an analysis of the process of curtailment by both Catholic and Anglican churches see: Thomas, Keith. *Religion and the Decline of Magic*. London:Weidenfeld & Nicolson, 1971. pp. 577-578.

around a multi-colored Maypole. The flower laden streamers, and the pole are symbolic of the spiral forces of nature leading to fertility. [175]

In the period after the fall of Rome, the Celtic festivals came back to life in the form of mystery play. These ceremonies continued the gnomon and shadow dials of the megaliths as the Maypole while adding elements of the Roman Saturnalia, the Greek Orphic mysteries — surrounding the Green Man — and of course Christianity. In the maypole spiral, the players follow a lunar course, first "widdershins" or contrary to the sun, then with the sun, then against it again on and on, weaving the ribbons as they go. The Hobby Horse was also used and numerous pagan masks were worn. These parades grew in intensity and popularity well into the Middle Ages. The Abbots of Glastonbury and the builders at Chartres could hardly have been ignorant of such festivities and the troubadours encouraged them as part of the reform movement hidden within the Cabala and the writings of Hermes. [176]

The continuity of proto-Celtic Atlantic rites went on throughout the centuries. The plays of Shakespeare — whoever he was — were performed in the Globe, a temple-like theater which was a model of the universe in miniature. Plays such as *The Tempest* were greatly influenced by the Fairy Faith, which was a kind of stylized Shamanism defined in in fantastical terms. As mentioned earlier,

---

[175]The totem poles of the Northwest serve a similar purpose. To the Tlinket and Kwakautil people the poles are the pillars of heaven. They point to the Pole Star and to the abode of the ancestors.

[176]Bonser, Wilfred: *Survivals of Paganism in Anglo-Saxon England.* Oxford: Monograph, 1934. For a full discourse on Pagan survivals see: Wind, Edgar *Pagan Mysteries in the Renaissance.* rev. ed. New York: W. W. Norton, 1968. And: Seznic, Jean *Survival of the Old Gods.* New York: Harper & Row, 1961. For a discourse on the Green Man see: Anderson, William *Green Man.* San Francisco: Harper/Collins, 1990.p-38-43

Falstaff's stag transformation — Falstaff is the Celto-Saxon Hern the Hunter; a combination of Nodens and Hu Gadran — in *The Merry Wives of Windsor,* was first performed for a Garter initiation. Additionally, a few of the plays were written for Elizabeth's visits to the country estates of her courtiers. *A Midsummer Night's Dream* was clearly inspired directly by the old pagan faith, Hermetism and Mithraism. In this play within a play, Titania, Queen of the Fairies, laments:

> *"...the fold stands empty in the drowned field, And crows are fatted with the murrion flock. The nine men's morris is fill'd up with mud, and the quaint mazes, in the wanton green for lack of tread, are undistinguishable. The human mortals want their winter here. No night is now with hymn or carol blest. Therefore the moon (the governess of floods), Pale in her anger, washes all the air."* [177]

Here again the Hermetic theme appears at the center of human events. [178]

In rural societies of Shakespeare's time the population, as a whole, could fall from grace in a few weeks if famine, pestilence or war caused a violent change in the flow of daily events. To harmonize humans with nature mazes and labyrinths, such as the Nine Men's Morris mentioned in *A Midsummer Night's Dream,* were traversed by everyone in the village. These plays and mummeries are initiation tableaux while the stag dance, the maypole, the hobby horse and the Jack-O-Lantern are obvious carry-overs from Paleolithic hunting rituals, rituals which provide a firm basis for the quest for the Grail. (Plate xxiii)

---

[177]Evans, G.B. (ed.) *The Riverside Shakespeare,* New York: Houghton-Mifflin, 1985. p. 227 Line 95-104.
[178]A ceremony called "Blowing the Stag," is still performed at Canterbury, each year.

In other words, both the play and the peregrination around the temple are intrinsic parts of the overall ceremony. At Brug na Boinne in Ireland, pilgrims gathering on the banks of the Boyne river were lead on a snake like journey, first across the river then to one or more meditative groves or nature sites and finally into the precinct around Newgrange or Dowth or Knowth (depending upon the time of year) wherein a theatrical presentation was made and the lightbeam was observed. Similar ceremonies were performed at Eleusis, outside Athens. Likewise, the Nazca Indians on the high deserts of Peru drank a potion made from the juices of an hallucinatory cactus and traced huge animal effigies to commemorate the constellations. Incas, Mayans and Aztecs did the same with their own jungle animals.

This spiral peregrination theme was carried through over thousands of years to the Arthurian literature and the quest of Grail knights. In one classic example, Sir Gawain travels for many days and nights only to reach the castle of the Fisher King where he sees a processional with the Grail at the center. The Grail is filled with a life giving substance, probably an organic psychedelic.

There are many examples of the quest ending in the consumption of a mind altering drug. In Navajo tradition the drug is Peyote. In Africa the Dogon use Ibogaine after a quest initiation. In Polynesia the quest ends and begins with a drink from the Kava-Kava bowl. The quest sequence takes place today in urban environments as fans make their way through many reversals and difficulties to take part in massive hallucinatory celebrations called rock concerts. In each case the pilgrimage or quest and the final epoptic vision bear uncanny similarities to the quests undertaken by the knights, particularly Gawain and Perceival. Mummeries and pageants of a pagan nature reached a peak in the Italian and English Renaissance where they caused a furor in the church, but they must have possessed some long-range impact since our present holidays, based on the changing light of the year, remain true to the pagan mysteries. [179]

Three Treasures at Chartres

The quest over a spiral maze now brings us to the greatest cathedral of all time. It has long been rumored that the grand Gothic cathedral at Chartres is built upon three secret treasures. What these treasures are and whether or not they are real or supernatural remains to be seen, but a larger mystery does emanate from Chartres. Chartres, located in the virtual center of France, can be seen for miles when approached from the north. It too houses a spiral maze. No one could enter from the main portico without crossing the labyrinth, and, it is said, that by traversing the labyrinth the pilgrim could lift his or her spirits to a state of grace, especially when accompanied by chanting. [180]

Chartres, like other cathedrals in the Gothic network, seems to incorporate direct influences from the megaliths and from Tarot, alchemy and Cabala. The belief that most abbeys and cathedrals were located over ancient wells, and were built above Star Temples, has been borne out by excavations. Unpublished digs sponsored by the diocese and the Vatican have found ancient megaliths beneath the original foundation. This supports the idea that the cathedrals were, at least in part, evidence of the survival of megalithic ideas in Christianity. [181]

---

[179]The next time you eat a fish you caught yourself, or your dog barks at an intruder, or you pick an apricot from a tree, or you spice a dish with Tarragon grown in your window box, try to remember your roots as a hunter-gatherer.

[180]The state of grace I speak of here is equivalent to what Abraham Maslow called "Peak Experience." Maslow, Abraham. *Religious Values and Peak Experience*. Boston: Brandeis Press, 1962.

[181]Charpentier, Louis. *Le Jacques et le Mysteries del la Compestella.* (Paris: Laffont, 1972.

The official name of the cathedral is *Notre Dame du Chartres,* indicating the influence of the Virgin on the builders, but the structure is not entirely Christian. The name "Chartres" is an anagram for Cathars, the ancient pagan sect that later became known as the Albigensians. Chartres is traditionally known as the "Bishop's Seat," but this is a Christian gloss and a political definition. The creation of another Bishopric or a special house for the Bishop could hardly have been the sole intention of the builders, since the cathedral is one of the most elaborate and costly in Europe. Chartres is more architecturally significant than any castle in the area and could easily house a king, and although Medieval Bishops often wielded the power of kings, they were none the less under the secular control of the Vatican whereas a king answered to no one, at least in theory. This small sociological discrepancy leads one to take another look at the place name. [182]

The French word "charter," is derived from the Latin *carrus*, meaning "wagon." Adding the "s" makes the word plural. The suffix *tres* in old French means great or huge, while in Latin it means triple. Here then we have a bilingual pun meaning "triple great wagon." Why would architects, who were obviously inspired by the highest ethics, call their finest creation a treasure wagon ?

One answer may appear in a *bas relief* on a column supporting the south porch at Chartres. Here we see an actual treasure wagon, pulled by oxen, carrying The Ark Of the Covenant with its top open. The contents are visible: a Grail-like monstrance, scrolls or tablets, said to be the tablets brought down from the mountain by Moses, and a rod, possibly Aaron's Rod used for magic and as a measuring standard. One Masonic legend tells us that the

---

[182]Sede, Gerard. *The Treasure of the Cathars.* Paris: Jullier, 1957.

treasure chest sacred to the Hebrews was brought to Chartres by a group of Knights Templars who located it buried beneath the stables of Solomon's Temple in Jerusalem, but is the Ark buried at Chartres or is the legend a metaphor for an esoteric initiation? [183] (Plate xxiv)

These questions cannot be answered superficially, but clues do exist. Every statue and carving at Chartres, and at any of the Gothic temples, was placed with extreme care. No carving or panel was simply thrown up at random. The saints are in sequence, the kings and queens are in their proper chronological order and the philosophers are located in one area. We can also assume that the Templars, if they did return the Ark and the cup given to Abraham by Melchizedek, would not advertise it directly. It was not, even then, designed for public consumption. What better way to display it than to have it depicted on the porch adjacent to the summer solstice sunbeam event.

The sunbeam does enter Chartres, precisely at noon on the summer solstice and just after dawn on the Winter Solstice. This has been observed by thousands of people. The summer beam is created by the admission of light through a lead wedge acting as a lens. The window stands above two empty columns, said to be Masonic in nature and representing Joachim and Boaz. The right column is decorated with a *fleur-de-lys,* the left with a three-leafed shamrock, both updated versions of the triple spiral motif. These columns stand at the end of a colonnade which supports an iron keyhole sundial, once decorated with gold, silver and quartz crystals. As the beam enters, the pilgrim sees that it is angled downward by the Earth's motion and strikes the floor near a brass stud — once a large sundial or inscribed plate — and then moves slowly across the floor toward the

---

[183]Horne, Alex. *King Solomon's Temple.* Los Angeles: Wilshire, 1974.

south porch. In the winter orientation the entry window for this beam is situated immediately adjacent to the south porch, and the now diffuse beam actually strikes the column displaying the carving of the treasure wagon as it leaves the cathedral. Evidently we are looking at an ancient architectural language cast in stone.

At Chartres the builders, some with well documented reputations like Villard de Honnecourt, are unquestionably trying to send us coded messages across the centuries. The lightbeam phenomenon, traceable to the Star Temples and to the painted caves, can also be seen at cathedrals in Florence, Bologna, and dozens of other locations on summer solstice and equinox dates. (Plate xxv)

Since Chartres was built on a known megalithic ring, we can assume that a Solstice and/or equinox beam has been leading pilgrims to that site for at least five thousand years. This is not a mere fantasy. As mentioned earlier the French word *tresor* translates as treasure, and by a slight stretch, it is a pun meaning "the wagon with three treasures." The English word "map" translates into French as "carte" so, by combining *carte* with *tres* and making the "h" silent we solve the rebus as "The map to the triple treasure." Could the lightbeam at Chartres be one of the treasures? Could the cathedral of *Chartres* be a triple map of the inner human universe, a map of consciousness, an early map of the human mind based on number and proportion? Could this be a link to the inner teachings of the Atlantic cosmology and the triple spiral at Newgrange or the triple layered labyrinth on the tor at Glastonbury, the tricephalic god of the Celts or even a link to all of these mysteries? More importantly, could it be a clue to the identity of the strange

134

ikon worshiped by the Templars or the triple crown worn by Hermes Trismegistus and Arthur? [184]

Critchlow and others have argued that the Gothic cathedrals, especially Chartres, are scale models of the universe, at least the universe as perceived by the architects of the Middle Ages. At Chartres, the triple spiral starts with the two main towers, one dedicated to the Sun, the other to the Moon, while the floor plan reflects the Tree of Life from the Cabala. Here also, we find the alchemical marriage between the moon Goddess and the God of light, consummated in the midst of the temple. The third dimension, the womb of the Goddess, the consciousness of the *supra-celestial void,* is symbolized by the massive vaulted interior of the cathedral, just as it is at Newgrange and Knowth. [185]

Although it is not the largest Gothic cathedral — Amiens owns that distinction — Chartres is a direct extension of the literary riddles and initiations of the Middle Ages and is, in every respect, a treasure house. [186]

The Quest Through the Labyrinth

Cathedrals like Chartres were designed to bombard the human senses and to lift the spirits to the ultimate

---

[184]Fulcanelli. *The Mystery of the Cathedrals.* London: Neville-Spearman, 1973 and Johnson, Kenneth Rayner. *The Fulcanelli Phenomenon.* Jersey: Neville Spearman, 1980. Fulcanelli contends that the secrets to alchemy are carved into the stones and stained glass of the cathedrals.

[185]Critchlow, Keith.*Time Stands Still.* New York: Saint Martins Press, 1982

[186]The zodiac is depicted in quatrefoils on the main porch. A number of Asian philosophers, perhaps Buddha, Lao Tsu, Confucius and Manes, may have been prominent sculptures on the main facade until they were destroyed by the Inquisition. The face of Baphomet, the Templer's guardian angel, (the lion headed Mithra) appears in the hexagram at the center of an inverted pentagram in a rose window in the left apse.

realization of God — or the Goddess — as a divinity of void, light and color. Visitors often report hearing colors and seeing sounds as music or light reflect from the scalloped surfaces of the columns. These synesthetic experiences are most frequently reported by those who have stood at the center of the great maze in the narthex, formed by black and white tessellated pavement stones in alternate settings. On the Spring and Autumnal Equinoxes, the huge radial window in the main transept at Chartres filters both morning and evening light through twelve fabulous glass panels, twelve windows which, by their number, suggest the signs of the zodiac. If one were able to visit the cathedral each day for a single year and draw a chalk mark on the floor near the maze, where the sun's rays strike the pavement, at year's end the marks would form a spiral, imitating the dance of the planets as they speed through the zodiac. [187]

Further similarities between the megalithic temples and the cathedrals can be noted. During certain solar events the radial window, like the roofbox at Newgrange, takes on a function unnoticed at other times. On these special occasions, the light shines through the stained glass, shifts spectrum, projects different colors and dances across the floor in a narrow beam which exactly strikes the maze. The window becomes a focal lens. Is this not identical to the light-beam at Newgrange and Knowth? Is this a coincidence or did the architects take inspiration from the megalithic builders? (Plate xvi)

The pilgrim's coil at Chartres, like many Gothic spirals, was called *La Lieue* or *The League* by its designers. The

[187]Critchlow, Keith, Jane Carroll and Llewylyn Vaughan-Lee. *Chartres Maze: a model of the Universe?* London: RILKO, 1975. I must stress that the sun does not rise or set and that the idea of a sunset is a misnomer.
—*Order in Space.* London: Thames & Hudson, 1970. p. 27-41 and 111-119.

exact center of the maze was often thought of as Jerusalem, a reference to the goal of the crusades and a certain "New Jerusalem," meaning the re-establishment of the old harmony between earth and heaven as defined in *Revelations,* the final book of the Bible. How old can only be guessed at, but there is room to investigate the possibility that the architects were addressing the concepts of Neoplatonic and Gnostic thinkers like Philo of Alexandria, Origen and other early masters, who were, in turn, addressing themselves to the builders of the pyramids and the megaliths. Is it a coincidence that the huge temple of Karnak in Egypt and the stone alignments at Carnac in Brittany have the same name?[188]

At Chartres and Amiens, to name just two magnificent examples of maze architecture, the quest for spiritual perfection reached a high point when the pilgrim walked through the Royal Portal, pausing to see Christ, surrounded by the animals of the zodiac and the New Testament, emerging overhead from a Vesica Pisces in the tympanum of the central bay. Once inside he or she would walk through the pastel lightbeams cast by the great circular windows on the way to the center of the labyrinth. Once at the center, the pilgrim was allowed to pause briefly to view a shrine containing a scene of cryptic beauty, something from Greek mythology, the Minoan minotaur in brass, gold, silver and jewels on an inscribed disk or the sacred chalice used by Christ. This same ritual took place at Glastonbury as the

---

[188]The French word *Lieue* is derived from the Gallo-Celtic, mile or *Lieuva* consisting of fifteen hundred paces. By the time the spiral floor at Chartres was laid the Lieuwe was no longer used in France. The architects must have used this measurement for a specific reason, namely to reestablish and preserve the old Celtic measurements which were probably based on the Neolithic measurements made permanent by the Star Temples and the distances between them.

pilgrims climbed a spiral to the chapel at the top of the tor, there to view a scene of remarkable mystery. (Plate xxvii)

Although commonplace today, the idea that the sun was at the center of the planetary system was very mysterious in the twelfth century. Apparently the architects of Chartres knew the sun stood still at least four hundred years before Copernicus. Is it possible that a simple teaching, having to do with a semi-heliocentric model, manifested in temple architecture, was carried through Western Europe for more than five thousand years? Was this the secret teaching of the Grail at Chartres, or is there more?

The labyrinths in the Gothic cathedrals were put in place for a specific initiation, probably a ceremony derived from an extremely esoteric and ancient rite. We might call this the Grail rite but it was forced underground as the suppressive forces within the church grew. Only the most militant Knights Templars were able to practice their version of Mithraism — wherein the Celtic tricephalic god was transformed into a cat-like creature known only as Baphomet. Yet even the powerful Templars were forced underground after the tragic death of their charismatic leader, Jacques De Molay, at the close of the fourteenth century. But all was not lost. The legacy of the Grail and the influence of the Templars remained on display for each and every citizen.

By the mid-fifteenth century, books derived from manuscripts mentioning both the Grail and King Arthur, were printed and circulated far and wide. Wandering monks taught reading and mathematics while on pilgrimages to megalithic shrines taken over by the church. [189]

As the fifteenth century drew to a close, millions of liberated citizens, newly empowered by their reading and

---

[189]Barber, M. *The Trial of the Templars*. Cambridge: Cambridge University Press, 1980.

mathematical skills sought upward mobility. Most became merchants, creating a burgeoning middle class, but a few adventuresome souls progressed into the higher realms and read forbidden material, even with the threat of the Inquisition, hanging over them. And the Inquisition was not without its stultifying effects. As each new generation of readers came on line a new rationale for suppression was invented. In the fifteenth century the spiral labyrinths of the cathedrals became so disused, and the public leaders fell so deeply into spiritual ignorance, that one Canon Jacquemart ordered the octagonal maze at Amiens torn up because it encouraged children to play hopscotch during mass.

From this point on the initiation within the church, the worship of the Christian Grail and the aboriginal Grail in the same ceremony came to an end. The gradual processional within the mass would be purged, if possible, of any pagan meaning. The maypole dance would be separated from the church rituals by time and mileage. The spiral quest — the megalithic journey, and ultimately the imitation of Christ's journey to Golgotha — could no longer be conducted in the cathedral. But elsewhere, in special rooms built within private houses, or on special occasions in rural villages, the quest — the spiral dance, the nostalgia for the Celtic cattle raid or Tain — continued, ofttimes as a children's festival, somewhat like a rock concert.

Totenkopf

Many game forms originate in spirals found in the cathedrals which, as we have seen, took inspiration from the snake-like processionals of the Druids and Bards around oak groves. In ancient Ireland, a "pattern" or large spiral migration to the Star Temples (later supplanted by pilgrimages to holy wells and shrines) took place every year around Lugnasad or November first (Samhain or

Halloween). This pilgrimage would begin in hundreds of villages, taking on larger and larger groups as it pressed closer to the shrine. Both adults and children met, fought, exchanged gifts. They also danced, drank and sang as they went. One of the central attractions at these meetings was tap dancing, a game not unlike hopscotch. In the tap dancing events, the players would cast a die or toss a bean bag to determine the number of skips required. The player would then literally tap dance around the scaled down maze. [190]

The spontaneous play of children in the treading path, or maze, such as the Nine Men's Morris or around the Maypole, represents the folk memory of extremely ancient rituals. Even today the children of Europe and America play hopscotch games which can be traced, under slightly different names and circumstances, to the megalithic processionals of the Bronze Age and earlier. In France, a game called *Escargot du Paradis* — Paradise Snail — is played along a spiral laid out in chalk or sand. In Germany, the identical game is called *Totenkopf* — Deadhead. [191]

The Secret of Westminster Abbey

The labyrinth of Westminster Abbey in London, also known as the "Presbytery Pavement," built by the Cosmoti Masonic brotherhood in the thirteenth century, presents a number of riddles similar in nature to the Chartres maze. The Cosmoti specialized in mosaic inlays and spiral staircases, and their work, especially in Italy, is masterful. An

---

[190]Joyce, P.W. *Concise History of Ireland*. Dublin: M.H. Gill, 1915. Awards were given to the best dancers. Other festivities like athletic contests and horse racing were included. Bare knuckle boxing matches held at these events were called "Pattern Fights." The fights were often little more than grudge matches between clans.
[191]"Double Ladder" and "Shoemaker" are also names for spiral hopscotch games, played on pavement stones and sidewalks.

early cadre of this order may have been the original builders of the Chartres labyrinth. In England, they were brought to Westminster to do special work by the Benedictine order, but no single Cosmoti craftsman was allowed to sign his own name to any project. The style was recognizable enough. [192]

Most of the monarchs of England have been crowned and anointed on the presbytery pavement since it was first laid in 1280. This is significant because the geometry of the mosaic floor at Westminster links the crowning ceremony to the quest around the Star Temples. In a manner similar to Chartres, the number of paces from the west portal of the abbey to the outer rim of the pavement is equal to the number of steps necessary to walk around the perimeter, and yet the floor is rectangular. To further emphasize the spiral nature of the ceremony and the rounding of the square, the mosaic encloses a triple layer of radial themes containing esoteric writing. Also, like the labyrinth at Chartres, the Cosmoti terrazzo is decorated with scenes suggesting zodiacal beasts and Celtic and Greek mythological ikons. The horse replaces Sagittarius, the Dolphin replaces Pisces, the eagle replaces Scorpio, but the relationships remain fixed.

It is difficult to describe this pavement more fully because it is covered up and is rarely seen by tourists or researchers, but one can get a general idea from old texts. Undoubtedly the Westminster Pavement is based on a sky myth or cosmology prevalent in esoteric circles in the Middle Ages. We know it is both a night sky scene and a creation scene, for at the center of the entire pavement,

---

[192] A 3/9 mystical numbering scheme is common to Cosmati floors. The mystical "9" is derived by dividing 36 into its integers, 3 and 6. These are added to yield 9. The number 9 associated with the spiral is extremely old, the triple spiral at Newgrange is displayed three times. A similar formula may exist for the pyramids, but with a 4 base and an erection of 3 yielding 12.

divided into three major sections (in keeping with the triple spiral motif), the Latin words *Primum Mobilis,* first cause, appear in bold letters. [193]

Labyrinths and topiaries, wherever they may appear, are often small models of the universe. The maze at Chartres is made up of twelve circles. The twelve rings are divided by eleven pathways and each of the twelve circles is divided into three segments of the spiral, making thirty-six modula called *dignities dei* in the tenth century system of the famed Irish monk and Neoplatonist John Scotus Erigena. The mosaic floor at Westminster contains a comparable numerical formula which reflects the medieval understanding of the universe as a prime force, leading to the conclusion that Erigena's writings made no small impact on the Cosmati. [194]

The floor at Glastonbury Abbey was similarly decorated long before the great fire. In 1126, the year Henry Blois was made abbot, William of Malmsbury in *Acts of the Kings,* Book I, Chapter ii writes:

> *In the pavement of the church at Glastonbury may be seen on every side, stones designedly inlaid in triangles and squares and figured with lead under which, if I believe some sacred enigma to be contained, I do no injustice to religion.* [195]

---

[193]The maze at Westminster may be similar to the missing floor at Glastonbury, said to have been radial and to have contained zodiacal figures. This missing floor is mentioned by John of Glaston, Malmsbury and others. Its existence, fifteen feet beneath the current ground level, was insisted upon by Frederick Bligh-Bond, an antiquarian writer who flourished around 1927.

[194]Yates, Frances. "John Scotus Erigena" in *Lull and Bruno.* Collected Essays Vol. 1. London:RKP, 1986.

[195]Stubbs, William ed. Malmsbury, William *Acts of the Kings (De Gestis Regum Anglorum)* London: (Rolls Series 2 vo.) 1887-89. And: Sharpe, John. trans. *The History of the Kings of England,* London: British Museum, 1815.

It is probable the builders of Chartres and Amiens, Strasbourg and Notre Dame de Paris, influenced by Philo the Alexandrian, Neoplatonism and the Hermetic doctrine, believed everything on Earth was a reflection of celestial events. These guild members probably knew the sun to be the center of the planetary system hundreds of years before Copernicus and put their ideas into their art. [196]

Villard de Honnecourt, one of a handful of Templar builders we know by name, incorporated alchemy, Cabala and the Grail saga into the walls and panels, sculpture and painting of his cathedrals. Most other builders from the order of the Knights Templars did the same. The results were striking, visionary and apocryphal, even to the most advanced theologians of the day. Religion and philosophy were combined with art and music in an almost perfect balance.

At Chartres, Plato and Socrates are depicted in close proximity to biblical scenes with no apparent break in continuity. Although they are now drab compared to their original gilded and bejeweled appearance, the cathedrals stand as books cast from stone, hand-hewn manuscripts containing most of the knowledge available at that time. So in a modern sense the great cathedrals, like the Star Temples before them, are nodes in a massive library network.

Because books are perishable some of the troubadour architects were inspired to include the spirit of Arthur, Guenevere and Gawain in permanent stone. The round table became the maze, and certain statuary, tapestries, and stained glass kept alive the hopes of the quest for the Atlantic cosmology in the midst of repressions from the church in Rome. At long last the secrets of the Star Temples

---

[196]Mackenzie, Norman. *Secret Societies.* New York: Holt, Rinehart & Winston, 1967.

and the old religion could be transmitted without fear of loss. Even the church could not destroy the cathedrals. Since the Grail mysteries were again etched in permanent stone, knowledge could be passed on through the orders of chivalry and the Knights Templars. Like Lazarus, the long-dormant megaliths were brought back to life in the very fabric of the Gothic Temples. [197]

A Pagan Continuity

Anyone who has made a pilgrimage to both a great Gothic cathedral and a Star Temple will soon realize that most of the major architectural elements seen in the Star Temples, are refined in the Gothic style. The buttress or kerb concept, the corbelled arch or Gothic vault, the tessellated pavement or flag stone, the baptismal font or cauldron stone, the maze or triple spiral — and above all the light-beam principle — are represented in both structures. Whether this is a coincidence or a direct influence is still being argued.

The fact that more than five thousand years separates the Star Temples from the cathedrals is not difficult to explain since both forms often exist in close geographic proximity,if not on a shared locus. The idea that the great cathedrals were inspired exclusively by the pyramids or the Temple of Solomon or the Arab world, or the Crusades in general is poppycock. The rituals carried out at both the Star Temples and the Gothic shrines was fundamentally the same throughout the millennia so there must have been a local contribution. Here again diffusionist thinking muddies the water.

---

[197]Charpentier, John *The Order of the Templars.* Paris: La Colombe, 1961. Lull, Ramon. *The Book of the Order of Chyvalry.* Caxton, William trans. & printer. London: Reprint 1483-1485. Early English Text Society ed. A.T.R. Byles, 1926.

In reality the Star Temple builders, architects who developed the cairn and finally the corbelled arch, are at the root of the Gothic structure. Not only did they leave us mythic foundations, in some cases they provided the actual stones for the foundations of more than one abbey or cathedral. It is ridiculous to assume that the Gothic and Romanesque architects did not survey every site carefully or that they possessed no knowledge of the old Star Temples, henge rings and standing stones that occupied the site upon which they were about to build.

Glastonbury Abbey, for one, was built at the foot of a spiral megalithic mound (Saint Michael's Tor) and was situated on any number of Neolithic, Bronze Age and Iron Age foundations. This was obviously done on purpose by the original builders. The exact extent of the abbey's early foundations may never be known because it was razed and rebuilt many times and because it grew to such complexity that it was almost as large as a cathedral at its high point in the thirteenth century, but we have sufficient evidence to conclude that Glastonbury, like Drogheda in Ireland and Vannes in Brittany, has been continually inhabited since the Neolithic period.

At Monasterboice Abbey, in Ireland's Boyne Valley, some of the great crosses were carved from stones removed from the Star Temple kerbs located less than one mile distant. It is difficult to imagine a situation where an artists as skilled as the cross carvers of Kells or Melifont could not have known the pagan significance of these huge stones.

It is well known in Southern France that the Knights Templars held ceremonies at a megalithic lightbeam site, possibly of early Bronze Age origin, called *L'Epee Roland* — the Sword of Roland, after Charlemagne's general, implying that the Dark Age knights also knew of it.

In Brittany, near Kercado, a number of archaeological digs, located on or near abbey grounds, have unearthed Dark Age habitations indicating that ceremonies took place on layers above the Neolithic artifacts and Star Temples that were entered by citizens of that period. In a well-documented case, a child of a king of Brittany was hidden in a megalithic cave to save him from the wrath of a Frankish king who saw him as a usurper. [198]

If these examples are insufficient to at least hint at a continuity of culture between the Neolithic and the Medieval settings, we can turn to the hundreds of ikons and tapestries generated between the rise of Charlemagne and the final construction Chartres. Illustrations from the *Book of Days of Catherine of Cleves,* for example, depict traditional Christian figures superimposed on megalithic sites. In a miniature, housed in the National Gallery in Washington, the nativity is shown in front of a grotto which is, on closer inspection, a megalithic mound. In the aforementioned book of Days a man is seen buried with an Oak tree growing from his chest. The entire scene, which looks much like a Tarot card, takes place before a cavernous megalithic mound.[199]

It is easy to believe European civilization began with the cathedrals because, prior to the twentieth century, no structures in Western Europe exceeded them in complexity, relative size or beauty, but an architectural link between

---

[198]Morris, John *The Age of Arthur*. New York: Charles Scribner's Sons, 1973. p. 256.

[199]It is important to point out that Henry of Blois, the brother of King Stephen and grandson and namesake of Henry I, was responsible for a great deal of construction and reorganization at Glastonbury. His plans came from Egyptian sources only in so far as the Egyptian Rite meant Mithraism. The day-to-day activities at Glastonbury were carried out by Celtic and Saxon Christian monks, not necessarily initiates into the Mithraic rituals.

146

Star Temple and cathedral does exist through a direct sociological transmission of culture in the same spot for thousands of years.

A primary assumption, or rather an almost embarrassing fallacy hangs over any discussion of Gothic architecture to wit, that the builders of Chartres and Amiens and Strasbourg and Rheims were inspired exclusively by Arabic influences brought back from the crusades. This is almost completely ridiculous. The Arabic influence theory, although obvious in part, assumes the architects were unaware of — and unimpressed by — the Star Temples in their midst, megalithic buildings of hoary antiquity which every Breton and Celt knew about from childhood. The Arabic influence theory further ignores the question of why so many cathedrals were built directly on top of Star Temple sites. So by the fundamental act of site selection, which was clearly linked to astronomy and navigation, the Gothic architects were, consciously or subconsciously, assuring the furtherance of the old religion and were, directly or indirectly, transforming the portly Venus of Lascaux, and the more abstract Star Temple Goddess into The Virgin Mary or Virge Noir. Even if the architects were not at all pagan and were simply carrying out the commands of Jesus who said to Peter, "On this stone — πετροσ — I build my Church," the end result is the same, the old Atlantic religion survives in the very stones of the cathedrals. Those who subscribe to this insightful stream of thought are logically forced to rethink a number of staid assumptions about how Western European civilization began and why the cathedrals were built in the first place.

At Chartres one receives the palpable impression that the cathedral is both a skyscraper and a city unto itself. True, the megaliths deep below are replaced by hundreds of carved gargoyles and statues, and only a few of the original

147

manuscripts remain in the scriptorium, but the knowledge is not lost, the entire edifice is a manuscript written in limestone. Once inside the cathedral, the spectator will encounter a glowing chalice pictured in a stained glass window — a clue to the mysteries of Holy Communion — in the possession of Melchizedek, the priest of Salem mentioned in Genesis. He holds a radiant monstrance at his *Solar Plexus*. This gesture or mudra, to use a Buddhist phrase, is entirely appropriate since the window radiates with an intense light at dawn on the Winter Solstice. [200]

Furthermore, the virgin birth — the essence of the Winter Solstice lightbeam ceremony, since the lightbeam is the primal impregnating source in the Atlantic cosmology — is worshipped in a dimly lit chapel in the catacombs at Chartres, but here, on the perimeter of what was once a recumbent megalith circle, the virgin birth is a rebirth experience, a catharsis, not simply a religious observance and the Goddess reverts to the shadow woman, *Le Virge Noir*. [201, 202]

---

[200] Robinson, James M. ed. "The Gospel of Melchizedek" in: *The Nag Hammadi Library*, San Francisco: Harper and Row, 1988. p. 440-444. The same chalice can be seen in the hands of the same priest in a portico sculpture at Chartres.

[201] Patai, Raphael. *The Hebrew Goddess.* New York: KTAV Press, 1967 and Koltuv, Barbera-Black. *The Book of Lilith.* New York: Nicolas-Hays, 1986. For an excellent photographic record of Chartres before World War I see: Houvet, Etienne, *Gardien de La Cathedral. Chartres: Editions Houvet,* 1916 available through the Chartres cathedral bookstore and museum.

[202] Begg, Ian. *The Cult of the Black Virgin.* London, RKP, 1986. See Also: Baigent, M., R. Leigh, and H. Lincoln. *Holy Blood and Holy Grail.* London: Jonathan Cape, 1982. p. 73. And: Feugere, Saint-Maxent and Georges Koker: *Le Serpent Rouge*, Paris: Bibliothèque Nationale, p.4. In this theory the Black Virgin is the conduit through which the Goddess and the Grail are transmitted into Christianity. The Mithra cult is the suggested vehicle. Mithra is often seen as the Leoncephalic Aeon with a snake wrapped around its body.

Next to the Great Rose window, the prophet Jesse is seen laying on his back asleep. A huge genealogical tree grows from his loins. In a dream he sees his descendants branching off at different levels. Jesus sits in radiance at the top of the tree.

By following the Winter Solstice lightbeam around and into Chartres, one may find other mysteries. Sculptures of Saint John and Saint Luke are surrounded by sculptures of medieval kings and queens. The tower of the sun is adorned with the angel Gabriel trumpeting to the winds. The tower of the moon is topped with a likeness of Saint Michael. A spiral staircase winds upwards within each tower — like a grapevine seeking the sun — and at each window the observer can make celestial observations and navigational reckonings. These are vertical labyrinths and each of these paths leads to the main labyrinth laid out on the floor under the constantly changing colors of the radial windows which reflect an alternative, sun-centered, cosmology into the soul of the traveller. (Plate xxviii)

Perhaps these Gothic treasure-houses were simple churches to the multitudes of orthodox Christian, mosques to the converted Crusaders, and temples to the pagan visitors, but to the Alchemists — the budding scientists of the Middle Ages, to the Cabalists and Tarot readers, and to the Hermetic scholars who frequented the cathedrals, they represented the accumulation of all knowledge, the fulfillment of the promise of the Grail mysteries, the cathedrals, even today, remain the final initiation of the Grail quest.

A Cosmic Dance

The concept of quest is firmly entrenched in the Hermetic literature, a body of writings claimed, by their editors, to be Egyptian, then proven to be authored by a great many people using the pseudonym Hermes Trismegistus.

Recent evidence suggests the *Corpus Hermeticum*, the basic texts of the Neoplatonic movement, were authored in the third and fourth centuries by anonymous masters, many of whom were inspired by the Greek philosopher Plotinus. The writings of Hermes contain unbelievably old elements culled from Celtic, Greek, Egyptian, Persian, and Hebrew sources.*The Divine Pymander of Hermes*, for example, came together in Alexandria in the fourth and fifth centuries after Christ, at a time when Western Europe was in a crisis of the spirit.

The arrival of the Hermetic stream in Narbonne in the south of France, for example — correlates neatly with the Welsh migrations to Brittany after the fall of the Roman Empire. The merger of Greek philosophy, Alexandrian Gnosticism, Neoplatonism and Celtic music and folklore lifted the spirits of the people of Brittany, Languedoc and the Dordogne across many cultural barriers to create a rich kaleidoscope of ideas. The localized troubadour movement, with it roots in the wandering minstrel shows, carried the development of the Grail myth into literature, so that by AD 450, the legends of the convex bowl, the Shaman's drum and the cosmology of the Paleolithic Goddess, were fluxed permanently into Middle eastern and Indo-European thought, and it is in this amalgamated form that they come down to us. Through them the clocks of Mother Nature were never forgotten. [203]

In the writings attributed to Hermes Trismegistus the ideas of transcendence and preparation for eternity are presented as dialogues, almost as if we were looking in on one of Aristotle's lectures. This tutorial style was carried forth to the quest literature. For example, in certain very early

---

[203]Festugiere, R.P. (O.P.) *La revelation of Hermes Trismegiste.* Paris, 1944. Reprint, Laffont, 1974.

variations, Gawain — The Green Knight to be — has a death-defying dialogue with the reigning Green Knight — Hermes. Certain ceremonial questions are asked and answered, implying that an initiation is taking place. Finally Gawain fights with and triumphs over the Green Knight. In the process the spirit of sanctity passes from the old knight, the old Grail Guardian, to the new. This entire tableaux takes place at the mouth of a cairn or Star Temple (now seen as an oracle and a prototype for the later cathedrals) referred to in the text as the Chapel Green. Similar initiations also took place in the catacombs of the cathedrals, this would be the natural place to find rites dedicated to Persephone the Queen of the underground, but here we find the rites conducted in the name of the Black Virgin. [204]

The Goddess was transformed, renewed, over and over again. In these ceremonies the Attic Greek literary dialogue was replaced by Judeo-Christian iconography, but the pagan emphasis was retained. Finally — over many years, and in a highly luminous state — the pilgrim was initiated into the secrets of the Grail and the labyrinth. Each Star Temple or megalith, lost to history by ignorance or savagery, has been replaced by a stone in the fabric of the Cathedral.

---

[204]The transfer of power from the Green Knight to Gawain has been interpreted severally by scholars. From a sociological perspective it is an initiation ceremony. However, the mythographic explanation is probably also valid in that many of the ceremonies of medieval chivalry were based on enactments of primordial myths. In this example, the Green Knight is the old god and Gawain is the reborn god. These rights are traditionally interpreted as arising from an Indo-European context (Tamuz-Adonis, and in an abstract sense Gilgamesh in the maze of Humbaba) but can also be traced to Atlantic myth as the reborn lightbeam god of Newgrange (Setanta who becomes Cu Cullen the warrior chief. In both east and west versions the dying god is the son of the great mother viz: (Ishtar=Summerian, Dectine=Irish).

"I have shown thee now everything
and the laws of all the stars
of the heaven is completed."
Enoch lxxxii

ANTHEM FOR THE END OF TIME

In *Parzival*, Wolfram von Eschenbach, makes mention of the Grail as a *stone.*, the philosopher's stone, an amulet that will take the owner beyond time. This simple interpretation takes us to a final understanding of the Grail ikon.

Ultimately, the rituals conducted around the Star Temples are early attempts to blend with the force of the lightbeam and the rhythms of "Mother Nature," particularly in her lunar manifestations. But the ritualization of perceived time was not original with the Star Temple architects — they seem to have inherited a calendar of sacred events, an ancient almanac, from their cave-dwelling ancestors, the legendary hunter-gatherers, the Dawn People of the Atlantic rim. These early magicians organized animal and natural magic to gain control of biological and celestial systems.

Evidence for transcultural similarities in prehistoric Occidental cultures — based on mapping lunar and celestial events — is being unearthed at a rapid pace. Each year new discoveries support the hypothesis that the earliest Atlantic people were highly intelligent and quite capable of learning from their environment, especially from natural and diurnal rhythms.

The lunar-oriented technology that went into the construction of numerous large stone "Medicine Wheels," built in the polar regions of Canada, approximately three-thousand years ago, compares favorably with the lunar counting system that drove the hand-held hunting calculators — used at Lascaux cave in France more than twenty-thousand years ago. The similarities, especially in lunar oriented cycles, also clearly extends to Maes Howe in the Orkneys and Newgrange in Ireland, two sites dating between the Lascaux cave technology and the North American Medicine Wheels. Whether there is a direct connection here or not begs the issue — the continuity in the foregoing examples lies in the universal human ability to accurately observe natural events and animal behavior then translate these observations to social rituals. The reckoning of perceived time, by sun, moon or planet-dialing, was probably one of the first ritualized measurement techniques ever to occur to human consciousness. [205]

Traditional interpreters argue rightly that amulets of totem animals worn on the body, even tattoos, acted as links between the human hunter and the souls of the animals painted onto the walls of cathedral caves, such as Lascaux. But recent scholarship takes the idea further. The work of Evan Haddingham hints that the animals depicted in the caves found counterparts in the constellations, (as precursors of Pegasus and the Ursine stars) and that the cave paintings represent evolving sky maps of the constellations as visualized by the first hunter-gatherers, a practice which changed only slightly as it moved out of the cave and onto the savannah which eventually supported the Star Temple cultures. [206]

---

[205]Briggs, John and David F. Peat. "Time's Arrow" in: *Turbulent Mirror.* San Francisco: Harper and Row, 1989. p. 134-152

[206]Haddingham, Evan. *Secrets of the Ice Age.* New York: Walker, 1979. Evidence for astronomy in the cave animals is only hinted at. Further research needs to be done, but I find this concept a reasonable and fascinating avenue for further research. See also Thom, Alexander.

At Newgrange and Knowth, monuments built some twenty-thousand years after the caves were painted, the same fertility cycles of animals were set into stone and correlated with the workings of the heavens. Clearly the Star Temple builders inherited the ultimate insight from their forbears. The proto-Hermetic insight that the sun and moon affect animal (and human) behavior by linking light, shadow, weather and the seasons was the ultimate kernel from which other megalithic assumptions flow. To them the mysteries of the Goddess were subsumed in the cycles of nature.

The medicine wheels in Manitoba, Canada, seem to have been built as pilgrimage centers quite like the centers found in the Atacama region of Peru and the Star Temples of Western Europe. The setting of the moon and the apparent rising of Sirius and the sun were intensely observed at the prayer wheels and at the related effigy systems so as to gauge the exact feeding and migratory patterns of the Canada Goose, bison, caribou and Killer Whale and of course to calibrate the spawning cycles of Salmon or elk, but they were also used to link heaven to Earth. Here we find the Hermetic philosophy at work five thousand years before Hermes. In most cases the wheels point to nearby ceremonial regions which contain huge animal effigies etched into the Earth's surface or built up with stones. As in the carvings of Newgrange, the ceremonialization of the fertility cycles of fetish animals has an amazingly practical application for navigation on land and sea. [207]

---

[207]Tyler, Larry. "Megaliths, Medicine Wheels and Mandalas," *The Midwest Quarterly*. XXI #3 Spring 1980. pp. 290-305. This may explain why the metallurgical pastoralists from Central Europe, such as Gimbutas' Vinca culture, were not overly impressed by ceremonial centers like Brug na Boinne when they arrived in Ireland circa 2500 BC. Although Gimbutas is probably correct in assuming the central Europeans were the first true agriculturalist in

To the shepherd the Goddess oversees the flocks, but to the hunter-gatherer the Goddess "drives the herd." This is a subtle, but significant, difference. To the husbandman the Goddess evolved into a time ghost, a companion spirit, almost amorphous in shape and function. But to those who remained hunter-gatherers the womb of the Goddess, represented by the dark interior of the cave or Star Temple, was the place of original creation, the *primum mobilis*, the dark mnemonic cell which operates the computers of life itself. To assure continued fertility, longevity and tribal well-being both the shepherd and the hunter-gatherer felt it imperative to track and record all possible rhythms and cycles. Knowing the exact geometry and iteration of each biorhythm, including that of humans, meant survival. Making the iterations permanent, by painting them onto cave walls, drawing them into effigies on the Earth's surface and eventually aligning stones in circles meant that the information would be passed on to successive generations. In this way the hunter-gatherer is a husbandman for the whole planet, whereas the cow herd or simple farmer looks out only for his own territory. This may explain why the civilizations who built larger mounds and Star Temples seemed to have less interest in absolute husbandry. They did not need corrals and farms. In essence the whole planet was their farm. (Plate xxix)

Because multiple observations are required at numerous stones to derive a predictive outcome, the Mound Builders

---

Western Europe, she misses the evidence from Ireland and the Atlantic rim which indicates a Paleolithic and Mesolithic lifestyle, which included pastoral domestication and crop rearing for animal feed, continuing in isolated Atlantic pockets well into the Iron Age. There are, for example, even today, small hardy island populations in the Hebrides, without electricity, that could easily do away with farming, and revert to hunting and fishing, weaving and carving as an exclusive lifestyle.

and effigy sculptors eventually took to carving geometric markings into the stones. This was a way of quickly identifying each setting to new initiates as the populations grew, and it was a way of assuring that the meaning of the stones would not be lost in future generations.

In most Star Temples the inner cell was a ritual chamber, an altar room, somewhat like a chapel, where human beings were initiated and tested. In the reduced stimulus density of the inner temple, the womb of the Goddess, shrouded in darkness, the only available rhythm is the human heartbeat and the breathing rate of the planet.

The baptism in light ceremony, held at Newgrange every year on December twenty-first, probably revealed the secret keys to the cycles of the Goddess. This same ritual, or variations of it, was practiced at thousands of stone rings and mounds located in breathtaking venues throughout Western Europe and along the Atlantic coastline. Each of these stone rings or passage mounds continues to track recurrent celestial events — a fact well-established by Ivinski, Hawkins, Lockyer, Thom and a host of others. — and yet the emotional experience of the Star Temple, and this can only be understood by visiting these magnificent sites, seems to go beyond time. The ritual of baptism in light, the ceremonial observation of the mating of the God and the Goddess, creates a timeless state in the onlooker, even to this day. Photographs can impart a literal picture of the solstice or equinox beam dial phenomenon, but to actually grasp the spirit of these places, they must be seen and touched.

The Illusion of Time

In order to understand the Grail ritual at the center of the baptism in light we must define what we mean by time and timelessness. In order to define "Time," scientists have labeled it "The Fourth Dimension," yet, if we label it any-thing it becomes more elusive and opaque. The very act of labeling it changes it. Then again the concept of "clock time," the time we use every day to regulate our lives, can be cut-up in any number of arbitrary ways since it doesn't really exist in the first place. It is an abstraction which has deviated from its foundation or "natural time." The Star Temples measure natural time but a wristwatch measures abstract or clock time. Both are illusions, but natural time-tracking makes more sense if you are attempting to harmonize yourself with nature. For example, psychologists use the term "perceived time" to measure stress in anxiety ridden patients, and yet, since it is an illusion, its whereabouts or rhythms are anyone's guess. The next best thing, even though it is an illusion, is to base perceived time on celestial events. That is what the Neolithic builders were doing when they built Star Temples like Newgrange and Stonehenge and that is what the cathe-dral architects were doing when they erected Amiens and Chartres.

Still, time is a complex illusion, and no matter how hard we try it remains inexplicable. Eventually we abstract it further and present contradictions as anomalies to Newto-nian physics or relativity theory. Sometimes we refer to the timelessness of the mystic state as "fifth dimensional" or even non-dimensional, but adding new adjectives to the menu does not make time any more real. The ancient Star Temple builders didn't have this problem. Their style of architecture and the precise orientation of each temple sig-nals that they believed in a spiritual recycling process. No pronouns or adjectives were needed. To the Neolithic mind, matter defined time and time dissolved with matter.

The technocratic mind measures time by the proximity or decay of material objects, however small or vast they may be. It takes so many units of distance — light-years or parsecs — to get from the sun to the nearest star at the speed of light; two minutes to boil an egg at sea level; a nanosecond to process a bit of data in a desktop computer. These "time-forms" are convenient, arbitrary distinctions because at the edge of matter there are voids defined only by the patterns the enclose and beyond these voids there are creations in which time and matter, space and distance simply don't apply.

It seems apparent that the Neolithic builders reached this point of contemplation. They too devised time-tracking units, something like minutes and hours, and certainly days and nights, but their artistic renderings in stone tell us that all of their time and distance events, all of their Solstices and Equinoxes occur within a framework of timelessness, or in a context where concepts such as time and space simply do not apply.

To make the entire framework operate they based their measuring units on natural events, moon rises, eclipse cycles and the arrival of planets or stars on the horizon. One could never become abstracted, alienated or forgotten by the clocks of mother nature. The object seems to have been to learn the Star Temple time-tracking system until one transcended it or until the system was so well integrated into the psyche that the flow of material and spiritual reality was combined, inseparable and constant.

So, the major intention of the Star Temple architects may have been to provide the shaman — assuming they were separate entities — with a place to observe the cycles of nature so that he or she could eventually teach the transcendence of time and space to the entire tribe. To do this consistently over many generations, cycles and intervals, measurements and standards were, of necessity, etched in stone and memorized until their understanding, and the transcendence of that understanding, was second nature. In short, the tenders of Newgrange, Stonehenge and Maes Howe were able to use the illusion of time to move into and beyond matter at will, something almost impossible to do with our modern technocratic mindset. To the shaman and sibyl of the Atlantic Star Temple, time and matter were only unified at the exact point where they no longer existed.

The Star Temple builders, like their ancestors of the caves and raised beaches, possessed a technique for producing the *non-moment* at will. In Zen, one meditates on an ice cube and tries to ascertain at what point it becomes water. In Shamanism, the heart rhythms of the dancers and the drum beats of the musicians produce a hypnosis which, in turn, creates a desirable null state. In this null state —what the Grail teachings called *nous* — the cosmos has a chance to work on the mind of the dreamer. In turn, the null mind provides a window into an astral world, a high-level internalized world, rarely explored by modern investigators, a world in which rain clouds can be controlled by ritual magic and where distant events can be viewed as if the seer were in flight.

In medieval alchemy and Cabala, both of which influenced the Grail prose authors, the externalization process was taken one step further. Alchemists who learned from the books of Basilus Valentinus, a monk living in Thuringia, believed the mind could be taught to influence chemical, metallic and metabolic processes through concentration, a process parapsychologists call PSI. The Christian alchemists believed that the missing secret ingredient, the true philosopher's stone, was the knowledge of control over chaos and the void achieved through faith and grace. Likewise, to the Rosicrucian brotherhood of the sixteenth century, "The God" was a lightbeam which penetrated a cave, a metaphor which mirrors the Atlantic Temple paradigm almost perfectly. In each of these examples the end result is a significant reduction of anxiety and a return to homeostatic balance. In other words, the process is one of healing both physically and spiritually. The finer the measurement the more control one has over the astronomical environment, at least in terms of predicting events. [208] (Plate xxx)

To be more illustrative, the fine vernier calibrations possible at Knowth and the precision of the lightbeams in the other Star Temples tells us that the builders were attempting to "tune in" to the cycles of nature, first to understand and master them, then to rise above them. Based on the labor required to build such magnificent temples, be they tombs or sky observatories or both, we can assume the Dawn People loved their environment. This is not wholly illogical. To the Dawn People the Goddess and the environment were identical, inseparable and causal realities. Because the Boyne Valley people, for example, lived in harmony with nature, they were incapable of polluting their environment. That they remained animistic, totemic and deeply involved with natural magic is not sufficient reason to categorize them as a subhuman life form. That they worshipped the Great Mother is no reason to wipe out their contributions or misinterpret their artifacts. They were not really primitive as characterized by Sir James Frazer in his misleading early work titled *The Golden Bough*. Perhaps we should think of ourselves as the

---

[208]Burland, C.A. *The Arts of the Alchemists*, London: Weidenfeld and Nicolson: 1967. pp. 179-180. Unfortunately the deception is often taken to extremes and the deceiver begins to charge money for the process. When this happens the secret society collapses as we have seen in Freemasonry, Scientology, *est* and Hari-Krishna. If this is to truly happen it must be done with no remuneration of any kind. The process can never be contaminated if it is "given."

barbarians and these time-transcendent mound builders as the more enlightened members of the human race.

Time Binding

The illusion of time has become an irksome convenience in our technological world. It seems to regulate our civilization because we agree on certain conventions, yet far too many take it seriously. Ulcers and headaches and conversion hysterias emanate from a mistaken sense of time, something therapists call "time-binding." Being on time and punctual is a matter of grave concern to grammar school teachers and drill sergeants. We are even paid by the number of hour units we contribute to our pay source. In the most punitive sense we are punished by being given more time. In our modern world we are sent to jail for a length of time, as if there is some kind of lesson to learn. Someone in prison is said to be "doing time," yet there is no such thing as time. Time is not real like peanut butter or a bee-sting, so one wonders how useful it really is. We seem to know it is an illusion and yet we are obsessed with it.

The Atlantic Neolithic people were also obsessed with time. Perhaps they too believed it was a real thing. They certainly built sufficient numbers of megalithic temples to track it and even regulate human behavior. But the abstraction they were using, however illusory, was at least built on purely natural observation. The force behind their clock was nature. The aim of the temple was to catapult the initiate beyond events and cycles into a higher state of consciousness or rather non-consciousness and therefore to get beyond the obsession. The kind of time twenty-first century dwellers are obsessed with isn't based on nature, yet it works about sixty per cent of the time because it overlaps with nature's light and dark cycles. When it is not based on nature, when you are forced to wake up by an alarm clock,

161

even though your body clock tells you to remain asleep, you are experiencing the devastating effects of unnatural time keeping. This means we are dysfunctional and opposed to nature about forty percent of the time — enough to drive anybody over the edge. Its amazing how any of us hang on. But that's all we are doing — hanging on. We are not experiencing the real thrill of living. You can spend a lot of money and go "Clear" but you won't get any fresh data.

When the Star Temples were built there was no need for arbitrary time. Although humans have used the candle, rope, wick and drip methods since the Paleolithic Age, most time-keeping was based on nature. Mechanical clock time, the agreed upon twenty-four hour division of the day as meted out by the Greenwich observatory, is an invention of the Newtonian world view. It was designed so that an elite class could regulate the activities of the under classes. As such it is inflexible and unforgiving. In the clock time world life can't be lived simply, it must be monitored and rewarded or punished. Until about two hundred years ago, most people woke up to the clarion cry of a rooster. The Star Temples tracked natural time, and even then, only large segments of natural time, such as days or months. [209]

In addition to time-pacing megalithic structures like Stonehenge and the Great Pyramids, Newgrange and Kercado illustrate an early method of meditation, an early *logos* or meta-language, which enabled the human psyche to enter a void or null state beyond time. Once in that state, one could drift beyond fear. The medieval Grail texts used the Greek word *Nous*: — Νουσ — meaning oblivion, (the knowledge of nothingness found beyond time). The Star

---

[209]One benefit to natural time-tracking is that it does away with an elite class. Since everyone has the same access to the time track form, viz. when everyone gets the same wake up call or hears the same rooster, the social organization tends toward dehierarchized.

Temple builders must have possessed a similar word or sign — probably the triple spiral — to indicate *Nous* and its transcendental states. [210]

Once the healthy human psyche is trained to see beyond time it automatically seals itself in a hermetic retort — the alchemist's glass bottle, sometimes called the Alembic. Moving beyond time can prove to be a lonely proposition. The timeless state becomes the hermit's retreat. Suddenly, the cryptic words of the hermit in the quest prose make sense. They are beyond time and beyond normal existence.

In the twentieth century, the existential philosophers, and most cosmographers, believed time was real and that time itself, like photons or gravity waves, carried artifacts of the original "Big Bang." Martin Heidegger was convinced humans were linked by a general agreement on time:

This dating of things in terms of the heavenly body which sheds forth light and warmth, and in terms of its distinctive "places" in the sky, is a way of assigning time which can be done in our Being with one another "under the same sky," and which can be done for "Everyman'" at any time in the same way, so that with certain limits everyone is agreed upon it.

It is the qualifying phrase "with certain limits" that allows for the forty percent dysfunction, without explaining it, and yet this self-same forty percent dysfunction causes alienation. Those who have transcended time, through

---

[210]Brennan, Martin. *The Stars and the Stones.* Thames and Hudson, London, 1982. While doing research in the Boyne complex and at Loughcrew, Brennan discovered vernier tracking based on celestial events. In other words, the megaliths display macrophenomenon, such as the annual lightbeam and microphenomenon such as the passing of a shadow twice each day, or even the closing of a shadow on a notch in one minute intervals. Brennan also found evidence of a sundial which counts in seconds by use of a pendulum.

normal means, experience no alienation. They are both aware and unaware simultaneously. Following Heidegger, Sartre thought the penetration of the time illusion would be a painful experience, but the psychic pain he spoke of, the alienation he defined in his classic work, *Le Nausee,* is not necessary, at least it was not necessary six thousand years ago. The Star Temple builders knew time was a complete illusion in the fourth millennium BC. The Star Temples were built, not to track time *per se,* but to link the human psyche to the astral clock. Actually, withdrawing from modern clock time dependency, and the anxiety caused by that dependency, is equivalent to withdrawal from drugs or sex; it is a temporary state. The pain evoked from timelessness comes only with the preliminary separation from family and the mundane world, from the withdrawal of social habits and family contacts. Timelessness is the true realization of freedom. [211]

Electronic media and designer drugs have spread the unnatural choices on the table next to the traditional skyward reaching sense of quest. For the first time in known history, human beings are learning to live without reference to Heidegger's "same sky" or any sky for that matter. Ours is a dangerous age. In the cities a person can live his or her entire life without once seeing a starlit night. It is almost as if we are reentering Plato's cave where most of the inhabitants believe in flickering images and shadows, secondary sensations instead of direct perceptions, derived data instead of hard research. With drugs — and the drug of television — people can withdraw completely from

[211]Heidegger, Martin *Sein und Zeit* 1927 translated Brock, W. 1949, Viking Press: New York, 1972. Sartre essentially clones Heidegger and adds only that man's lot is to be condemned to freedom. He does not explain fully why this should be necessarily painful. See: Sartre, Jean-Paul *Being and Nothingness*. Trans. and Intro Barnes, H.E. Harcourt: New York, 1957.

participation in the human drama. Unfathomable inventions have changed human consciousness for better or for worse. Soporificants seem to put a patch on the subtle wounds caused by anxiety. The anxiety seems to stop. But does it? How perfect is the synthetic world? Are there not rents in the fabric here and there? Does not the light of Heidegger's "same sky" peek in occasionally?

If one takes mind-altering drugs in unsupervised settings or in abusive, "loud," environments, or if one abandons the true nature of the self by following a fake guru or a rock band, or remains constantly stoned, he or she will emerge in an irreversible state of alienation. Nothing seems to work. The "right" husband can't be found. The "perfect" diet fails. In this sense Sartre, himself an incorrigible alcoholic and addict, was correct. If, on the other hand, one sees into the self after years of preparation and achieves a natural time-free perspective, no alienation occurs; in fact, quite the opposite happens. The fear of death — the fear of pain over the act of dying — evaporates and one finds oneself engaging in charitable acts based on a sound and healthy psyche. This compassionate alternative is well laid out in the Grail and alchemical literature of the Middle Ages and seems to be the case in the ceremonies held at Eleusis in Athens and at the Star Temples of the Neolithic Age. It is also part of the Mithraic initiation and that of the original Freemasons. To the writers of the Grail texts the quest for the Grail was not a quest for a simple vision, or even to touch a sacred object, no, to writers as gracious as Wolfram and Chretien, the Grail quest was a search for existence beyond alienation, a merger with the Goddess and her invisible consort and a pathway to the void. (Plate xxxi)

A natural sense of solitude is a recurring motif in the Grail literature. Hermits are everywhere seen along the knight's quest. The Grail stories are full of wise men and

165

women happily living out their lives in retreat, perhaps in an Oak grove, a chapel, a cave or grotto. The king suffers from a magical malaise (involutional melancholia), the land goes barren and the knights on the quest suffer great hardship (alienation) but they press on, see the vision of the Grail, and obliterate their pain.

The fairy tale ends in a kind of never never land, because that is precisely the way the Dawn People, the Star Temple builders and their children's children saw life, death and reality. To them death was simply another transition. To the specific, and as yet unidentified, tribe who built the third stage of Stonehenge, the fairy world, inherited from the cave dwellers and the earlier megalith builders, really was a world beyond time and death. [212]

To fictional knights like Perceival, seeing the Grail was only the first phase of the cosmic quest, but Perceival's vision of the Grail allows us to follow the quest and achieve a similar peak experience. This, in turn, allows us to move beyond the lower orders of time consciousness. The reader's observation of the knights as they progress through their trials also provides us with a clue to the greater mysteries. While watching the knights progress we progress.

Both the anonymous author of *The Perlesvaus* and the echoed voices of the Atlantic and Indo-European ancestors seem to be telling us that although two journeys along the quest may seem identical, each is as unique as the person

---

[212]Belief in fairies and supernatural spirits was common in peasant and children's lore for hundreds of generations, but once Christianity entered the picture, especially after the crusades, even the most harmless superstition was taboo. The belief in the power of fairies as guardian spirits was carried on in those regions dominated by Gaelic speech and customs. An urban nostalgia for fairy lore came again briefly under the Tudor dynasty, but it would always be a forbidden practice in the eyes of Catholic and Protestant reformers.

who takes it. Once the first time-barrier is penetrated we immediately begin another leg of the journey — it may be toward another illusion or it may provide us a glimpse of the geometric order that contains chaos and the void. [213]

Judging from the permanence of the Star Temples, the Star Temple builders must have understood the need for a gradual education into the secrets of timelessness and chaos. They constructed temples so permanent that the learning process would not need to be hurried. The permanence of the temples enabled certain individuals in each generation to achieve a full awareness of the levels of illusion and reality in the natural world. Some of these students were capable of moving back and forth between the illusion of time and the reality of no-time. Some of them, like the shaman or sibyl, must have lived in a state of surrender to the void, enabling them to do what Ho Tai and Bodhidharma, operating thousands of years later in Asia, called "Entering the city with bliss-bestowing hands." Still others must have taken on the task of teaching the philosophy of timelessness to others.

---

[213] I find it interesting that the word for the most consciousness raising date in the Indo-European Celtic calendar was Samhain, what we now call Halloween, and that the Sanskrit term for enlightenment is samhadi, pronounced Saam-ha-dee, yet the Star Temples which delineate the moment for the worship of Samhain are easily dated to a period long before the arrival of the Indo-Europeans. Clearly, the Indo-Europeans merged their festivals with the aboriginal people. In Buddhism, which was derived from the Asian version of the Paleolithic shamanism that spawned the Grail, each hermit must discover a unique way to go back and forth into the world of people and things, preferably to teach and render aid. To make the trip even more treacherous, this transition must be achieved gradually, without destroying the void consciousness and without credit to the ego. See Oxford English Dictionary under "Sabbath."

Passage Beyond Time

The triple spiral is not unique to the Occident, but at Newgrange it became the central symbolic motif. It is found on the stones guarding the Grail or basin stone in the interior of the mound, and it is carved on the huge stone guarding the entrance. Since Newgrange was the last light-beam mound to be built in the Boyne Valley, and since the triple spiral only occurs at Newgrange, we can conclude that the other mounds interact with Newgrange and that the builders wanted future generations to know that the three mounds were linked, perhaps as a unified initiatory theater. Additionally, the triple spiral signifies that at least three levels of initiation were conducted in the Boyne complex. And, although we do not have an absolute insight into the initiation, we can reconstruct it with some degree of confidence. Clearly a processional was part of the ceremony, and one would not be too unscientific to assume it meandered from the river to all three mounds in a triple spiral course.

In the first stage the "elders" probably taught sacred geometry and ritual astronomy. This was done through dance, song, chanting and storytelling. Each song probably included a meditation on the megalithic structures and their carvings.

In the second stage, the pilgrims were undoubtedly shown how the cycles of the Goddess could be used in Geomancy, landscaping, farming and husbandry to harmonize the world and to focus on the precise moment when order returns from chaos or when chaos begins from order, the precise moment when the day is shortest or longest and so forth. But in the third and final stage, the initiate was probably taught how to go beyond any perception of time or chaos and merge with the Goddess. To do this the initiate was isolated for long periods. This third stage was probably

168

accompanied by a rite of passage and a mystery ceremony involving the consumption of a psychotropic substance such as a mushroom or refined ergot alkaloid.

In this expanded state, the initiate was probably left alone in the darkness within the Star Temple, the womb of the Goddess not unlike the inkiness of interstellar space — until the light poured in. This was most likely taken as a simile for death and rebirth. Now the initiate knew death was not a passage into a beautiful heaven full of bright and happy things, but a passage into the void, a passage beyond time. This would predictably be followed by a rite of rebirth and social reintegration.

To the Atlantic Star Temple people, the Goddess was a rational deity. She kept track of the harvest seasons and marked out the proper times to plant and reap. Since her temple was made of solid stone, she could continue her teachings for many generations, and since the temple was a model of her anatomy, it was not empty. Her cosmic soul filled the void and absorbed the fears of the entire tribe. Oneness with the great mother enabled the clan and tribe, as well as the individual, to go on living in an almost anxiety-free state.

Time And The Dawn People

Time as we know it, as measured by a ticking-pulse device, has only been kept by individuals for about four hundred years. Prior to the pocket watch, humans were forced to employ water drips, sand-clocks, burning candles, or beam-dials often in a public setting to tell the so-called "time-of-day." In lieu of a sundial or water clock, most farmers tuned into the cycles of nature. [214]

---

[214]Bhattacharya, D.K. *Palaeolithic Europe*. Princeton, New Jersey: Humanities Press, 1977. Bhattacharya's survey points out numerous flint industries

The concept of temporal standardization probably began in the Upper Paleolithic phase. However, two thousand years before Newgrange, in an era referred to as Mesolithic, the people of the Atlantic dawn, the Western European version of the North American Maritime Archaic people, evolved large structures so that they could track and worship celestial events. The fertile plains and rolling hills along the polar rim, and down either side of the Atlantic shore, offered food and shelter in abundance. The ice sheets were melting. Huge boulders were left in ready-to-use quarries. The rivers and seas were teeming with fish. Fruit and nuts grew in wide variety. Wood was available for burning and building. [215]

Hundreds of raised beaches provided safe harbors. In Maine, along Penobscot Bay, small megalithic temples and tools can be found identical to cairns and tools in Ireland and Sweden. Yet, in spite of the abundance, the Atlantic hunter-gatherers grew nostalgic for the security and rituals practiced under the vaulted interior of the ancestral caves. The stories and legends of the painted caves dedicated to the Great Bear or the Great Mother were passed down to them. Perhaps life on the savannah made them appreciative of the permanence of the sheltering caves. Only the great caves could provide the void timeless state. The opportunity to

---

and cave carvings in England and a few in Ireland dating to an inter-glacial period. This is almost revolutionary. A technological continuity seems to exist and a strong argument is made for a flourishing late Magdalenian tool assemblage in pre-Celtic Atlantic Europe. Examples come from Mother Grundy's Parlor, Swanscombe (Thames Valley), Creswell Crags, Pinhole Cave, Hengistbury Head and a number of Mendip sites overlooking the Glastonbury-Bath region. For Irish Paleolithic habitation see: Charlesworth, J. "The Palaeolithic Implements of Sligo," *Proceedings of the Royal Irish Academy,* # 39c 1929. p. 18.

[215] See Appendix C and D for a tutorial on the traditional time periods and nomenclature.

build a structure as solid as the caves was provided by the melting ice sheets. Huge stones were laying about the landscape — the perfect building material for the Star Temple.

The surviving songs and legends of the horned dancers and hunters were designed to evoke magical feelings in the hunters prior to a hunt and in the fishers setting off to sea. The hunting and fishing stories may have changed slightly from tribe to tribe, and over the centuries, but the intention and results were the same. The caves and stones worshiped by the ancestors remained constant, the stars remained in order, even if the planets shifted and moved with perplexing regularity, and the stories about the stars remained consistent. Shifting the pole star changed the axis of the legends, but not the legends themselves. Eventually the legends were captured in the Star Temples.

Lascaux and Altamira, two cave temple, decorated with the most brilliant art on Earth, were abandoned, but not forgotten. The totality of cave art from the Lower Paleolithic in France and Spain represents an Atlantic cosmology, an early explanation of the creation of the universe unconnected, except by coincidence and the universal mind, to anything going on in Central Europe, Asia or Africa. To the cave artisans and their children's children and to the Star Temple builders, the universe — and all event cycles within — were born from the Goddess. Once enthroned she was impregnated by an invisible lightbeam, not a sun God *per se*, but an emanation of light defined as that which can be seen only during the exact moment of impregnation.

The proto-Celtic cosmology, a belief system which permeated the Atlantic sphere, when fully understood, parallels the most probable *actual* case for creation as we know it. According to the world's most advanced visionaries, thinkers of the level of Stephen Hawking and George Gamow, the universe is constantly creating itself from nothing — something from nothing — a miraculous thought now and most certainly a forceful vision to hunter-gatherers. At a very early period the peoples of France, Ireland, Britain, and the Iberian peninsula caught hold of the idea that harmony and disharmony between "heaven" and "Earth" was close to an ultimate understanding of reality and that all creation stems from this balance or imbalance. To insure the system would stay intact for future generations, they built larger, permanent and more complex temples dedicated to a quest for timelessness. [216]

The cave-Star Temple sequence progressed, in relative isolation, for thousands of years in the Atlantic sphere and, as we realize by observing Newgrange and Knowth, the interior vault, the basis for the Gothic arch, was achieved at an early phase of development. Once the Grail Stone was put into place in the inner temple sanctuary, the "machine" was complete. The dynamic ritual of bowl and arch, cavern and lightbeam could continue. The light and shadow elements at Newgrange, or even earlier at Lascaux, are no different, in essence, than the ones we worship as we enter our churches and synagogues on the Solstice and Equinoxes. [217, 218]

---

[216] Actually, the system I perceive as known to the cave painters and Star Temple builders was a five pointed one as follows: Nature is either in balance or out of balance or on it's way to being balanced or on it's way to being out of balance or integrated in a fifth state viz. myriad combinations and multiple states of the above. This theorem is represented on many occasions at Newgrange, Knowth and Dowth as a circle with multiple spokes radiating from a center.

[217] It appears there is a continuity in the ritual of light enacted in both the man-made Star Temples and the much earlier caves, such as those at Lascaux in France.

[218] Gourhan-Leroi, A. *Treasures of Prehistoric Art*. New York: Abrams, 1967. This huge book is of special interest for its collection of horse's heads with bridles and its very fine computer-ready correlation charts. Based on what we now know and on what turns up each year it is not overly idealistic

172

The birth-death metaphor is fundamental to evolution and life itself, so why should the worship of light not be similar throughout human history? It seems we have inherited more than we thought possible from our ancestors, the Dawn People. Their wisdom has survived through the Star Temples to inspire later historical groups such as the Dionysians, the Druids, the Neoplatonists and the mystic Christians. [219]

The stone cauldron and lightbeam rituals that were obviously conducted inside the Star Temples were adopted and modified by the Celts, Mycenaeans and early Greeks. Each of these eventually combined with the massive power of the *Torah* and the Mithra cult to influence the Christians of the Middle Ages, the citizens of Europe, who handed the cathedrals and the Grail literature down to us. In the transformation between generations and disciplines, the basin stone became the baptismal font and the beaker became the chalice of Holy Communion. Nothing was lost.[220]

---

to assume that the Ice Age cave painters were from an artisan class who were wanderers traveling from community to community telling stories, singing songs and offering objects for barter. One might even call them the first troubadours.

[219]Kahane, Henry, and Rene Kahane. *The Krater and the Grail Hermetic Sources of the Parzival.* Urbana: University of Illinois Press, 1965. Without question this single work is the most important piece of American scholarship ever conducted on the Grail as part of the Dionysian sub-culture. The Kahanes continue where Lazzarelli and Hippolytus left off. They convincingly link the Grail of the Medieval literature to the Krater Hermetis and to Christ. It is therefore reasonable to connect the Celtic and Atlantic Neolithic basin stone and cauldron to the Krater, thence to Christianity and the Medieval Grail.

[220]Nasr, S.H. "Sufism and the Perenniality of the Mystical Quest," *Studies in Comparitive Religion*, Autumn, 1970. See also: Ponsoye, Pierre. *Islam and the Holy Grail.* Paris: Donoel, 1958. Also: Talmud Sanhedrin. eds *The Babylonian Talmud.* Berlin: Hebrew University of Germany, 1842. The medieval Grail literature reveals important information about the Tarot cards wherein The Grail is the Ace of Cups. The Grail also resides at the center of

The Stone Book

Everything one can see in a Gothic cathedral can also be found in a painted cave or carved megalithic temple. The entire Western European pageant can be traced from the caves to the cathedrals. The quest and pilgrimage is the same in both cases. Each temple complex represents a permanent record, a stone *book* containing clues to the decipherment of early Occidental magic and ritual. [221]

The horse and bison, fish and oxen painted so perfectly on the walls of the grottos at Lascaux are identical in function to the carvings on the megaliths of the Star Temples in Brittany or Ireland and to the stained glass windows and sculptures of the cathedrals and abbeys in France and Germany.

In the Gothic cathedral, the ikon of the beast of burden, the huge Ox called the Aurochs still exists, except it is now depicted as a domestic ox pulling the carts that hauled the stones to the site. In the cathedral, the semi-domesticated pony of the cave is transformed into the fully domesticated noble steed carrying a knight to the crusades. Both cave and cathedral embody the gestation cycle of the horse, human, lamb and goat. At Chartres, John the Baptist holds the Lamb of God in his arms, symbolizing the spring sacrifice. At Amiens, a mysterious lion head, reminiscent of the head of Mithra as fashioned in sculptures for the temples of the

cabalistic magic, where it is the mystery found in the cup of the Seder, but both of these subjects are so vast they exceed the focus of the present work.

[221]Isikowitz, Karl. *Primitive Views of the World*. New York: Columbia University Press, 1964. Also: Munitz, Milton. *Theories of the Universe*. New York: Macmillan, 1957. If the reader will take the time to scan the first twenty-six verses of Genesis as if they were a redaction of the Atlantic cosmology and replace the word Og or Ogdoad, Ogmios, Oc, Och, Lugh and other variants, for the mosaic anagram: GOD, the entire chapter would take on an Occidental tone. That it was democratic is patently obvious. Gender isn't a factor in this cabalistic account of creation until Chapter 27.

Roman legions, can be seen in the center of an inverted pentagram in a huge radial stained glass window.

In the painted cave each wild animal is represented by a direct totemic image. If painted representations or carvings, or tapestries were used in the Star Temple ceremonies, they have faded down the centuries, but we still have the placement of the stones and the zigzag and spiral carvings which tell us that the Star Temple builders were counting the fertility cycles of domesticated animals. In the Star Temple the pictoglyph is gone, replaced by an alphanumeric ikon, but the initiatory journey or quest through the cave — from dark to light — remains. [222, 223]

The idea of initiation through the agency of a Virgin Goddess is also evident in each case. In the painted caves, the Goddess is present as the cave itself, but also as an obese Venus, a pregnant mare, or a fertile salmon. In the Star Temple, she is still the very structure of the building, and she remains in the form of the Grail Stone and as the markings on the walls. The inner chamber is her womb, while the basin or Grail Stone is the focus for the lightbeam and eventual birth and rebirth. Here we see the fundamental elements for what Christians would later call immaculate conception and resurrection.

At Notre Dame in Paris, the cathedral is a shrine to the Virgin Goddess. At Chartres, also dedicated to the Goddess, women with painful menstruation or infertility problems

---

[222]Sanders, N.K. *Prehistoric Art in Europe*. Baltimore: Penguin, 1968.

[223]Marschak, Alexander: *The Roots of Civilization*. New York: McGraw-Hill, 1972. pp. 431-364. Marschak indicates great advances in consciousness witnessed by the fabulous murals painted on the cave walls of Lascaux, in France, or Altamira, in Spain, as well as a concerted effort to organize a numbering scheme more than 20,000 years ago. To fuel the Atlantic debate, I feel it necessary to report that wall paintings of hunting scenes with possible lunar counting motifs dating to 50,000 years ago have been found in South America. See: Mysteries of the Ancient Americas.

pray at the shrine of the Virgin's veil. At Amiens the *Virge Noir* is seen in statuary and as Virgo of the zodiac. Each of these buildings and others, not the least of which is Strasbourg, is named after the mother of Christ, but there is a hint that the cathedrals are also dedicated to the aboriginal mother — the Great Goddess. During a span of at least twenty-thousand years, her influence has remained constant, probably because the human spirit has sought communion with nature, in the same locations, throughout the years. [224]

But, as pointed out earlier, the Virgin is not the only element in Gothic architecture adopted from the Star Temples. The solar dial is in evidence at every cathedral. In the examples thus far investigated the Gothic arch shows the way to the beam dial. The ogive allows for the interior height and strength necessary to position the windows at various angles so the beam can be controlled with precision over the centuries. The proportions have grown on a miraculous scale, but the Star Temple is alive within each Gothic shrine. Light continues to enter the inner chamber at Winter Solstice and the Atlantic Genesis lives on. [225]

By the same process, the basin stone found in almost every Star Temple became the baptismal font. The cauldron

---

[224] Although the Catholic church does not advertise it, many of the cathedrals were built over megalithic sites. Chartres was built over an ancient henge circle which featured a sacred well, about 150 meters deep and Strasbourg was built over a Roman temple dedicated to Mars. It is rumored that the foundations of Amiens were moved several times to accommodate the stones dug up from an ancient temple.

[225] The main porch at Amiens, portal to the tallest complete Gothic cathedral in existence, exhibits an entire zodiac in quatrefoils, including the representation of the Virgin as Virgo mentioned earlier. A perfect cross-section of the ogive found on Malta at the Treasury of Artius and in Ireland at Knowth and Newgrange can be seen above the doorway at the end of the main aisle at Amiens.

is still very much in residence, but now the Grail has become a book of unending pages cut from stone. Glass fired with red gold, emerald dust and powdered sapphire make up the fabulous windows. The cathedral itself becomes the Star Temple. Light is still worshipped and the lightbeam still enters on cue. Carvings of the saints, philosophers and poets, kings, queens and biblical figures replace the hyper-text notation on the megaliths, and the portraits of sacred horses on the cave walls. Polished crystals incorporated into golden reliquaries, replace the crystals used to conduct the lightbeam into the Star Temples, but the purpose for the Gothic cathedral and the Star Temple remains constant over the millennia, each edifice continues to join heaven to Earth. [226, 227] (Plate xxxii)

Authors and Architects

During the earliest Crusades, the Knights Templars developed an extensive esoteric network. Many of these knights were also princes and religious clerics and many were initiates into various craft and secret guilds (forerunners of the Freemasons) influential in the construction of the Gothic cathedrals. It is not coincidence that many of these same knights were busy penning esoteric manuscripts precisely linked to construction plans and fund raising for the great work — the new Star Temples.

---

[226]Polished crystals can still be found in the cathedrals in many settings. The famous shrine of Lourdes is a grotto used in ancient times as a temple for blessings from the water spirits. Many crystals and magic stones as well as wooden artifacts, effigies of the river Goddess and votive effigy dolls, dateable to the Neolithic, have been located at the river confluence near the grotto.
[227]Krupp, E.C. *In Search of Ancient Astronomies.* London: Charlotte and Windas, 1979. Cincinnati: Meridian Books, 1980. For other examples of cave dwellings taken over by Christian chapels see Charpentier, Louis. *Saint James and the Route to Compestelle.* Paris: Laffont, 1972.

For those who could read, the manuscripts told of the marriage of the old and new religions. To those who could not read, the cathedrals themselves stood as textbooks. Royalty and commoners alike came to the cathedrals to perform the lowliest of mason's tasks. The knights were building the Grail Temple in stone precisely as the Dawn People did on a smaller scale. The minstrels and monks were placing the events on parchment with quill pens exactly as the Star Temple carvers did with flint points. The connection between the Star Temples and the Gothic Temple, the continuity between the megalithic corbelled arch and the Gothic arch has remained one of their most inviolate secrets. Each structure predicts events and captures the same astronomical elements. These elements and events, in turn, balance the human world.

By the twelfth century, the troubadours, operating from Southern France, and the trouveres operating in the north and in England under the Norman franchise, passed information along a complex underground network. Each node in the network made certain the messages were distributed in an undistorted fashion. Through this grapevine the Atlantic Genesis, and its rebirthing secrets, became known as the Holy Grail quest. Rituals and passwords pertaining to a sacred manuscript, sometimes known as *The High History of the Holy Grail*, were incorporated into public and religious life though architecture, song, drama and elaborately illustrated manuscripts. [228]

The Knights Templars, the troubadour groups and other organizations with military power lived on for a while longer, but eventually they too were brought to their knees

---

[228] Copies of the closest approximation of this manuscript currently available are located in Belgium and in Switzerland under the name *The Perlesvaus. See:* Evans, Sebastian trans. *The High History of the Holy Grail.* (Perlesvaus) London: Reprint 1927. James Clark, 1969. p. ix.

by the Inquisition. The late thirteenth and early fourteenth centuries were times of struggle for Grail initiates. Only the cathedrals and a few manuscripts managed to survive, but the syndicate was not broken. Powerful princes in Italy and England supported new ideas, and the movement towards freedom of expression, long promised by Solon in Athens and the bards of Ireland, remained alive.

Baptism In Light

An astronomy ritual in the form of a baptism in light is evident at Newgrange. The lightbeam enters the temple mound and strikes the basin stone on December twenty-first each year. As the lightbeam crosses the basin stone any fluid contained in the concavity of the stone, (blood, berry juice, or water) is sanctified. This fluid can then be distributed to the participants waiting outside the temple entrance. It may have been used to anoint infants and perhaps to make bread for a Eucharist, or, it may have contained rye wort (ergotomine) or psychedelic mushrooms on special occasions.

This lightbeam ritual is the major key to most Occidental mysteries, especially those associated with Hermetism, Gnosticism Neoplatonism and the Celts. Evidence for a water or psychedelic baptism ritual surrounding the lightbeam event is plentiful. The triple spiral at Newgrange maps out a processional which probably followed a spiral path. [229]

More than six thousand years ago the sacred chambers of the telescopic Atlantic temples were built with corbelled ceilings by intuitive architects who were also astronomers,

[229]Nutt, Alfred. *The Mabinogion*. London: Dent and Sons, 1927. Nutt's extensive bibliography is critical reading for any Grail scholar seeking Celtic connections. Also see: Jones, Gwyn and L. Thomas. *The Mabinogion*. New York: Dutton, 1950 and Nutt, Alfred. *Studies on the Legend of the Holy Grail*. New York: Cooper Square, 1965.

men and women who linked their behavior to celestial events. This observation casts an eerie glow on the Grail mysteries. There is a deeper meaning here. The Grail manuscripts and the cathedrals, the troubadours and the Templars are linked to the geometry of the old stones and to a mystic root within Christianity, but just how was this link established? Perhaps it was never broken. Was Christ an initiate, born to fulfill, not only the prophecies of the Hebrews, but of the Celts and Greeks as well?

The inner chambers of many of the Star Temples, while acting as scientific instruments, were also symbolic of the fertility of the Goddess. In her name the basin stone of re-birth was penetrated by a divine beam of light. The basin stones, often hidden many meters inside the passages, must have been mirrors of the heavens, beam dials, and prisms designed to synchronize everyday life with the annual birth-rebirth cycle made accurate to the minute, possibly even the second, by the architecture of the Temple itself.[230]

Watching the lightbeam enter the mounds at three Boyne Valley sites, at Loughcrew in the mountains about twenty miles to the west, at Maes Howe in the Orkneys, at Epée du Roland near Arles in France, at Kercado in Brittany and at Los Milares in Spain, elicits an awestruck response in everyone who sees it. (Plate xxxiii)

The lightbeam is the lasting symbol of the old religion. Obviously, the people who practiced this religion were able to navigate on land and sea in a wide lens. It is therefor not stretching the truth to assume that the Dawn People conducted rituals based on astronomy. The central cer-emony in the Star Temple was the observance of the

---

[230]The equality of women in the Goddess religion, is rarely addressed by historians or archaeologists. The concept of being reborn within the womb of the Goddess is fundamentally unchanged in architecture and ritual over a seven thousand year span in direct Occidental tradition.

lightbeam. In the Boyne Valley the event took place at least four times each year. Each citizen was given ample opportunity to participate in one or more exposures. Nothing much beyond reverence was required. Merely seeing the event "is" the initiation. The observation of the event "is" the essence of the ritual. Any consequent enlightenment may come immediately or gradually. Like people everywhere some "get-it" on the first exposure, others require multiple exposures. [231]

The same sense of gradual and public enlightenment is evident in the painted caves of Lascaux. If you are lucky enough to visit the caves, and perhaps catch a glimpse of a pregnant mare one hundred feet long running fifty feet above your head, you will get a sense of direct contact with the painters, men and women who were initiated into the mysteries of light and shadow. To them the great mother of the cathedral, the Paleolithic "Sophia" was a horse, the prototype of the Goddess Danu or Epona. A similar immediacy with the artist is witnessed when looking up at the huge inverted pentagram in a stained glass window at Amiens or when observing the lightbeam enter Dowth at twilight.

An increasing roster of modern scholars, especially those who have actively visited the sites listed above and Glastonbury Tor, agree: the answers to the long-secret Grail mysteries, especially those that come to the surface in the Arthur and Guenevere story, are finally revealed. The quest legends and the rituals described in the prose narratives are in significant measure derived from pre-Celtic ceremonies associated with the megaliths. The idea that the Grail is somehow a Christian artifact is a gloss.

---

[231]Brennan, Martin. *The Stones of Ancient Ireland.* Archives Press: San Francisco, 1992.

Christ obviously inherited the Grail ritual or it was grafted on long after Christianity came into the Celtic territories.

More than five-thousand years ago, *light,* the life-giving essence, was directed through stone and crystal apertures to pierce the blackness of the megalithic temple, but why? A fertility ritual is the most obvious answer, but why such elaborate architecture? If the Star Temple complex was built to support a simple fertility ritual, could not the whole affair have been conducted outdoors under the boughs of a sacred oak? Yes, it could have, but the ritual would not have been permanent enough for growing tribes with burgeoning economic and logistic problems. Only stone would be permanent enough to survive through the ages, and only stone would seal the mystery for later generations.

In the opinion of a growing group of modern scholars the Star Temples can be thought of as gifts to us from the Dawn People. Places like Newgrange and Stonehenge are large scale moon driven computers which represent an entire canon of Neolithic ritual astronomy. [232]

Time and the Goddess

The shaman's compulsion to totemize the Goddess as a deer, bear, horse or fish was gradually replaced by the Star Temple structure itself. Fertility cycles of the animals, including human beings, were constantly correlated with

---

[232]Knowth features an oval shaped, stone lined, reflector pool approximately six inches deep. The courtyard pool was originally situated in front of a large phallic stone which was originally located directly in front of the east passage where, as a gnomon, it cast a shadow on the entrance stone at Spring Equinox. I believe this pool and gnomon are quite similar, albeit on a smaller scale, to the Washington monument and the moon pool adjacent to the Jefferson memorial. The gnomon was a sundial while the pool was used to precisely define the transit of various stars and orbital bodies. The pool and foresight were unearthed by Professor Eogan in 1981, but were not reported on, mainly because the professor broke the foresight and buried it beneath the east wall, even as he diverted the course of the entrance passage.

182

sky events. The Athenians humanized her into Diana, but the Celts accepted her in aboriginal form as a horse and as a woman who rode a horse. To the Celts of various tribes she was Epona, Guenevere, Tara or even Rhianon, each a separate social mask for the White Goddess of antiquity.

The Star Temple people were skilled in farming and animal husbandry. They were energetic builders, who tilled, planted and raised pigs, sheep, goats and ducks, but they were also fishers on the high seas and in rivers. Their diet was rich in nutrients and protein. One of their favorite meals was a breakfast of bread, gulls eggs and scallops or limpets. They also ate seaweed, picked herbs and made salt with which they seasoned a wide variety of shellfish and snails. They continued to hunt deer and wild boar, but they augmented their hunting with gathered goods such as wild berries, nuts, and mushrooms. They weren't above robbing a wild beehive. There is even speculation that they enjoyed pollen, wax and honey from domesticated bees. All of this bounty was watched over by the ephemeral shepherdess, the Goddess of what the Greeks called Arcadia.[233]

Lucius Apuleius, the Hermetic initiate and poet, wrote of the Goddess in the first person as if he was taken over by her spirit which was, in turn, speaking to an audience in an amphitheater:

I am she that is the natural mother of all things, mistress and governess of all elements, the initial progeny of worlds, chief of the powers divine, queen of all that are in the underworld, the principle of them that dwell in the cosmos, manifested alone and under one form. [234]

---

[233]The Boyne is dotted with ingenious Neolithic salmon weirs.
[234]Graves, Robert. *The Golden Ass of Apulius.s New York:* Basic Books, 1972.

Once cattle and sheep were domesticated, large monument construction would be the next logical progression. Life grew serene.They survived for centuries by staying in tune with nature. They watched the stars and heavenly objects both night and day just as we watch television. The sundial and the shadow clock were of extreme importance for these purposes. Judging from their refusal to adopt metal tools they probably resisted change from the Middle European world for a very long time. Their society was regulated and it was, by many standards, a true civilization, isolated from the Orient and Africa. They dressed in skins and used leather-covered boats to ply the waterways.

Gradually, the people of the Atlantic dawn were able to refine their hunting and fishing skills by tuning themselves to the work-a-day rhythms of domesticated animals which they kept track of with great precision. The construction of the Star Temples and henge monuments helped focus the wandering bands into a cohesive cultural lens.The scattered families began to unite into settled tribes. The people of the Boyne, Somerset and the Bay of Biscay stopped using the direct effigy of the salmon as a talisman and began worshipping the cycles of the salmon etched in stone. They did not cease worshipping the great mother in her many manifestations, the sacred mare, for example, but the worship did change focus. The horse was no longer a wild animal. Once the Star Temples were established the populace could track the eleven-month gestation period of the horse with extreme accuracy. [235]

The mounds and henges are public and clearly observable from hills and cliffs and from every lane and *boreen*.

---

[235]Brown, Peter Lancaster. *Megaliths and Masterminds*. New York: Scribners, 1979. p. 165

Labor enough to manipulate the huge stones was probably communal. The Celts, living as they did around the megaliths, must have realized that the Star Temple builders intended them to be used for a very long time by anyone who could decipher their meaning. This is why there are so many references to the megaliths in Celtic lore. A public initiation indicates an absence of suppressive factors in the political environment and a sharing of wealth or at least an equal distribution of responsibility. If we study the set and setting around Newgrange, Stonehenge and the other Atlantic temples we will plainly sense this openness. These structures appear to have been built by free societies seeking transcendence from world alienation in a climate of virtual democracy. [236]

The arrival of Bronze Age populations and Christianity did not stop the process of ritual astronomy. The linguistic, cultural and genetic momentum was too great. The migrations between Ireland, Wales, England and France did not start with the fall of the Roman Empire. The post-Roman migrations were continuations of the aboriginal migrations heralded in song and legend. Heroic sagas were memorized and retold generation after generation. The creation of the world in the womb of the Goddess, the Atlantic Genesis legend, was retold to each generation and at each retelling the stars and the stones were used as verification.

---

[236]Herity, M. and G. Eogan *Ireland in Prehistory* p. 17. Larnian, Mesolithic tree clearance cultures in Ireland are judged, before calibration, to be of a fifth millennium date. Corrected dates would indicate advanced habitation by 6000 BC, or earlier. This would correlate for dates in the Canadian Maritime Archaic lens. The land bridge between England and France was inundated around 7000 BC.

185

Rebirth

At Newgrange, and in hundreds of mounds in the Atlantic zone, the lightbeam, a moving finger of light, squeezes through a prepared lens. This could be a space between two stones or a hole bored into a stone. No two monuments are identical, but in every case the lightbeam touches the markings or the dressed edges carved into the stones as if to retrace them. Once the beam has illuminated the chamber or standing stone it moves on, unable to return until the same date one year hence.

A similar lightbeam event occurs in cathedrals and Star Temples throughout Western Europe. In Bologna, the light makes its way across the tessellated pavement and strikes the baptismal font on Christmas day. At Amiens, the lightbeam enters through the center of an inverted pentagram in a stained glass rose window above the north portico. At Chartres, on Summer Solstice, the lightbeam appears through windows adjacent to the southeast side of the porch, passes two pillars, one marked with a *fleur-de-lys,* the other with a shamrock, and finally enters the cathedral through a special window, dedicated to Saint John, the patron saint of Glastonbury and the Summer Solstice. [237]

To the Star Temple builders the common model of the universe was not a hypothetical construct or an abstraction. The power and symbols of the Goddess and her consort were everywhere. Each time a farmer looked at a rainbow he or she was reminded of the Solstice and Equinox cere-

---

[237]Neuman, Erich. *The Great Mother.* Princeton: Bollingen Series, 1955. What is occult in puritanical societies is often traceable to tribal sources. The old Goddess is difficult to expunge in Occidental tradition because she is clearly a forerunner of most theocracies regardless of where they are found. Astarte, Cybele, Diana and the Cathar Widow should perhaps be thought of as later developments of the Paleolithic Goddess originating in the Atlantic theater and progressing through different tribal avenues.

monies. Those pilgrims who flocked to the Star Temples were absolutely convinced they were observing the process of an actual and real God and Goddess operating within an actual and real cosmic model. The parabolic reflector stones (or Grail Stones) contained within the mounds were undoubtedly used for ritual observations having to do with rebirth and the annual reappearance of fertility represented by the mating of the old God and Goddess. It may not have been entirely accurate by our present standards, but it came close to what we now perceive as the way the universe works. If a shaman architect of the seventh millennium before our era, could intuit the idea of a black hole and the condensation of light as a beam having something to do with cosmic and human conception, and further that the universe grew from blackness as if it were a living embryo, then how far have we really progressed?

When we compare our current view of creation — which for lack of a better phrase is called "The Big Bang" hypothesis — with the megalithic model we can but marvel at the similarities. The Star Temple model of heaven and Earth is close to what we now think of as "the scientific real thing." The Star Temple people were guessing at first, their's was a naive approach to be sure, yet they based their wisdom on many centuries of painstaking observation. [238]

A Megalithic Hypertext Deciphered

At Newgrange the slightly concave basin stone in the west chamber takes the form of a grinding surface. A similar concave stone is found broken in the rear (north) recess. The east basin stone seems dedicated to an early baptism ritual. It is part of a complex water collection system, (similar to the baptismal fonts in the Gothic cathedrals.) This

---

[238]This is far more practical than anything we are currently planning.

concave stone is oval in shape, holds about twenty gallons of liquid and was set in place before the mound was built. It is not inscribed or decorated, although the white quartz stone above the east basin, probably the most decorated stone in existence, would be reflected in the lower basin when it was filled with water, again bringing the paradigm of the mating of heaven and Earth into a human scale. In other words, the large basin stone does not need to be carved since it is a receptacle for the heavenly carvings overhead.[239]

This arrangement is quite straightforward to anyone who will take the time to visit Newgrange. The interpretation of the arrangement should be obvious: "that which is above is reflected in that which is below" — the ultimate Hermetic riddle, expressed in stone nearly four thousand years before the writings of the Neoplatonists.

At last we see the conditions for teaching and expressing the ultimate lesson in permanent stone. These carvings, once thought of as doodles by the local tavern keepers, can only be described as star maps used in a birthing ritual. When the child was baptized by water touched by the light-beam, he or she saw an entire, almost scientific, notation system carved on the stone overhead. [240, 241]

The downfall of the Victorian world would amount to little more than a normal passage of an age if it had not rotted the very core of Occidental history. What we now

---

[239]If this is the case then the carvings on the white quartz stone above the east chamber, which has been broken by shoddy reconstruction techniques, cannot be read unless they are seen in a mirror.
[240]O'Kelly, Michael J. *Newgrange. Archaeology, art and legend.* London: Thames & Hudson, 1982.
[241]When the overhead stone in the east chamber was replaced after reconstruction it cracked due to stress on the cement pilings, but the markings are still clear. The excavators claim the stone was cracked before work began, but locals who entered the temple in living memory swear it was intact prior to 1960.

believe about the ancient past has been greatly influenced by people with a narrow view of the ancient world. [242]

Many antiquarians invaded Atlantic temples specifically to dig for buried treasure when in fact the true pre-Celtic treasure was in the sky. These same antiquarians, often armed with royal permits of extraordinary scope, frequently used the mass media to exaggerate the importance of finds and commonly posed as scientists when they were often mere glory hunters. [243]

Unfortunately, an academic reliance on prehistoric time barriers and hidebound theories about sudden attacks and invasions has created an impression of discontinuity where none exists. In truth, and the evidence supports this view, a long period of experimentation and gradual change was the norm. The hunting and gathering cultures of Western Europe did not suddenly cease hunting and gathering. The Stone Age people did not abruptly swap off their hunting sagas for a new pastoral legend. Stone writing did not suddenly appear. The transitions from Paleolithic to Mesolithic thence to Neolithic were slow and smooth. The Star Temple builders and the later Bell Beaker people were either natural groups who evolved in place, or friendly outsiders who gradually absorbed the ways of the indigenous people.

In any case, the traditional idea that the architects of Maes Howe or Kercado were cannibals and barbarians has fallen. This assertion is supported by the research of Alexander Marschak, a respected American scientist who has made many studies of the controversial Paleolithic horizon. One of his finds, a calculator made from an animal

---

[242]Pochoda, Elizabeth. *Arthurian Propaganda*. Chapel Hill: The University of North Carolina Press, 1971.
[243]Michell, John. *Megalithomania*. London: Thames& Hudson. p. 122.

bone, was used to predict lunar cycles with accuracy more than twenty-five thousand years ago. [244]

The people who built Newgrange actually did possess a written symbolic and scientific language. It may have not be identical to trigonometry or algebra, but it got the job done. Could a truly backward culture devise such brilliant and accurate architectures? Furthermore, writing alone can hardly be the best criteria for judging the degree of civility in a given culture. Ebla, a major city in the Middle East and the "developmental center" for the first forms of writing — was sacked and burned at a time when Kercado in Brittany and Knowth in Ireland were already one thousand years old and supporting peace-loving astronomers. [245]

The clay tablets from Ebla told us very little except that a language did exist at an early period in Mesopotamia. The tablets were basically granary and treasury inventories which would have been lost if they hadn't been baked by a fire started when the city was raided by an aggressive neighbor, probably the Babylonians. There was nothing in Ebla built to last six thousand years, even though the Babylonian calendar can be projected thousands of years into the future. In other words, there is no evidence the average Babylonian or Eblite placed much store in these macrocycles.

---

[244]Marschak, Alexander. *National Geographic* v. 147, #1, Jan. 1975. p. 65.
[245]Piggot, Stuart. *Ancient Europe.* Chicago: Aldine, 1970. Piggot estimates there were at least 10,000 people in England in 7500 BC. This is conservative, but adequate to ask what happened to those people? In my opinion they became the Star Temple builders. Jack Roberts estimates that there were about 200,000 people in Ireland during the late Neolithic and early Bronze Age, while Castleden conservatively estimates the Neolithic English population at 1.5 million. The discrepancy derives from the head count of graves and remains. This is not a good index because the majority of remains were scattered. A better method is to extrapolate on the number of farm sites.

Conversely, the stone carvings of the Boyne Valley were not exposed to violence until the mid-twentieth century when tourists and archaeologists started hacking on them. They counted huge calendrical cycles and were designed to last thousands of years. The carvings on the stones — and the placement of the stones in precise locations — continue to accurately predict eclipse cycles, moon dials and calendars of many types. The builders of the Boyne, who could have easily built a temple from sticks and gravel, decided to reach out to the future by using cyclopean building stones upon which to display there writing and astronomy. In this way they were unique in all the ancient world. (Plate xxxiv)

No matter what else they may turn out to be, the Star Temples are time capsules. Each precinct contains gifts from an ancient civilization to us. Anyone who visits these sites suddenly realizes the megalithic astronomers did possess a form of picture writing, a brilliant hyper-text which described their insights into the cosmos in clear-cut terms. This may have evolved into the language known to the Greeks, Romans and early Christians as *The Logos*. [246]

The early Indo-European writings found in Ebla were notations regarding economics, the size of a crop for taxation or the degree of wealth of a given merchant. There was no astronomy in that particular example. The Eblites, like most Indo-European groups, possessed a male dominated, almost military and almost vertical chain of command. Their's was a paternalistic culture with distinct chiefs and kings ruling segmented and hierarchical lower castes, probably including a slave class. They were not Goddess worshipers, at least not in a primary sense, and the female Goddesses they did worship were destructive like Kali,

---

[246]Bermant C. and M. Weitzman *Ebla*. New York: Times Books, 1979.

Astarte and Lilith. By contrast, the etched Star Temple notation, especially the snake-like sinusoidal and curvilinear carvings, seem to be based on the moon and the orbit of the planets as they correlate with the spawning cycle of salmon or the gestation period of swine.

After viewing these comparisons one can only ask why oriental writing, such as cuneiform, is still used as a standard to judge the intellectual abilities of ancient Occidental cultures. Clearly the Star Temple builders developed an architectural logoscript at a very early period. They may have worn skins, but they were not guided by extra-terrestrials and they did not have wars. Actually, they were more than simple farmers or husbandman, hunters or poets. Like their ancestors — living in the painted caves or following the trail of the snow goose — they were also astronomers with ample reason to drag huge stones over miles of rough terrain. [247]

In the Atlantic tradition the abstract writing on the megaliths continued the legends of the heroic maritime hunting and fishing cultures into historic times. In essence, the stones preserved their own legends. This is easily demonstrated in Ireland, Scotland and Brittany, less so in England, perhaps because more evidence was destroyed in England, but the flint-using tribes of the Star Temples did evolve the corbelled arch and their sophistication in agronomy, astronomy and art is irrefutable. The markings carved into the megaliths are not simple doodles and the juxtaposition of each stone to every other stone in the complex and to specific astronomical events indicates that the builders did possess a symbolic notation system. [248]

---

[247]Renfrew, Colin. *Before Civilization..* New York: Knopf, 1973. p. 120

[248]Morris, John. *The Age of Arthur.* New York: Scribners, 1973. p. 71. Morris is of the opinion that "There is almost nothing to show that Christians in Britain and Ireland were aware of Saint Austin. His so-called tri-

The Collapsing Wall

Newgrange, mentioned by Arthur C. Clark as the oldest stone building in the world, is one of the easiest Star Temples to visit because it is less than an hour's drive from the Dublin airport. When you approach Newgrange, an eerie feeling takes over. The first sight that strikes the visitor is its glistening art-deco facade. This southeast facing white quartz wall shimmers with reflected color by day and casts an orange glow by moonlight, as if it was designed by an anonymous Bauhaus architect. Professor O'Kelly assures us that both the small quartz and large, river rolled, stones were replaced exactly as they were found, so we must assume the temple looked somewhat as it does now. [249]

Professor O'Kelly and his wife Claire were in charge of reconstructing Newgrange from 1962 to 1975. During that period they observed the midwinter lightbeam on many

umphant conversion of the British can be attributed to the well-known comment that when he arrived he found them already worshipping the cross. This may imply that something akin to Christianity, that is the quest for Chi-Rho, the quest for the lightbeam and the basin stone, the quest for the cross of light was in place long before the historical Christ. The cross he spoke of was the Celtic cross still common throughout Ireland, Wales and Scotland. It is also entirely possible that a small circle of apostles knew of this religion when Christ was alive, but that the more esoteric nature of the rite was forgotten or expunged by the time it traveled to Rome and certainly by the time Saint Austin made his way to Britain.

[249]Clark, Arthur C. *Mysterious World*. London, Voyager Press/Granada Television, 1981. Clark was almost correct Actually, Newgrange is only one of the oldest stone buildings in the world. Kercado in France is older and Knowth and Dowth, less than a mile from Newgrange, are older by at least five hundred years. The dates for the Irish passage temples range between 4200 and 3200 BC, but recent cairns in Labrador have been dated to 4500 BC and a stone hearth was unearthed in Sligo dating to 6000 BC. In any case, the carved megalithic monuments of the Western European Atlantic cultures, as a group, are the oldest stone buildings on Earth.

occasions, although they were not the first to observe it, since it was common knowledge to the locals of the regions for at least three centuries, or, if you prefer, since the temple was built.

Martin Brennan has attempted to bring Professor O'Kelly's discoveries (and oversights) to world attention, but the issue is so calumnious, that an entire book could be written on the politics alone. Opponents from the Catholic church, various political parties, and the official Irish Board of Public Works feel Professor O'Kelly exaggerated the facade during his reconstruction, but others feel he did not go far enough. Suffice it to say O'Kelly followed almost every lead and went about his work with scientific rigor. Still, regardless of criticism, O'Kelly did play a stupendous role in the Atlantic drama. He was truthful to his intuition about Newgrange, in spite of pressure to avoid "pagan" interpretations, and he rebuilt Newgrange within reason. If it were not for his diligence in these matters Newgrange may have gone the way of Knowth, it's nearby companion mound, which will probably lay in an eroding heap for centuries to come. [250]

A study of the O'Kelly's construction techniques indicates that he was not closed minded. O'Kelly and a number of students built an experimental wall from temple stones designed to reveal just how the mound collapsed. Much to his amazement the many stones in the twenty-four-foot high revetment wall fell systematically, like a lava flow, almost as if the wall was designed to slip at a precise angle, sealing the temple in the process.

---

[250]Brennan, Martin op.cit. *The Stones of Ancient Ireland.*

In her *Illustrated Guide To Newgrange*, Claire O'Kelly, who worked side by side with her husband on the project, blames the slippage on bad construction techniques on the part of the Neolithic builders, but just the opposite is true. Not only was the Neolithic construction superb, the mounds were probably designed to collapse! [251]

From analysis of currently available data, there is little doubt the collapsed temples at Gavrinis, Kercado, Newgrange, Dowth, Knowth, and dozens of other locations around the North Atlantic rim were purposefully designed to "hermetically seal" their secrets. This means the people who built the temples knew their system could be misinterpreted and probably realized how temporary their form of enlightenment could be. They must have known their form of worship could be profaned if misunderstood and yet they used huge stones as building blocks. One can only assume they wanted their most important secrets to be encapsulated for a very long time. [252]

---

[251]O'Kelly, Clare. *An Illustrated Guide to Newgrange.* Cork: Cork University Press, 1977. Although O'Kelly did a defective job of reconstruction, his insights into the temple structure and the lightbeam were significant, even though he denied that astronomy could be the underlying motive for the mounds construction. O'Kelly's major mistake was in using uncoated iron reinforcement bar and badly mixed cement behind the walls. This is currently leaching iron oxide and is deteriorating some of the stones. He also used an inferior grade of cement which expanded and caused a large fully engraved capstone, located above the east chamber, to crack.

[252]Eogan, George. "A Neolithic Habitation Site in Townly Hall County Louth." *Journal of the Royal Society of Archaeology for Ireland.*, # 93. 1963 pp. 37-81. 1963. Eogan's speculation on dates was conducted three years before O'Kelly began excavating Newgrange. In fact Eogan found radiocarbon dates very close to those of Kercado in Brittany (4250 BC) from one sample of charcoal, but rejects them as anomalies and far too old. Actually 5000 BC is not an outlandish date for the earliest Atlantic rim cairn monuments and stone hearths.

But how was this achieved? As unbelievable as it may seem, the Star Temple builders may have allowed their sanctuaries to collapse with the aid of a well-placed hydraulic system. Before excavation, the mounds were composed of layers of gravel and charcoal built upon layers of mud and turf so that if the drainage system were to clog, a gradually increasing hydrostatic pressure would force the weight of the mound outward, collapsing the walls evenly around the circumference of the temple. In this process the entrances would be sealed and the stones in the kerb would be protected. In other words the Star Temples — the world's oldest stone buildings, containing the proto-Grail religion and the basic teachings of an entire aboriginal civilization — would automatically seal themselves from the eyes of the world if there were no initiates to clear the drains. This theory has at least one powerful factor on its side. If a famine or drought or a snap Ice Age struck the population, or if the work force shifted emphasis — as it seems to have done after the introduction of copper and bronze — the constant repairs required in the various temple sanctuaries would cease and the walls would collapse on their own, sealing the *logos* and the Atlantic Genesis for hundreds of generations to come.

The legends, including the proto-Grail legend, probably lived on, but the rites of the lightbeam and rebirth at these locations, would be sealed until more enlightened minds could unearth them. This explanation implies further that the Star Temple builders were what we would now call "futurists," and supplies the first solid evidence that ancient

196

Atlantic peoples were capable of formulating a concept of cultural destiny as well as a cultural past. [253]

Unbroken Chain

Not only did the Star Temples collapse and seal themselves, it is probable that the Boyne monuments are linked for terrestrial and oceanic navigational purposes to Maes Howe to the north in Scotland, Avebury to the south in Britain and Kercado to the east, in Brittany, because the alignments and situations of these major centers are very similar and very precise. The use of the corbelled ceiling and certain other building techniques, in areas far removed from one another, are too similar to attribute all of them to spontaneous developments. It seems as if these Star Temple complexes acted as ports of call or cargo hubs for a vast trading network that we are only now beginning to uncover. To see this hidden pattern, we need not assume the builders were flying saucer people or anything but practical fishers and husbandmen wishing to fix the hunting and planting calendar for purposes of survival and navigation. If we reject the idea that the temples have astronomical significance the linkage will not be seen, but when we assume, simply for the sake of argument, that the mounds do have lunar and solar connections beyond the lightbeam phenomenon or perhaps rooted to it and branching out from it, then the linkage becomes apparent.

The Boyne Valley structures, for example, operate interactively both between themselves and in conjunction

---

[253]Probably within a few centuries after the sanctuary was abandoned the pressure from backed-up rain water would build to push the upper material outward so that it would eventually "ooze" downward forming an almost airtight seal. Cattle, mankind and time would do the rest.

with a number of remote temple complexes. Contrary to local beliefs, and the denial of the archaeologists who misinterpret the data, they are celestial observatories. As the lightbeam enters Newgrange on the Solstice morning so does it enter Dowth on the same evening. It also enters Maes Howe, some four hundred miles away at sunset on the same Mid-Winter eve. This has been proven, filmed and published by numerous observers including the highly respected archaeologist Colin Renfrew. [254]

Clearly, the civilization which built the Star Temples needed them for navigation. If this transoceanic meshing of gears, this great stone network, were to be diminished in priority by difficult times or the rise to dominance of a less enlightened society, the continuity between the architect and the shaman of the ice caves — represented by the mounds and the shamanic rituals conducted in them — would also be broken. Rather than have the temples desecrated by vandals and disbelievers, the architect-navigators who built them thought it better to bury the Grail Stone and the other signs of the old religion under tons of stone and turf. Even so, the chain might not be entirely broken. Evidence of later cultural arrivals (the Bell Beaker people) and tolerance between groups in shared living circumstances exists in the Boyne, at nearby Tara and at Avebury in England. So the rudimentary Grail religion and legends may have been carried on by storytellers wending their way between these remote pocket cultures. By the time Occidental history, however biased, was placed on parchment by the Greeks and Romans, the songs and rituals of the

---

[254]Renfrew, Colin. *Investigation in the Orkneys.* London: Thames & Hudson, 1982.

Star Temple builders were faint whispers. In Plato's time, the visions of the isolated Atlantic culture grew into a ghostly wind from a place he called "Atlantis."

Philo the Alexandrian warned that a delicate balance exists between heaven and Earth, between light and dark. This is the basis for the modern science of ecology, but the idea is as much Megalithic as it is Hopi, Alexandrine or modern. The desire for harmony and peace is universal. The first surfaces to be ritualized under the illumination of lunar-reflected light, sunlight and firelight were the walls of the communal cave. The painters of the caverns and the builders of the Star Temples — artisans who existed ten thousand years apart — must have seen the same relationships between earthly events and skyward forces. They must have accumulated millions of hours collectively meditating on the proper ritual astronomy to match each event. These rites, ikons and legends were then handed down from priest to sibyl, from mother to son, from father to daughter until they were finally set into stone. The survival of the Star Temples meant the clocks of mother nature, the Paleolithic mother Goddess, would be kept in perfect order. Under her care the incoherent was made reasonable, the wild was tamed. Those initiated into her secrets must have developed a natural balance.

In the proto-Celtic world, the Goddess presided over the Grail Stone ritual. She supervised the ablutions, the public ceremonies, the construction of the shrine and the "mixing of the medicine" — probably an ergot and mushroom combination — a liquid which reflected the stars and the transits of the planets as it settled into its concave stone. The contents of this Grail Stone or cauldron meant a great deal to the participants in the ritual. The same held true five-thousand years later when the same rituals appeared in medieval illuminated manuscripts, one of which was to become known as *The Book of the Holy Grail.* The muted peasant populations of Western Europe, the ancestors of most North Americans, have carried the secret books of the Grail in their hearts for thousands of years. Those who serve it are rewarded. Its democracy and its feast of love did survive. It is the Ace of Cups in the Tarot, the Dionysian ritual quest, a secret book, a communion chalice, a baptismal font, but more importantly it is, as the megalith people saw it, an inexhaustible basin full of light waiting for enlightened minds to peer into its secrets.

Apparently we are those enlightened minds. But are we ready for what we have before us? Are we enlightened enough to cast off our stereotypes and our obsolete notions about the beginning of the human race? Are we as enlightened as the Dawn People or the Star Temple builders?

APPENDICES

Appendix A
A Chronology of Star Temple Sites

	Location	Description	Age
1	L'Anse Amour, Labrador, Canada.	Oldest uncarved cairn as yet discovered. Small trilithon arch. Possible lightbeam.	5000 BC
2	Sliabh Gullion, Sligo, Ireland.	Oldest uncarved court cairn and cruciform chamber in Europe.	4700 BC
3	Loughcrew, Oldcastle, Ireland.	Oldest known carved cairns. Multiple lightbeams.	4500 BC
4	Kercado, Vannes, France.	Oldest uncarved Passage Temple and cruciform chamber. [1]	4200 BC
5	Dowth, Boyne Valley, Ireland.	Oldest, combined cairn and Passage Temple. [2]	4000 BC
6	Knowth, Boyne Valley, Ireland.	Oldest fully excavated complex Passage Temple. [3]	3800 BC
7	Newgrange, Boyne Valley, Ireland.	Carved cruciform chamber.	3400 BC
8	Avebury, Wiltshire, England.	Largest uncut stone circle.	3200 BC
9	Carnac, Vannes, France.	Largest linear stone alignment	3200 BC
10	Stonehenge III.	Largest Trilithons known. [4]	1800 BC

All dates are recalibrated to ±500 years. Many sites remain unexcavated.

[1] Lightbeam not established at Kercado due to subsidence, but alignment indicates Winter Solstice beam and heel stone arrangement.

[2] Winter Solstice sunset beam. Possible sunrise beam. Multiple basin stones.

[3] Spring Equinox sunrise lightbeam and Autumnal Equinox sunset beam, plus eclipse predictor. Multiple foresights and gnomons. Multiple carved basin stones and reflecting pools.

[4] Summer Solstice dawn lightbeam if occluded.

Appendix B

Transformations of the Grail Ikon

The fundamental premise of this work, in fact the entire Grail Trilogy, is that a sacred chalice or concave ritual object, symbolic of the Great Mother spirit, has evolved in the Atlantic Mysteries through various stages since its inception and that this ikon, known earlier by various names, became The Holy Grail.This implies that the Grail was not originally Christian and that elements of the religion we know call Christianity were incorporated and imported from the early cauldron worship practices.

In other words the Grail, the chalice we think of as the cup used by Jesus at the last supper, is only one manifestation of a much older and archetypical ikon which can be traced to Paleolithic Shamanism in Western Europe, to Neolithic astronomy centers in Ireland and to sources in Africa and Asia. Worship of a concave object is probably traceable to the earliest practices of our species.

The transformation of symbols is well established in Jungian psychology, and it is well known that symbols often change in meaning during their transformation. Oddly enough the Grail symbol, while changing outwardly, as a skull, a horn, a clay pot or a cauldron stone, has remained consistent in meaning over time. Since we have no way of knowing what the shaman or sibyl called the bowl or chalice we must select a name for it.

I have selected the modern evolution of the word — "Grail" to mean any concave ritual object used in a temple context and in conjunction with shamanic ritual, astronomy, beam dialing or lightbeam activity. Calling it the Grail or proto-Grail, even though the word "Graal," was proximally coined in the Middle Ages, is not a misnomer.

The following chart tracks the evolution of the lesser and greater Grail ikons in Atlantic Europe.

Era	Ikon
Paleolithic and Mesolithic (200,000-5000 BC)	Skull Rams Horn or Gourd
Neolithic (5000-2500 BC)	Basin Stone Scallop Shell
Bronze Age (2500-800 BC)	Copper Cauldron Bell Beaker
Iron Age and Dark Ages (800 BC- AD 800)	Illuminated Manuscript Baptismal Font and Chalice
Middle Ages (AD 900-1400)	Gothic Cathedral
Renaissance (1400-present)	Alchemists Retort

Table of progressive Grail Ikon Transformations as correlated with the known historical progression of Western Civilization

The Paleolithic
and Mesolithic Grail   *200,000-5,000 BC*

The first version of the Grail ikon was probably a skull. Skulls have been located in ritual contexts at Neanderthal and Cro-Magnon sites. In some cases a human skull was used, but in many cases the cave shaman preferred a bison, bear or other large animal skull because it held a larger quantity of sacramental fluid, probably a mushroom mixture or some other vision producing compound. In almost every case, the worship of the concave object is a variation on the worship of the Goddess. Here Goddess worship is fundamentally defined as worship of the void.

As our species evolved into the Mesolithic era in Western Europe the skull was replaced by the drinking gourd or goats horn fashioned into a cup. Even at this early stage a dichotomy between the lesser and greater vessels can be seen in ritual use. By 8000 BC, the scallop shell was in use as a personal spoon or ladle while the skull itself was reserved for the role of the cauldron. So here the cauldron is the central ikon or Grail, not the chalice, although both appear necessary for the entire ritual.

The Neolithic Grail   *5000-2500 BC*

After the Ice Age, as pastoral settlement and tree clearance begins, the cauldron, once a skull, becomes a solid concave stone, but the smaller Grail remains a scallop shell or rude clay cup. For the first time the world of man takes precedence over the celestial world and for the first time in human evolution the cave is replaced by stone buildings built and designed for ritual purposes.

Here, probably for the first time, the lightbeam and basin stone are linked in a permanent sanctuary setting. Populations are larger, land is parceled out and tribes begin to form.

The Bronze Age Grail   *2500-800 BC*

The cauldron stone gives way gradually to the art of metallurgy. The cauldron is now fashioned from copper and bronze. The skilfully crafted ceremonial beaker begins to make an appearance in the Bronze Age, giving precedence to the chalice over the cauldron.

205

There is an extensive overlapping period between 3000 and 2500 BC in which numerous tribal identities were merged in Western Europe, the proto-Celts were formed in this period, for example, and yet the Goddess and the Grail-Cauldron construct remain central to all religious practices and most legends. The scallop shell is still in use in some rituals especially in Spain.

The Winter lightbeam ritual migrates to Stonehenge and Avebury although it is not as central as it was in the Irish and French temples of the proceeding era.

The Iron Age and Dark Age Grail   *800 BC - AD 800*

The Grail grew into a chalice in the period of Atlantic tribal formation immediately preceding the rise of the Greek State and the denouement of the Roman Empire. The chalice was now cast in silver and gold and decorated with precious gems, the Ardagh Chalice from Ireland being a classic example.

The chalice took on a double meaning as Mithraic and Dionysian rites continued to influence nascent Christianity. The Chalice became the most critical aspect of the communion ceremony. By drinking from it one could be transfigured or at least be empathic with the spirit of Christ. But the basin stone was not forgotten; it evolved into the baptismal font, located in every church.

Romanesque architecture and numerous illuminated manuscripts crafted by monks, some of which were heretics, resurrected the Star Temple ceremony by including the lightbeam ritual and the processional around the cathedral or maze (the gradual, the choir processional, the rosary, and the fourteen stages of the cross for example) as part of the normal activity of Christian worship. The old religion was now transparent.

Appendix B

The Gothic Grail   *AD 900-1400*

In the Middle Ages, marked between the reign of Charlemagne and the tenure of Duns Scotus Erigena to the final construction of Chartres and Ameins, the Grail becomes a literary abstraction, deeply linked to Christianity as the cup used at the last supper and the cup used by Joseph to collect the drops of blood from the wounds of Christ. The Grail is the chalice used at communion and, in the larger sense, the baptismal font, but it now evolves into a larger more all embracing construct.

The Grail remains central to Christian ritual, but its roots in the ancient Celtic legends and in the mythical personas of Arthur and Guenevere and the knights of the Round Table are emphasized in a parallel and alternative form as defined by the literature and poetry of the troubadours. But more than this the Grail religion, the idea that heaven is reflected on Earth, the idea that the Goddess is manifest in everything in nature — symbolized by the Virgin Mary — manifests itself as the abstract reason behind the construction of many Gothic cathedrals. In other words, the Gothic cathedrals are dedicated to the Goddess and through her to the Grail, which is an abstraction of her sinuosity as the vessel of the void. At last the Grail and the Cathedral are reunited. The lightbeam continues to enter the illuminated sanctuary of the Great Mother.

The Renaissance Grail   *1400 to Present Era*

The word "renaissance" literally means rebirth. Once the Grail religion, the old religion, the hermetic doctrine, was reborn in permanent stone, and in the stained glass and sculpture that make up the Gothic cathedrals, the final manifestation of the Grail was possible.

207

As more and more people became literate and enlightened, the Grail could easily be seen as the retort or alembic of the alchemist. New medicine and new political schemes, actually old ideals like democracy, manifested for the first time in Western Europe emerged, with the alchemists and the Rosicrucians or Knights of the Temple or other secret societies leading the way. The legendary promise that the Grail was a cauldron or cornucopia of health and spiritual nourishment would now come true. The transformation of the human race — from frightened and ignorant savages to reasonable and tolerant measurers of time and goods — was now complete.

In the renaissance the Grail evolved within the science of alchemy, causing a revolution in art, architecture and medicine. All modern chemistry and nuclear physics took root in the alchemical movement and, if the Rosicrucian enlightenment is any indication, so did the idea of freedom of speech and action for the common citizen.

Appendix C
The Atlantic Cultural Continuum

Anyone seriously interested in a stream of inquiry leading to a new definition of The Holy Grail is well advised to study the various phases of early architectural development in Western Europe. The three pre-Christian phases most interesting to the Grail theme are the Final Paleolithic, the Mesolithic and the Neolithic.

The Final Paleolithic or Old Stone Age

The time frame known as the Paleolithic or "Old Stone Age" covers prehistory in Western Europe from the first walking tool users to the ascent of true *Homo Sapiens* and is itself generally subdivided into three sections as follows: Lower Paleolithic — encompassing proto-humans, our earliest ancestors, about four million years ago, Middle Paleolithic — including most of Neanderthal and Cro-Magnon evolution in Western Europe and the Final Paleolithic — starting about forty thousand years ago and ending with the last glacial, or Wurm, epoch. A few poets have argued that we are still in this phase and will not leave it until we do away with violence, but this is speculation.

There is much controversy, but the Final Paleolithic is considered the first era of modern humans in Western Europe. Here we discover widespread standardization of tools, art techniques and probably speech patterns. Denizens of the Final Paleolithic generally looked and walked like contemporary people. We have been brainwashed about their savage appearance. Some were tall, some short. Some were red headed some dark. Some claimed Mediterranean ancestors and some migrated from Ethiopia or other parts of Africa. Bones of every shape size and description have been found and yet, until recently, no single computer system has been fast enough or large enough to sort the finds as to shape and size, blood type and gender. Even so, a factual picture is emerging. The human beings we once thought of as ugly, monkey-like and primitive, would not, if properly clad, be out of place in a New York subway.

The Final Paleolithic was dominated by a human type sometimes referred to as *Homo Faber,* man the manufacturer, the creator beast. They were fascinated by technology and made implements for ceremony as well as hunting. Although the great cave paintings at Lascaux are from this era, abstract art was also used. Zigzags, spirals and other geometric marks are commonly found on tools of that era, tools often so finely produced, and so standardized in size, that they can only be thought of as ritual objects.

The interactive populations at the end of the last great Ice Age are identified by advanced blade tools and increasingly elaborate cave art which included counting and tally marks as well as geometric and, according to some researchers, celestial decorations. Counting tools such as the hand held lunar calculators, used to predict salmon and red deer migrations, also played an important role.

The Mesolithic or Middle Stone Age

Next, in school book order, comes a difficult to define prehistoric layer called the Mesolithic or "Middle Stone Age" created by the withdrawal of the glaciers about 8300 BC. This period, typified by hunting and gathering from riverside encampments rather than caves, was supposed to have lasted about five thousand years, but some tribes in Western Europe may have evolved quickly from the cave to agriculture, without a well defined intermediate period, while others may have remained hunter-gatherers well into the

Roman occupation of Western Europe. Here again a few humanists and poets believe we are still in the hunter-gatherer period and that agriculture is merely a logical extension of the gathering process, while husbandry is a logical extension of early hunting technology.

In the Mesolithic era hunters, still operating in the Ice Age fashion, buried their dead in red ochre-lined graves and sailed along the ice rims to Greenland and beyond following the killer whale and other migratory animals, including geese. The oldest site in Labrador is dated circa 7500 years before the present era. In Bosulan, Sweden a date of 5300 BC is well established and a similar date has been derived by analyzing charcoal from a stone hearth in Sligo, Ireland.

On the island of Jura, conical round huts became wood and stone houses covered with skins and thatch. Around the same time in Portugal, Sligo and West Cork, kitchens were built from stone slabs incorporated into the walls of similar round houses. Most importantly for the Grail, many carved megaliths began to appear in isolated alignments. Each Atlantic maritime village or tribe possessed its own stone ring which acted as a node within a complex communications network.

The Neolithic or New Stone Age

The sheer majesty of monuments such as the Star Temples and Stonehenge, hints that the Neolithic era was colored by a culture-wide quest for enlightenment through architecture, but this quest, once achieved, led to a quest for individual enlightenment. The Star Temple builders developed a spectacular architectural model that allowed ritual astronomy to enter the life of every citizen, every day. Their's was a quest for a temple precinct which would bring back the musical resonance and social security of the tribal cave and the hunt while capturing the new rhythms of the sea and pasture.

The Atlantic Genesis cosmology can also be detected in the positioning of the stones and in the progress of architectural themes. In the Star Temples we see the reconstruction of the cave environment, but we also see a catalog of abstract art — the oral traditions of the Paleolithic — carved in petroglyphs for Neolithic audiences. In the Star Temple, representational paintings are no longer imperative. Totemic magic *per se* is no longer absolute. The geometric talisman augments the animistic totem. Both are used. The old ways were never discarded, but like many transitions, the new forms — spirals and counting devices — are relied on more heavily as they become accessible.

Once the legends of the hunt and the measurements of nature are cast in stone, the tribe gains the ability to anticipate cyclic events identically over many generations. Anxiety is reduced because everyone in the culture can see into the future with a degree of accuracy only dreamt of by the hunter-gatherers of the Maglemosian era. Still, the hunting rituals are commemorated in legend. The sagas and treks of the ancestors are made into myth and memorized by association with the stars and the stones. In the Atlantic Neolithic Genesis, the science of number and the predictability of events took precedence over sympathetic magic, but the shaman and sibyl were still necessary as spiritual guides and medicine makers, midwives and storytellers.

Appendix D
Atlantic Architectural Styles

There are a number of architectural styles in the Atlantic biome that have evolved along with the evolution of the Grail ikon.

The Dolmen

Dolmen and tripod structures, translated as "table stones" French: *quoit,* Welsh: *cromlech*, seem to mark the fuzzy line between the Mesolithic wanderers (the Dawn People) and the Neolithic settlement folk (the Star Temple builders). Dolmen were constructed throughout the Neolithic horizon well into the Bronze Age. They may be associated with death rituals because they were probably used as exposure platforms in the excarnation process, but they are also astronomy platforms as it was believed the human soul could only achieve oneness with the universe by going back to nature on a specific solar, lunar or planetary alignment. Like the Star Temple architects, the dolmen builders were attempting to bring the sky to Earth. They may have exposed a body in ritual fashion on top of the dolmen, but rarely under it and the Dolmen should not be confused with a "Wedge Tomb," pit burial or saucer mound.

Dolmen are stone arches composed of three or four megaliths capped with a massive boulder or flat rock. The capstone feature appears in Maine, along Penobscot Bay, and again at Stonehenge and in the corbelled ceilings of the Star Temples of Brittany and Ireland. Some dolmen were more labor intensive, designed with as many as twenty-four upright stones called "orthostats," obviously leading the way to the cairn idea, the next evolution of architecture.

Others used as few as two orthostats, the whole leaning against a hillside for support. Structures using three support uprights are sometimes called tripod structures.

These famous monuments are common in Brittany, Ireland, Wales and Scotland and often mark trade routes. They are also significant along specific straight tracks which connect villages and habitation settlements to trackways.

Dolmen are often part of larger precincts dedicated to astronomical observations and seafaring navigation. The observer could sit inside and meditate or simply observe the passage of a planet or the sun or moon. Fires could have been set alight within a dolmen to create a lighthouse effect when viewed from the sea.

Like native North American tribes, the elements of the human form would be taken from the top of the Dolmen skyward to the spirit world. Ravens and other animals carried away the bodies leaving little to cremate or bury. The tripod dolmen, found all over Western Europe, is actually an intermediate form between the small trilithon found in early cairns about 5500 BC and the huge trilithons at Stonehenge.

Since the triple stone monument was so well known they may have some mathematic symbolism beyond architecture. They may have even been an early influence on Greek mathematics. Look closely at the symbol π, the symbol we know from basic geometry as part of a formula for determining the circumference of a circle and for erecting triangles within a circle. It looks like a megalithic arch or the portal to one of the dolmen. Is this coincidence?

The Cairn Temple

Cairns, essentially small stone mounds used for ritual astronomy, are the next natural progression in the building technology of Atlantic Europe and North America. Contrary to popular belief only a small percentage of these structures were used for burial.

Cairns are older than the dolmen in Labrador, but seem to have been completely integrated with the trilithon or orthostat and weighted slab technique at a very early period in Ireland, Scotland and Norway. This may someday be explained by the possibility that a cultural merger between Amerindian peoples and European Aboriginal peoples took place shortly after the end of the Wurm Ice Age. The dolmen comes before the full-blown Star Temple in the architectural sequence and yet it can also be seen in use in the Bronze Age, almost as if it were a symbolic alter to the old gods and magicians, a kind of local Star Temple in miniature.

From an architectural viewpoint, piled stone cairns have aspects in common with the dolmen including astronomical alignments, but unlike dolmen they often appear adjacent to permanent housing settlements and were probably used as public chapels.

Cairns, especially court cairns, incorporate the first cyclopean stone temples constructed anywhere on Earth and are excellent indications of an early date for settled religious practices in the Atlantic interactive sphere. Early cairns date to about 4500 BC in Portugal at Evora, but Irish dates can exceed the fifth millennium and North American cairns may be older.

Many cairns contained basin stones or ritual ceramic bowls and many show a distinct trilithon feature, either as a small pit in the interior as in Labrador, or as an actual architectural member to give height to a chamber as at Loughcrew in Ireland.

The inner chambers of the more complex cairns are often cruciform, and most of them incorporate beam-

215

dialing in some form indicating a systematic progression between the cairn builders and the full-blown passage temple builders. The Carrowkeel Cairn in Sligo dates to about 4500 BC and is built in the shape of the "Fat Goddess" as are the temples at Tarxien on Malta. The difference being that the Carrowkeel cairn is at least one thousand years older than the Maltese temples.

The cairn at Fourknocks, near Dublin airport, built in the Bronze Age after the Star Temples collapsed, or roughly 1800 BC, is pear-shaped like the uterus of the Goddess and appears to be composed of elements brought to the site from other Star Temples These two sites mark building designs on either side of the passage temple period.

The Irish, French and Portuguese cairns are two thousand years older than the Maltese structures. Here the trend seems to have moved from West to East over a very long period of time with only minor changes, probably because most of the cairns and settings are almost identical in terms of ritual astronomy. Obviously, there was some kind of philosophy, some creation myth, behind the construction of these structures — a deep and consistent idea.

Cairns on the island of Anglesea, off the coast of Wales, exhibit the typical large stone kerb or circular bumper wall of the true megalithic Star temple filled in from behind with alternate layers of gravel and turf. They display very few inscriptions, and we can assume they are a transitional phase between the simple cairn and the Star Temple, but these structures look more like beehives or astronomy sites than tombs. Again, few original inhumations have been located.

Carved Megaliths

Some of cairns show evidence of symbolic carvings which represent a hypertext or meta-language we are only now beginning to understand. The cairns which use the hypertext seem to begin at the first phase of the Neolithic, at the exact point where the cairn grew into a larger more complex temple. The best example of this is located on a small mountain top at Loughcrew near Oldcastle, again in Ireland.

Loughcrew is a Neolithic hilltop site located about fifty miles northwest of Dublin and in direct line with the Boyne Valley monuments. The hill is dotted with cairns and standing stones and the view rotates three hundred and sixty degrees. Each of the cairns is located in such a way as to catch the apparent rise and set of the sun and the activities of the moon and Venus in a huge X pattern at different times of the year. The entire year is represented at Loughcrew, indicating its importance for the Atlantic people.

The entire hilltop — *Sliebe Na Kalligh* in Irish; literally translated to "Witch Mountain" — is an observatory standing eight hundred feet above sea level. This location features a number of huge stones, one recumbent alter called "The Hags Chair," weighing twenty tons or more, and a number of smaller stones many with carvings. The Loughcrew markings are similar in style to those found in Portugal and France, in Britain and Southern Ireland and any experts feel there is a direct cultural connection.

An intrepid astronomer will marvel at this fabulous site. The climb up and the observations take at least a day, but the most amazing observations take place at night. If the observers body is positioned into one of the many sighting cairns the totality of the void, the black of space and the twinkle of the planets as they wander by their marker stones, can be experienced. An overnight stay is recommended.

At Loughcrew the clear night skies reveal an unbelievable view of the moon in its phases, and every star and planet alignment visible to the naked eye is easy to spot. On a new moon night one gets the feeling the stars are close enough to touch. In Spring, the visitor can see the Atlantic to the west and the Irish Sea to the east. In October, bonfires can be seen blazing across the countryside and at Winter Solstice, the sunbeam enters a number of cairns. At this height, a signal system could have been set up to convey messages across Ireland and to fishing craft at sea. No false horizons were necessary on the Witches Mountain as they are at Newgrange in the valley below.

Cairn T, the major cairn, and the only intact structure, was once thought to be the tomb of the legendary bard, *Ollamah Fodlah*. Although the bardic habitation of the place is mythical, it remains a site of enormous importance and a place of breathtaking beauty, at least as impressive, in an Atlantic sense, as Machu Picchu in Peru, especially when we realize it is five thousand years older than the Peruvian site. Its status as a tomb is also unlikely as no skeletal remains dating to the construction date have been found. Cairn T, which is rich in spirals and zigzag markings, is calibrated to the fourth millennium making it one of the first carved astronomical observatories on Earth.

Passage Temples

The Passage Temple, also known by the outdated phrase "Passage Tomb," is the third and final development in pre-bronze Atlantic architecture and is, without doubt, the most controversial.

To be true to the ancient cultures, cairns are actually Star Temples, but unlike cairns, which feature short passages and grotto like chambers, Star Temples feature long passages leading to an interior ceremonial chamber often large enough for human entry. Both cairn and Star Temple can display beam dials and shadow clocks, and both certainly display elemental signs of ritual astronomy, but the Star Temple seems to be the high mark of Neolithic architecture.

There are thousands of carved megalith sites in Atlantic Europe, and yet they appear no where else on Earth, at least not in the fourth millennium time frame. Some early Star Temples have cairn-like grottos which can be thought of as truncated passages since they do admit a beam of light, such as those at Dowth. Others have long narrow tunnels, such as those at Knowth, and a few take sharp angles, such as the passage in the mound on the Island of Gavrinis off the Quiberron Peninsula in Brittany.

Star Temples are designed to admit sun, star or lunar light at certain times of the year and to exclude it at other times, implying they were designed for specific rituals and cycles.Contrary to the beliefs of many elder archaeologists, these mounds, regardless of what else they might have been, were observatories for astronomical events.

Appendix E
Illustrations and Maps

National Gallery, Washington, D.C.

Plate i. *Chalice of the Abbot Suger of St. Denis.*

Plate ii. *Drombeg Circle, West Cork, Ireland.*

Jack Roberts

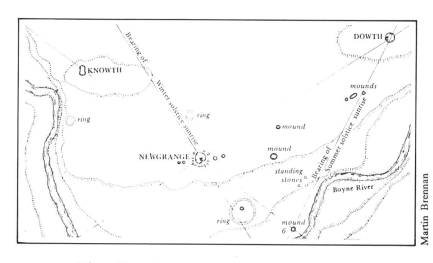

Martin Brennan

Plate iii. *The Boyne Valley showing the
location of mounds in the Star Temple complex.*

The Cauldron and The Grail

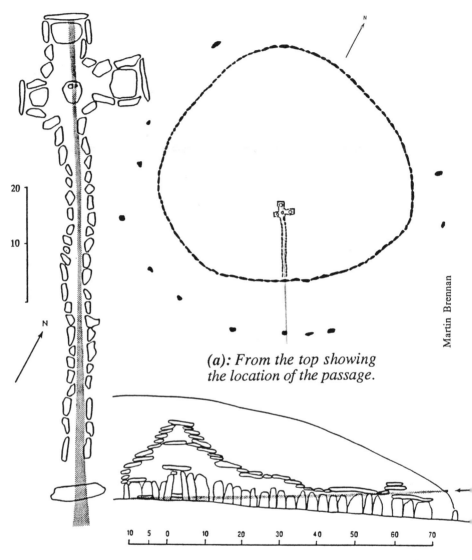

(a): From the top showing the location of the passage.

(b): Enlarged detail of the passage showing the location of the Grail Stone.

(c): From the west side showing the direction of the sunbeam at Winter Solstice.

Plate iv. *Newgrange ground plan.*

222

Appendix E

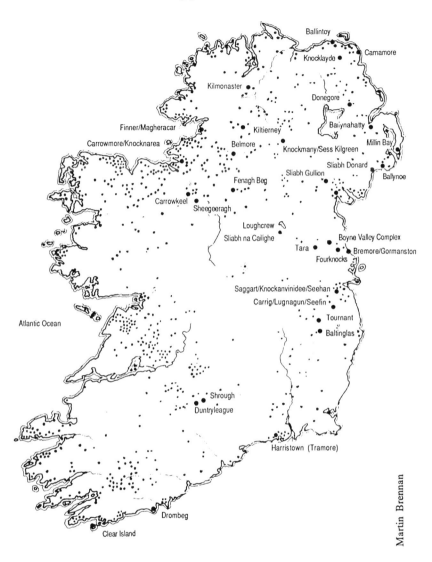

Plate v. *Location of major Irish Star Temple sites.*

223

Manly P. Hall

Plate vi. Mithra in the form of the leontocephalic Kronos.

224

British Museum

Plate vii. Interior detail. Dionysian ritual bowl
(Krater), Goddess at center holding Grail.

225

Jack Roberts

Plate viii. Newgrange entrance stone and roof box.

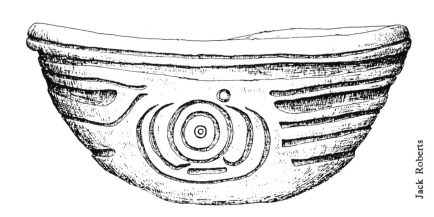

Jack Roberts

Plate ix. Knowth Grail Stone.

226

Appendix E

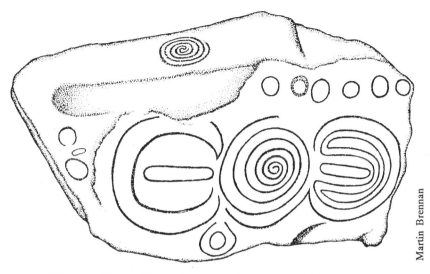

Martin Brennan

Plate x. Top: *Knowth carved stone c. 4000 BC.*
Bottom: *Christiaan Huygens' drawings of the planet Saturn,
eighteenth century naked eye observation. For comparison.*

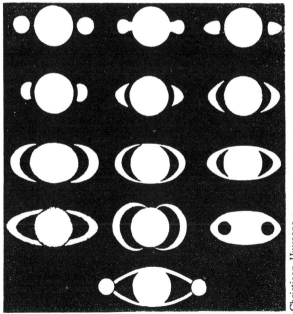

Christiaan Huygens

227

Joffra Boschart

Plate xi. *The angel appears to the alchemist with the secrets of the Grail. A Rosicrucian metaphor for the lightbeam.*

228

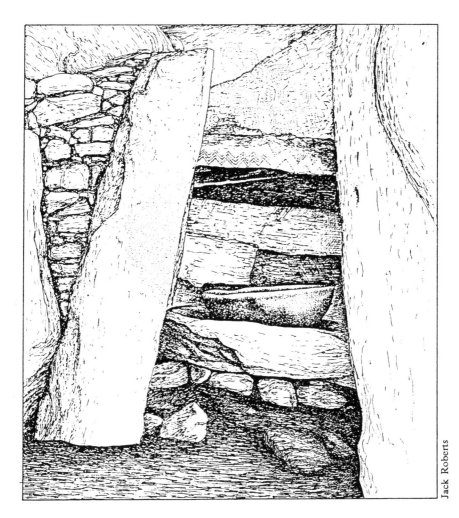

Jack Roberts

***Plate xii.** Interior chamber, east recess, Newgrange,
showing Grail Stone.*

Martin Brennan

Plate xiii. Triple spiral carving from Newgrange passage.

Irish National Museum, Dublin

*Plate xiv. Elaborately carved macehead,
found in the east chamber at Knowth.*

230

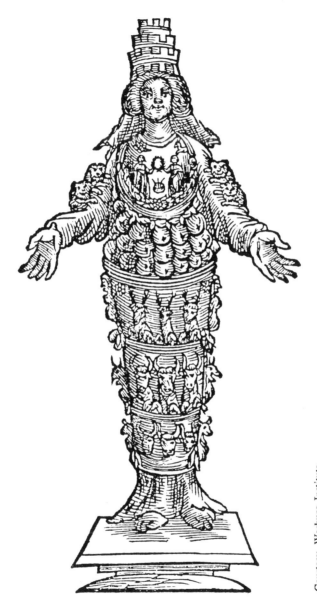

Plate xv. Isis Multimammia.

Courtesy, Warburg Institute

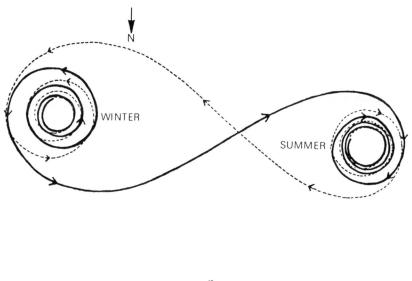

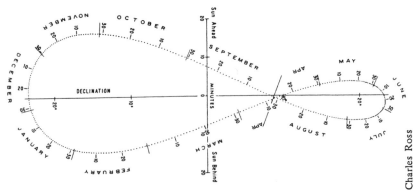

Plate xvi. *The Analemma: the declination of the sun relative to the earth's orbit. The curved ends represent the Solstices the center represents the Equinoxes.*

Plate xvii. *Aerial view of Glastonbury Tor c. 1920.*
The clearly delineated spiral labyrinth cut into the
slope is now eroded almost beyond recognition.

K.E. Maltwood

Courtesy, Warburg Institute, London

Plate xviii. *Jacques de Molay,*
the last Grand Master of the Knights Templars.

233

Courtesy, Warburg Institute, London

Plate xix. The Roman goddess, Cybele, emerging from the
sea indicating her influence over the tides and fertility.

Courtesy, Bibliothèque Nationale, Paris

Courtesy, Time Life, Inc.

Plate xx. *Bronze poppy-headed pins from Switzerland, c. 1800 BC, compared to opium pods prepared for harvest.*

235

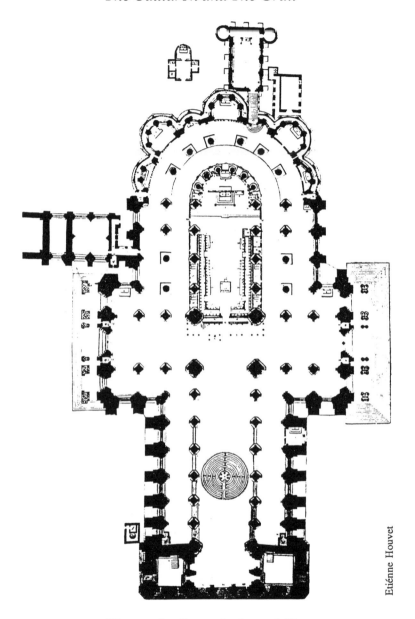

Plate xxi. Ground plan of Chartres Cathedral showing the narthex and maze.

Etiénne Houvet

236

Plate xxii. *Armillary Sphere. Woodcut from*
Textus de Sphaera by Johannes de Sacrobosco, 1538.
Note the entire universe emerges from the
Grail-like object in the center.

Courtesy, Warburg Institute

Plate xxiii. *Morris Dancers c. 1580. Note Maypole,
Hobby Horse and other pagan symbols.*

238

Courtesy, RILKO

Plate xxiv. *The portal of initiation at Chartres cathedral showing the Ark of the Covenant containing the Grail and Aaron's Rod, brought by ox cart to Chartres from Jerusalem.*

Plate xxv. Virgin as Grail Bearer from the sketchbook of the Templar architect, Villard de Honnecourt. Thirteenth century.

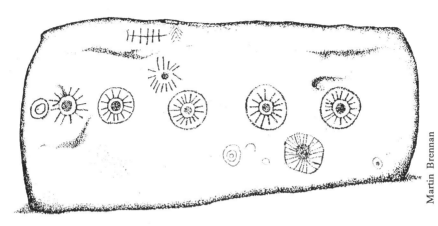

Martin Brennan

Plate xxvi. *Stone of the Seven Suns, Dowth.*

Plate xxvii. *The Royal Portal, Chartres cathedral,*
Christ emerging from a vesica symbolizing the
womb of the prepatriarchical Great Mother
surrounded by zodiac animals and angels.

Courtesy Warburg Institute

Plate xxviii. *St. Michael with an Excalibur-like sword slaying the dragon, a metaphor for changes in the pole star.*

242

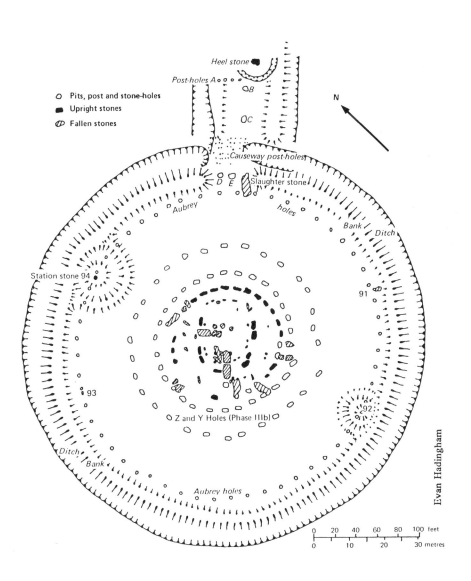

Plate xxix. *Radial, computer-like layout of Stonehenge.*

243

Plate xxx. *Mons Philosophorum, Rosicrucian depiction of creation and evolution. Note that the hermit is located in a mound cavern similar to the Star Temples.*

Plate xxxi. *The title page of Athanasius Kircher's seventeenth century opus Ars Magna Lucs et Umbrae. (Great Book of Light and Shadow). Kircher, a Rosicrucian initiate, shows the two basic methods of studying light used in the Star Temples. Note the arrangement of reflected lightbeams entering the stone mound.*

Plate xxxii. *Neolithic Hypertext notations.*

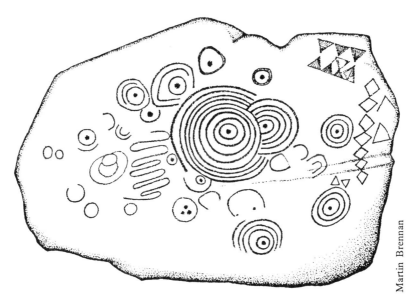

Plate xxxiii. Carved stone, Loughcrew.

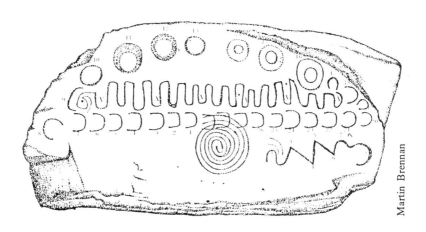

Plate xxxiv. The Calendar Stone, Knowth.

247

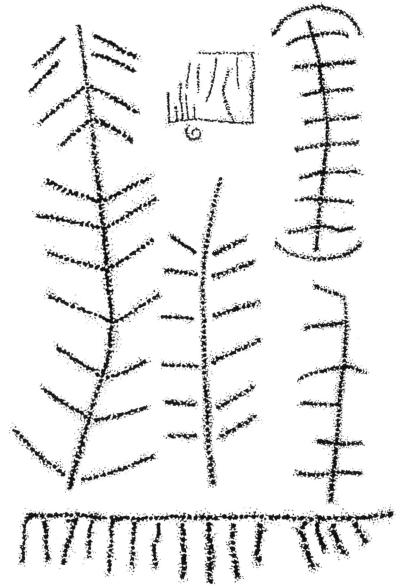

(a) Irish Neolithic offset "words."

Plate xxxv. *Atlantic forerunners of modern writing.*

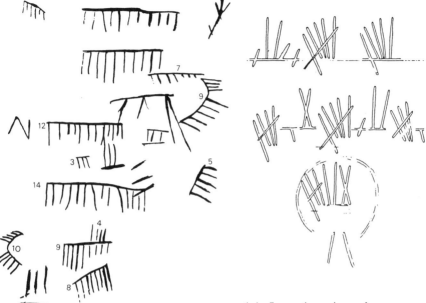

(b) Cro-magnon cave tally marks.

(c) Iron Age American cave notations, Wyoming.

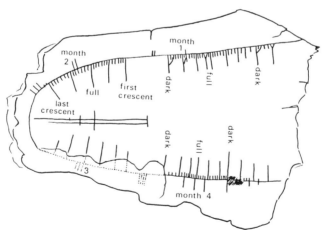

(d) Neanderthal moon phase calculator.

Plate xxxv *(continued)*.

SUBJECT BIBLIOGRAPHY

The following references are listed by topic to allow specialists and students to seek specific avenues of inquiry in related areas. The entries are not exhaustive but should provide essential reading in each area. As much as possible the listings are in keeping with the cataloging system used at the Warburg Institute, London.

Alchemy

Ashmole, Elias. *Alchemical History of Britain*. Berkeley: Shambala, 1973.

Bacstrom, C. Hamilton and J. W. Jones ed. *Bacstrom's Alchemical Anthology*. London: John M. Watkins, 1960.

Burland, C.A. *The Arts of the Alchemists*, Weidenfeld and Nicolson: London, 1967.

Eliade, M. *The Forge and the Crucible*. second ed. Chicago: University of Chicago Press, 1978.

Fulcanelli (pseud. anon.) *The Mystere de la Cathedral*. London: Neville Spearman, 1972.

Johnson, Ben. Limited ed. *The Alchemist*. London: The Kings Library De La More Press, 1951.

Johnson, Kenneth Rayner. *The Fulcanelli Phenomenon*. Jersey: Neville Spearman, 1980.

Magnus, Albertus *Secrets of Albertus Magnus' Herbal*. London: Warburg Institute, 1954.

Pachter, H. *Magic Into Science: The Story of Paracelsus*. New York: Henry Schuman, 1951.

Archaeoastronomy

Aveni, Anthony F. "Archaeoastronomy." *Advances in Archaeological Method and Theory*. Vol. 4. Princeton: Academic Press, 1981.

Baity, Elizabeth Chesley. "Archaeoastronomy and Ethno-astronomy So Far." *Current Anthropology*, #14. 1973.

Bass, George F. ed. *A History of Seafaring*. (early navigation) London: Thames & Hudson, 1972.

Brown, Peter Lancaster. *Megaliths and Masterminds.* New York: Scribner's Sons, 1979.

Colin, Rodney. *A Theory of Celestial Influence.* New York: Universe Press, 1957.

Gleadow, R. *The Origins of the Zodiac.* London: Jonathan Cape, 1968.

Harrison, Hank. 6000 Year Old Computers, *Dr. Dobb's Journal-Software Tools.* Palo Alto: December, 1982.

Hawkins, G. *Stonehenge Decoded.* New York: Doubleday, 1963.

— "Stonehenge, a Neolithic Computer," *Nature,* #200, 1963 p.92f.

— *Beyond Stonehenge.* New York: Harper & Row, Publishers, Inc., 1972.

Heath, Sir Thomas. *Aristarchus of Samos, The Ancient Copernican.* 1913. Reprint. New York: Dover, 1981.

Heggie, Douglas C. "Highlights and Problems of Megalithic Astronomy," *Archaeoastronomy* JHA Supplement 3, 1981: S17-S37.

Johnstone, Paul. "Stern First in the Stone Age."*International Journal of Nautical Archaeology and Underwater Explorations.* #21. 1973 p. 3-11.

Krupp, E.C. *In Search of Ancient Astronomies.* London: Charlotte & Windas, 1979.

— *Echoes of the Ancient Skies.* New York: NAL-Meridian, 1983.

Langley, Samuel P. *"The New Astronomy."* Washington: Smithsonian Institute, 1889.

Lockyer, Sir J. Norman *Stonehenge and Other British Stone Monuments Astronomically Considered.* 2d ed. London: MacMillan, 1909.

Maltwood, K. E.*Glastonbury's Temple of the Stars,* London: James Clark, 1964.

— *The Enchantments of Britain* first ed. Victoria, B. C. Canada: The Maltwood Estate. 1942.

— *Airview Supplement.* London:John Watkins, 1935.

McCreery, T. "The Kintraw Stone Platform," *Kronos* # 5: April, 1980. 71-79.

251

Michell, John *A Little History of Astroarchaeology,* London: Thames & Hudson, 1976.

Plunket, Emeline M.*Ancient Calendars and Constellations.* London: John Murray, 1903.

Santillana, Giorgio, and Hertha von Dechend. *Hamlet's Mill.* Cambridge: M I T Press, 1968.

Wernick, Robert. "An unknown lady of Vix and her buried treasures." *Smithsonian*, March, 1986, pp. 140-159.

Wood, John Edwin. *Sun, Moon and Standing Stones.* London: Oxford Press, 1978.

Arthurian Studies

Ashe, Geoffrey. *The Quest for Arthur's Britain.* London: Paladin, 1971.

— *The Discovery of King Arthur.* London: Paladin, 1974.

Brodeur, Arthur G. *Arthur Dux Bellorum.* (Monograph) Berkeley: University of California, 1939.

Chant, Joy. *The High Kings: Arthur's Celtic Ancestors.* New York: Bantam, 1983.

Clemens, S. L. Pseud. Mark Twain. *Connecticut Yankee in King Arthur's Court.* Reprint 1889. New York: Heritage Press, 1942.

Jaffray, Robert. *King Arthur and the Holy Grail.* New York: G. P. Putnam's, 1928.

Jarman, A.O. *The Legend of Merlin.* Cardiff: University of Wales Press, 1960.

Lewis, C. S., and William Charles. *The Arthurian Torso.* Grand Rapids: Eerdmans, 1973.

Morris, John. *The Age of Arthur.* New York: Charles Scribner's, 1973.

O'Sharkey, Eithne. "The Maimed King in Arthurian Romance". *Etudes Celtiques,* VIII, Fasc. 2 1959.

Pochoda, Elizabeth. *Arthurian Propaganda.* Chapel Hill: The University of North Carolina Press, 1971.

Snell, F. J. *King Arthur's Country.* London: Dent & Sons, 1926.

Wace, D. and Layamon. *Arthurian Chronicles.* London: Longmans-Green, 1937.

British Archaeology and Legend

Atkinson, R. J. C. *Stonehenge*. London: Pelican, 1960.

Balch, H.E. *The Caves of Mendip*. London: Folk Press, 1927.

Barber, T. *Speculation of the Ancient Britons*. London: Soho, 1854.

Bhattacharya, D.K. *Palaeolithic Europe*. Princeton: Humanities Press, 1977.

Blackie, C. *A Dictionary of Place Names*. London: John Murray Press, 1887.

Branston, Brian.*The Lost Gods of England*. London: Thames & Hudson, 1957.

Burl, A. *Prehistoric Avebury*. New York: Yale Press, 1979.

Burn, A.R. *The Romans in Britain, An Anthology of Stone Inscriptions*. Columbia: University of South Carolina Press, 1969.

Castleden, Rodney. *The Stonehenge People*. London: RKP, 1987.

Clark, D.V., T.G. Cowie and A. Foxon. *Symbols of Power at the Time of Stonehenge*. Edinburgh: National Museum of Antiquities of Scotland, 1985.

Clifford, Elsie. "The Cotswold Megalithic Cultures."*The Early Cultures of Northwest Europe*. Cambridge: Cambridge University Press, 1950.

Coles, John and Bryony Coles *Sweet Track To Glastonbury*. London: Thames & Hudson, 1986.

Collinson's History. *"Antiquities of Somersetshire."* Bath: Wells Cathedral, 1794.

Cutts, A. *Works of Saint Augustine*. (Austin) London: Westminster Abbey Library, 1895.

Dames, Michael. *The Avebury Cycle*. London: Thames & Hudson, 1977.

—*The Silbury Treasure. London:* Thames & Hudson, 1976.

Ellegaard, Alvar. "Stone Age Science in Britain." *Current Anthropology*. Vol. 22 #2: April, 1981. p. 99-125.

Graham, Rose. *English Ecclesiastical Studies*. London: McMillan, 1929.

Graves, Robert. *The White Goddess*. London: Farraux, Straus & Cudahy, 1948.

Hadingham, Evan. *Circles and Standing Stones*. New York: Walker & Co., 1975.

Hawkes, Jaquetta *Mortimer Wheeler, Adventurer in Archaeology*. London: Weidenfeld & Nicolson, 1982.

— "God in the Machine," *Antiquity,* Vol. 41, p.174.

Hoppe, H. trans. Tertullian *Quintus Septimius Florens Tertulianus*. New York: American Library Association, 1903.

Jackson, Jeanette, ed. *Britain: A Study in Patterns*. London: RILKO Press, 1973.

Mattingly, G. trans. *Tacitus: Agricola*. London: Richard Clay, 1948.

Mercer, R. J. A "Neolithic Fortress and Funeral Center." *Scientific American*. 1985, March.

Monmouth, Geoffrey: Thorpe, Lewis trans.*The History of the Kings of Britain*. Baltimore: Penquin, 1968.

Pearce, Susan M. *The Archaeology of South West Britain*. London: Collins, 1979.

Renfrew, Colin *Investigation in the Orkneys*. London: Thames & Hudson,1982.

Richmond, I.A. and Crawford, O. *The British Section of the Ravenna Cosmography*. London: Oxford University Press, 1949.

Ritchie, Graham and Anna *Scotland: Archaeology and Early History*. New York: Thames & Hudson, 1981.

Smith, G. *The Cassiterides*, an inquiry into the commercial operations of the Phoenicians in Western Europe. London: Longman, Green, Longman and Roberts, 1863.

Thom, Alexander *Megalithic Sites in Britain*. Oxford: The Clarendon Press, 1967.

— Megaliths and Mathematics. Antiquity, 40, 1966 121-8.

— *Megalithic Lunar Observatories*. London: Oxford, 1971.

— "The Standing Stones in Argyllshire," Glasgow Archaeological Journal 6 1979: 5-10.

— "A New Study of Lunar Sightlines," *Archaeoastronomy* JHA Supplement 2, 1980: S78-S89.

Vatcher, Faith. *The Avebury Monuments Wiltshire*. London, Her Majesty's Stationery Office, 1976.

Subject Bibliography

Dating Technology

Burr, H.S. "Tree Potential and Sunspots." *Cycles* #243, October 1964.

Case, H.J. "Beaker People, The First Metallurgists." *Palaeohistorica* Vol. 12 1966. p.141.

Hall E.T. "Dating Pottery by Thermoluminescence." In: Brothwelld and Higgs E. eds. *Science in Archaeology.* London: RKP, 1963.

Lanting, J.N., W.G. Mook and J. D. van der Waals. "C-14 Chronology and the Beaker Problem." *Helinium,* #13 1973. p.38f

Lavell, C. ed. *Archaeological Site Index for Radio-carbon dates for Great Britain and Ireland.* London: Council for British Archaeology, 1971.

Libby, Willard. *Radiocarbon Dating.* Chicago: University of Chicago Press. 1955.

Mackie, E. and H. Suess. "Thoughts on Radio Carbon Dating." *Antiquity,* XLV 1971, 197-204.

Renfrew, Colin. *Before Civilization:the radiocarbon revolution and Prehistoric Europe.* New York: Alfred A Knopf, 1973.

Suess, H.E. "Bristlecone Pine calibration of the radiocarbon time-scale 5200 BC to the present, in radiocarbon variations and absolute chronology," *Proceedings of the Twelfth Nobel Symposium,* 303 Vol. 12. New York: Wiley, 1970.

— and E. Mackie. "Thoughts on Radiocarbon Dating." *Antiquity*, XLV 1970, 197-204.

Sacred Geometry, Cabala and Gematria

Blau, J. L. *The Christian Interpretation of the Cabala in the Renaissance.* London:Warburg Institute,1960.

— and Thomas, Simcox-Lea, *Gematria.* London: RILKO, 1977.

— *A Preliminary Investigation of the Cabala.* London: Reprint 1919. RILKO, 1978.

— *The Apostolic Gnosis.* London: Reprint 1919. RILKO, 1979.

Charles, R.H. ed. "The Book of Enoch." In: *The Apocrypha and Pseudepigrapha of the Old Testament.* Vol. II. Oxford: Clarendon Press, 1913. pp.163-281.

Deacon, R. *John Dee*. London: Frederick Muller, 1968.

French, J. *John Dee: The World of an Elizabethan Magus*. London: RKP, 1972.

Huntley, H. E. *The Divine Proportion: A Study in Mathematical Beauty*. New York: Dover Publishers, 1970.

Michell, John. *City of Revelations*. London: Garnstone, 1974.

— *The New View Over Atlantis*. New York: Thames & Hudson,1983.

— *Megalithomania*. London: Thames & Hudson, 1981.

— *City of Revelation*. London: Garnstone, 1975.

— *Ancient Metrology*. Bristol: Pentacle Books, 1981.

Schwartz, Stephan ed. *The Secret Vaults of Time*. Grosset and Dunlap. New York, 1978. p.1-56.

Stukeley, William. *Stonehenge, a Temple Restored to the British Druids*. London: 1740.

Weinraub, Eugene. "Cretien's Jewish Grail." *Essays* #2, Chapel Hill: University of North Carolina, 1976.

Cathedrals and Labyrinths

Adams, Henry. *Mont-Saint Michelle and Chartres*. New York: Houghton-Mifflin, 1933.

Adolf, Helen. *Visio Pacis, The Holy City and Grail*. Philadelphia: Pennsylvania State University, 1960.

Bowie, Theodore. *The Sketchbook of Villard de Honnecourt*. Bloomington: Indiana University Press, 1959.

Charpentier, Louis. *Le Jacques et le Mysteries del la Compestelle*. Paris: Laffont, 1972.

— *The Mysteries of Chartres*. London: Rilko Press, 1972.

Critchlow, Keith, Jane Carroll and Llewylyn Vaughan-Lee. *Chartres Maze: a model of the Universe?* London: RILKO, 1975.

Fulcanelli. (pseud.) translator unknown. *Le Mysterie de la Cathedrale*. London: Neville Spearman, 1970.

Houvet, Etienne. *Gardien de La Cathedral*. Paris: Ecole de Beaux Arts, 1916.

Johnson, Kenneth Rayner. *The Fulcanelli Phenomenon*. Jersey: Neville Spearman, 1980.

Lethaby,W.*Westminster Abbey and the King's Craftsmen*. London: Duckworth, 1954.

Matthews, W.H. *Mazes and Labyrinths*. Reprint 1922. New York: Dutton, 1970.

Pulver, Max. "Jesus Round Dance and Crucifixion according to the Acts of Saint John" In: Campbell, Joseph *The Mysteries*. Bollingen Series XXX.2. Princeton: Princeton University Press, 1955. 169f.

Stahl, W.H. trans. *Commentary on the Dream of Scipio*. New York: Columbia University Press. 1966.

Van Pelt, Robert. "Philo of Alexandria and the Architecture of the Cosmos." London: *Architectural Association Journal*, July, 1983.

von Simson, Otto. *The Gothic Cathedral*. New York: Pantheon Books, 1956.

Ward, Anne. G. *et al. The Quest for Theseus*. New York: Praeger, 1970.

Celtic Studies

Anderson, William *Green Man*. San Francisco: Harper, 1990.

Chadwick, Nora. *The Celts*. London: Pelican, 1970.

Cunliffe, Barry. *The Celts*. New York: McGraw-Hill, 1979.

Dillon, Miles and Nora Chadwick. *The Celtic Sphere*. London: Palladin, 1972.

Evans-Wentz, W. *The Fairy Faith in Celtic Countries*. New York: Universe Books, 1966.

Guest, Lady Charlotte. *The Mabinogion*. London: Bernard Quaritch:1877. Reprint, Cardiff: John Jones, 1977.

Harrison, Hank. *The Quest For Flight*. New York: Bobbs-Merrill, 1976.

Herodotis *History*. George Rawlinson trans.London: 1880. Warburg Institute mss.

Jones, Gwyn and Thomas, L. *The Mabinogion*. New York: Dutton, 1950.

Nutt, Alfred. *The Mabinogion*. London: Dent and Sons, 1927.

Parry, Thomas. *A History of Welsh Literature*. Oxford: Clarendon Press, 1962.

Sharkey, John. *Celtic Mysteries and Ancient Religion*. London: Thames & Hudson, 1975.

Spence, Lewis. *Magic Arts in Celtic Britain*. New York: Weiser, 1968.

Stone, J.F.S. *Wessex Before the Celts*. London: Thames & Hudson,1958.

Tierney, J.J. "The Celtic Ethnography of Posidonius." *Proceedings of the Royal Irish Academy LX C5,* Dublin 1960.

— *De Bello Gallico de Julio Ceasare*. Dublin: Gill-MacMillan, 1961.

Continental Megaliths and Antiquities

Arlette V. "The Archaeology of Lascaux Cave," *Scientific American*. Vol. 246, June 1982.

Bom, Fritz. *The Mystery of the Hunebedden*. Deventer: Ankh-Hermes,1978.

— *East Netherlands Hunebedden Grids*. Deventer: Ankh-Hermes, 1979.

Breuil, Abbey H. *Four Hundred Centuries of Cave Art*. Reprint. Paris: Montignac, 1952.

Briard, Jacques. *The Bronze Age In Barbarian Europe*. London: RKP, 1979.

Clark, Grahame. *Prehistoric Europe: the Economic Basis*. London: Methuen, 1952.

Cole, Sonia. *The Neolithic Revolution*. London: British Museum Natural History Series, p. viii. 1970.

Coles, John. "The Archaeological Evidence for a Bull Cult in Late Bronze Age Europe." *Antiquities*, #39 1965. 217-219.

Edwards, S.W. "Non-Utilitiarian Activities in the Lower Palaeolithic." *Current Anthropology*. Vol 19. #1 1978. p.135.

Eliade, M. *A History of Religious Ideas*. Vol. 1. *from the Stone Age to the Eleusinian Mysteries*. Chicago: University of Chicago Press, 1969.

Evans, Sir A. *The Shaft Graves and Beehive Tombs of Mycenae*. New York: MacMillan, 1929.

Fagan, B. "Prehistoric Times." In: *Readings from Scientific American,*. New York: Freeman, 1983.

Gimbutas, Marija. *The Goddesses and Gods of Old Europe, 6500-3500BC*. Abridged. London: Thames & Hudson, 1986.

Giot, P.R. *Brittany:* Ancient People and Places, Vol.13. New York: Praeger, 1960.

Gourhan-Leroi, A. *Treasures of Prehistoric Art.* New York: Abrams, 1967.

Hadingham, Evan. *Secrets of the Ice Age,* New York: Walker, 1979.

— "Carnac Revisited," *Archaeoastronomy* Maryland III, #3 July -August - September, 1980: 10-13.

Hubbard, L.*Neolithic Cattle-ways.* London: Methuen,1921.

Jacq, M. *Carnac-Morbihan.* Vannes: Museum of Archaeology, 1989.

Mahe, Abbe. *Essay on the Antiquities of Morbihan.* Paris: Faqualle, 1825.

Maranger, J. and H.G. Bandi. *Art in the Ice Ages.* New York: Houghton-Mifflin, 1953.

Mellaart, James. *Catal Huyuk.* New York: McGraw-Hill, 1967.

Pardo, Antonio. *Ancient Spain.* Geneva: Minerva, 1976.

Piggott, Stuart. *Ancient Europe: A Survey.* Chicago: Aldine, 1965.

— *The Druids.* London: Thames & Hudson, 1984.

Reinach, S. "Art and Magic of La Ferrassie Cave." *L' Anthropologie* Vol.14, 1903. p. 257.

Renfrew, Colin ed.*The Megalithic Monuments of Western Europe* London: Thames & Hudson, 1983.

Sanders, N.K. *Prehistoric Art in Europe.* Baltimore: Penguin, 1968.

Scarre, Christopher Ed. *Ancient France, 6000 - 2000 BC.* Edinburgh, University Press, 1986.

Service A. *et al. A Guide to the Megaliths of Europe.* London: Palladin Books, 1981.

Shee-Twoig, Elizabeth.*The Megalithic Art Of Western Europe.* London: Oxford University Press, 1981.

Souriau, E. "Art Prehistorique et Esthetique du Movement La Ferrassie." In: Varagnac, A. ed. *Melanges Offerts.* Paris, Ecole Pratiques des Etudes, 1971.

Thom, Alexander and A. S. Thom. *Megalithic Remains in Britain and Brittany.* Oxford: Oxford Press, 1978.

Whishaw, W.E. *Atlantis in Andalucia.* London: Rider, 1922.

Ethnopharmacology

Allegro, John. *The Sacred Mushroom and the Cross*. New York: Doubleday, 1970.

Baille, Hugh. "Poisonous Fungi of South-Western England." *The Illustrated London News,* October 1978.

Furst, Peter T. *Hallucinogens and Culture*. San Francisco: Chandler & Sharp, 1976.

Hoffer, A., and H. Osmond. *The Hallucinogens*. Saskatoon: The University of Saskatchewan Press, 1966.

Mandell, Arnold J. "The Neurochemistry of Religious Insight and Ecstasy." In: ed. Berrin, Kathleen *The Art of the Huichol Indians*. New York: Abrams, 1978.

Pribram, Karl. *The Holographic Paradigm*. Boulder Colorado: Shambala, 1982.

Schultes, Richard Evans and Albert Hofmann.*Plants of the Gods*. New York: McGraw-Hill, 1979.

Wasson, Gordon *Soma*. New York: Harcourt-Brace-Jovanovich, 1972.

— and Albert Hofmann. *The Road to Eleusis*. New York: Harcourt-Brace-Javonovich, 1978.

— *The Wondrous Mushroom*. New York: McGraw-Hill, 1980.

Hart, Mickey with Jay Stevens. *"Drumming at the Edge of Magic."* San Francisco: Harper-Collins, 1990

Geomancy, Earth Art, Ley Lines and Dowsing

Bourdou D. "Megaliths." *Art in America*. 69:27. November 1981.

Behrend, Michael.*The Landscape Geometry of Southern Britain*. Cambridge: The Institute of Geomantic Research, 1975.

Critchlow, Keith. *Time Stands Still*. New York: Saint Martins, 1972.

— *Order in Space*. London: Thames &Hudson, 1970. p. 27,41, and 111-119.

Devereux, Paul. *The Ley Hunters Companion*. London: Thames & Hudson, 1979.

Gourhan-Leroi, A. *Treasures of Prehistoric Art*. New York: Abrams, 1967.

Guichard, Xavier. *Eleusis Alesia*. Paris-Abbeville: Francois Paillart, 1936.

Hadingham, Evan. *Ancient Carvings in Britain: A Mystery.* London:Garnstone, 1974.

Henry, Francoise ed. *The Book Of Kells.* London: Thames &Hudson, 1974.

— *Irish Art.* London: Thames & Hudson, 1940.

Leader, Elizabeth ed. *Earth Mysteries.* London: RILKO, 1979.

Mann, Ludovic, MacLellan. *Craftsmen's Measures In Prehistoric Times.* London: British Museum Guides, 1989.

Pennick, Nigel. *The Ancient Science of Geomancy.* London: Thames & Hudson, 1978.

Ross, Charles. "Solarburn."*Arts Magazine.* January 1973.

Sanders, N.K. *Prehistoric Art in Europe.* Baltimore: Penguin, 1968.

Setzler, Fran M. "Seeking the Secret of the Giants."*National Geographic.* September 1952.

Shee-Twoig, Elizabeth. *The Megalithic Art Of Western Europe.* London: Oxford University Press, 1981.

Soleri, Paolo.*The Omega Seed.* New York: Doubleday-Anchor, 1981.

Thom, Alexander *Megalithic Sites in Britain.* Oxford: The Clarendon Press, 1967.

— Megaliths and Mathematics. *Antiquity,* 40, 1966 121-8.

— *Megalithic Lunar Observatories.* London: Oxford, 1971.

— and A.S. Thom. *Megalithic Remains in Britain and Brittany.* Oxford: Oxford Press, 1978.

— "The Standing Stones in Argyllshire," Glasgow Archaeological Journal 6 1979: 5-10.

— "A New Study of All Lunar Sightlines," *Archaeoastronomy* JHA Supplement 2, 1980 S78-S89.

Underwood, Guy. *The Pattern of the Past.* London: Abacus 1969.

Watkins, Alfred. *The Old Straight Track.* London: Methuen, 1925.

— *Ley Hunters Manual: a Guide to Early Tracks.* Hereford: Watkins Meter Co., 1927. Reprint London: Simpkins-Marshall, 1927.

Glastonbury

Bligh-Bond, F. *The Company of Avalon*. Oxford: Blackwell, 1924.

— *The Gate of Remembrance*. Oxford: Blackwell, 1926.

Cook, G. H. *Letters to Cromwell*. London: John Baker, 1965.

Greed, John A. *Glastonbury Tales*. Bristol: Saint Trillo, 1975.

Harrison, Hank. "The Lady of Glastonbury." *Vancouver*: August 1974.

Howgrave, Graham. *Peter Lightfoot, Monk of Glastonbury*. Wells: Glastonbury Press, 1922.

Leader, Elizabeth. Ed. *Glastonbury: A Study in Patterns*. Vol. 1, ed. London: Rilko, 1972.

Maltwood, K. E. *Glastonbury's Temple of the Stars,* London: James Clark, 1964.

— *The Enchantments of Britain* first ed. Victoria, B. C. Canada: The Maltwood Estate. 1942.

— *Airview Supplement*. London:John Watkins, 1935.

Moon, Adrian.*The First Ground of God*. Glastonbury: Gothic Image Press, 1978.

Roberts, Anthony ed.*Glastonbury-Ancient Avalon*. London: Rider, 1977.

Scott, John. *William of Malmsbury, the Early History of Glastonbury*. London: Boydell, 1981.

Smithitt-Lewis, Lionel.*Saint Joseph of Arimathea at Glastonbury*. Reprint 1922. London: James Clark, 1978.

Treharne, R. F. *The Glastonbury Legends*. London: Cresset, 1969.

The Goddess and the Mysteries

Gimbutas, Marija. *The Goddesses and Gods of Old Europe, 6500-3500 BC*. Abridged. London: Thames & Hudson, 1986.

Graves, Robert. *The White Goddess*. London: Farraux, Straus & Cudahy, 1948.

Koltuv, Barbera-Black. *The Book of Lilith*. New York: Nicolas-Hays, 1986.

Markale, J. *Women of the Celts*. Vermont: Inner Traditions, 1979.

Meautis, George. *The Mystery of Eleusis*. Benares: Theosophy Press, 1932.

Neumann, Erich ed. *The Great Mother,* Bollingen, Princeton, 1955.

Otto, Walter. "The Meaning of the Eleusinian Mysteries." *The Mysteries*. Eranos Yearbooks, p.14. ed. Joseph Campbell, Bollingen Series XXX, Princeton, 1955.

Patai, Raphael. *The Hebrew Goddess*. New York: KTAV Press, 1967.

Stone, Merlin *When God Was a Woman*. New York: Harcourt-Brace-Javonovich, 1976.

Yates, Francis. *Astrea*. London: RKP, 1976.

Grail Legend and Literature

Bartsch, K. ed. *Parzival* by Wolfram von Eschenbach. Leipzig, Leipzig University, 1927. Reprint, London: Dent and Sons, 1929.

Brown, A.C.L. *The Origins of the Grail Legend*. Cambridge, Mass., Cambridge University Press, 1943.

Carter, H. H. *The Portuguese Book of Joseph of Arimathea*. Chapel Hill: University of North Carolina Press, 1967.

Comfort, W.W. trans. *Chretien de Troyes Arthurian Romances*. London: Dent and Sons, 1976.

Currer-Briggs, Noel.*The Shroud and the Grail*. London: Weidenfeld &Nicolson, 1987.

Denert, Wilhelm. *Astrology in Wolfram Von Eschenbach*. Munich: Deutz, 1960.

Evans, Sebastian. trans. *The High History of the Holy Grail*. London: Reprint 1927. James Clark, 1969.

Fox, J.C. "Marie de France." *English Historical Review*, XXV.

Furnivall, F. ed. *Seynt Graal les Sank Ryal de Robert De Boron*. London: Oxford Press 1861-63.

Guest, Lady Charlotte. *The Mabinogion*. London: Bernard Quaritch:1877. Reprint, Cardiff: John Jones, 1977.

Holmes, Urban T. and Amelia Klenke. *Chretien de Troyes and the Grail. (Li Contes del Graal)*. Chapel Hill: University of North Carolina Press, 1959.

Jung, Emma.*the Grail Legends*. New York: Putnam's 1970.

Kahane, Henry and Rene Kahane. *The Krater and the Grail: Hermetic Sources of the Parzival.* Urbana: University of Illinois Press, 1965.

Lumiansky, R.M. ed. "Mallory's Originality." Forward to: *Morte de Arthur.* Princeton: Princeton University Press, 1983.

Marx, Jean. *"Le Cortege du Chateau des Merveilles." Etudes celtiques,* IX 1960.

— *The Legend Arthurienne et le Graal.* Paris: Dupont, 1952.

Matarasso, P. M. trans.*The Quest of the Holy Grail.* London: Penguin Books, 1960.

Mustard, Helen M. and Charles E. Passage eds. and trans. *Parzival.* New York: Columbia University Press., 1961.

Nitze, W.A., T. Jenkins. and T. Anderson eds.*Le haut livre du Graal, Perlesvaus.* Chicago: University of Chicago Press, 1932.

— "The Fisher King and the Grail in Retrospect". *Romance Philology,* VI.

— ed. *Perlesvaus.* 1937.

— "The Siege Perilleux and the Lia Fail or Stone of Destiny". *Speculum,* 1956.

Nutt, Alfred. *Studies on the Legend of the Holy Grail.* New York: Cooper Square, 1965.

Parry J.J. *The Art of Courtly Love.* New York: Columbia University Press, 1941.

— "Vita Merlini". *Studies in Language and Literature,* August 1925, #3 University of Illinois.

Peers, E. Allison. *Blanquerna.* London: Warburg Institute, 1925.

Pokorny, J. *Der Graal in Ireland und die mythischen Grundlagen de Graalsage.* Mitt. der Anthropologie, Gesellschaft. Vienna, 1918.

Ponsoye, Pierre. *Islam and the Grail.* Paris: Denot, 1958.

Rathofer, Johannes. *Der Gral.* Darmstadt: Wissenschaftliche Buchgesellischaft. 1974.

Stone, B. *Sir Gawain and the Green Knight* London: Penguin, 1961.

Strassburg, Gottfried von. *Tristan: Masterpiece of the early thirteenth century.* London: Penguin Classics Series, 1967.

Tennyson, Alfred. *"The Holy Grail; In Memorium; Maud and Other Poems.* New York: Hurst & Co, 1912.

Thompson, A.W. *The Elucidation: A Prologue to the Conte del Graal.* New York: Schoken, 1931.

Tolkein, J. R. R. *Sir Gawain and the Green Knight.* New York: Houghton-Mifflin, 1975.

Warnke, M. ed. *Lais de Marie de France.* London: Oxford, 1944.

Webster, Deborah, Rogers. trans. *Lancelot, The Knight of the Cart.* New York: Columbia University Press, 1984.

Yates, Francis. *Valoise Tapestries.* 2d ed. London: RKP, 1977.

Hermetism, Neoplatonism and the Mysteries

Armstrong A.H. trans. Plotinus: *Enneads.* VI Vol. Cambridge, Massachusetts: Harvard University Press, 1966.

Boer, W. "Theseus. The Growth of a Myth in History." *Greece and Rome.* #16, 1969. p.1-13.

Campbell, Joseph. *Masks of God: Creative Mythology.* Vol. IV. New York: Viking, 1965.

Festugiere, R.P. (O.P.) *La revelation of Hermes Trismegiste.* Paris, 1944. Reprint, Laffont, 1974.

Graves, Robert.*Claudius The God.* New York: Harrison Smith and Robert Haas, 1935.

— *The Golden Ass of Apuelius.* New York: Basic Books, 1972.

Herberger, Charles F. *The Thread of Ariadne.* New York: Philosophical Library, 1972.

Herter, H. "Theseus the Ionian," Vol. I, "Theseus the Athenian," Vol.II and "Theseus and Hippolytos," Vol. III. *Journal of the Deutsch Museum of Philology.* #85. 1936.

Jonas, Hans. *The Gnostic Religion.* Boston: Beacon Press, 1968.

Klibansky, R. *The Continuity of the Platonic Tradition.* London: Warburg Institute, 1939.

Lazzarelli, Lodovico. facsimile.*Calix Christi et Crater Hermetis,* fourteenth century. New York: W. W. Norton & Company, 1968.

Lee, H.D.P. trans. Plato — *Timaeus and Critias.* London: Penguin Classics, 1971.

Pryse, James M. *The Apocalypse Unsealed, The Magical Message of Ioannes.* New York: Theosophical Press, 1909.

265

Scott, W. *Hermetica*. 4 Vol. London: Oxford Press, 1924. Reprint. Berkeley: Shambala. 1985

Stroup, Thomas B. *Microcosmos;The Shape of the Elizabethan Play*. Lexington: University of Kentucky Press, 1965.

Sutton, E.W. and H. Rackham. trans. *Cicero — De Oratore*. London: Penguin Classics, 1964.

Taran, Leonardo. trans. and comm. *Parmenides*. London: Faber &Faber,1965.

Taylor, Thomas. *Hymns of Orpheus*. London: Life and Theology Press, 1887.

— trans. Plato — *Timaeus and Critias*. revised ed. New York: Pantheon-Bollingen Series III, 1972.

Van Pelt, Robert. "Philo of Alexandria and the Architecture of the Cosmos." London: *Architectural Association Journal*, July, 1983.

Yates, Francis. *Giordano Bruno and the Hermetic Tradition*. London: RKP, 1966.

— *Shakespeare's Last Plays*. London: RKP, 1967

— *Lull and Bruno*. London: RKP, 1986.

— *Theater of the World*. Chicago: University of Chicago, 1972.

Irish Archaeology and Legends

Barber, John. "The Orientation of Recumbent Stone Circles of the South-West Ireland," *Journal of the Kerry Archaeological and Historical Society,* #6. 1973.

Benes, Brigit. "Shamanism in the Saga of Buile Suibne." *Journal for Celtic Philology*, Berlin, 1961.

Bieler, Ludwig. *The Works of Saint Patrick*. Dublin: Gill, 1953.

Brennan, Martin. *The Stars and the Stones*. New York: Thames &Hudson, 1984.

— *The Stones of Ancient Ireland*. San Francisco:Archives Press, Dolmen, 1991.

— *The Boyne Valley Vision*. Dublin: Dolman Press, 1980.

Campbell, J.L. "The Tour of Edward Lhuyd (Lloyd) in Ireland-1699-1700." *Celtica* #5, 1960. 218-28.

Charlesworth J.K. "The Palaeolithic Implements of Sligo." *Proceedings of the Royal Irish Academy*, 39c 1929.

Coffey, George. *Newgrange and Other Incised Tumuli in Ireland*. 1912 Reprint. Dublin: Dolphin, 1977.

Conwell, E.A. "On Ancient Mounds of the Loughcrew Hills." Dublin: *Proceedings of the Royal Irish Academy*, #9, 1864

De Valera. R and J. O'Nuaillain. *Survey of the Megalithic Sites of Ireland.*Vols. 1-3. Dublin: Irish Stationery Office, 1972.

Eogan, George. *Knowth*. Thames & Hudson, London, 1984.

— "A Neolithic Habitation Site in Townly Hall County Louth." *Journal of the Royal Society for Archaeology in Ireland.* #93: 1963.

— "The Knowth Excavations." *Antiquities*. #41: 1967, p.302-64.

Gallico, Paul. *The Life of Saint Patrick*. New York: Doubleday, 1958.

Griffiths, W.E. "Decorated Rotary Querns from Wales and Ireland." *Ulster Journal of Archaeology:* #14, 1951. 49-61.

Herity, M. *Irish Passage Graves*. Dublin: Dublin University Press, 1974.

— and Eogan, George. *Ireland in Prehistory*. London: RKP, 1978.

Joyce, Padraig Weston. *Irish Place Names,* 3 Vol. Dublin: Irish Stationery Office, 1897.

— *Concise History of Ireland*. Dublin: M.H. Gill, 1915.

— *The Wonders of Ireland*. Dublin: Longmans & Green, 1916.

— *A Child's History of Ireland. Dublin: Gill, 1896.*

Kinsella, Thomas. trans. *The Tain.*Dublin: Dolmen Press, 1981.

MacAlister R.A.S. *The Archaeology of Ireland*. London: Benjamin Blom, 1928. New York: Reprint; Arno, 1977.

— "Teamhair Breg: A Study of the Remains and traditions of Tara." *Proceedings of the Royal Irish Academy,* Vol. XXXIV, 1919, p.231.

Martin, Cecil. *Prehistoric Man in Ireland*. London: MacMillan, 1935.

Mitchell, G.F. and Sieveking, G. de "Flintflake, Probably of Palaeolithic Age from Mell Townland, Near Drogheda, Co.Louth." *Journal of the Royal Society of Antiquaries of Ireland,* #102. 1972.

— "The Siege Perilleux and the Lia Fail or Stone of Destiny". *Speculum*, 1956.

O'Brien, Henry.*The Round Towers of Ireland*. Dublin: Parbury & Allen, 1884.

O'Donovan, P. *Ancient Laws of Ireland,* 6 vols. Dublin: Four Courts Press, 1865-1901.

O'Kelly, Clare. *An Illustrated Guide to Newgrange.* Cork: 1977.

O'Kelly, Michael J. *Newgrange. Archaeology, art and legend.* Thames & Hudson, London, 1982.

Pilcher, J. R. *et al.* "Land Clearance in the Irish Neolithic: New Evidence." *Science.* #172: 1971 p. 560-562.

Pokorny, J. *Der Graal in Irland und die mythischen Grundlagen de Graalsage.* Mitt. der Anthropologie, Gesellschaft. Vienna, 1918.

Roberts, Jack. *Exploring West Cork.* Skibbereen: Key Books, 1989.

— *Sketches of Ancient Carbery:The Megaliths of West Cork.* Skibbereen: Key Books, 1991.

Rotherham, E. "On the Excavation of a Cairn on Sleive-na-Caillighe, Loughcrew." *Journal of the Royal Irish Society,* #25, 1895 p. 311-316.

Selkirk, A. "Newgrange." *Current Archaeology,* # 2, 297-300 1970.

Shee-Twoig, Elizabeth. *The Megalithic Art Of Western Europe.* London: Oxford University Press, 1981.

Thomas, Charles. *Britain and Ireland in Early Times, A. D. 400-800.* London: Thames & Hudson, 1971.

Tierney, J.J. "The Celtic Ethnography of Posidonius." *Proceedings of the Royal Irish Academy LX-C5,* Dublin,1960.

Vallancey, Charles. *Collectanea de rebus Hibernicis,* 6 vols. Dublin: Government Printing Office, 1770-1894.

Wilde, William, R. *Beauties and Antiquities of the Boyne.* Cork: Tower Books, 1978.

Woodman, P.C. "A Mesolithic Camp in Ireland, 7000 BC". *Scientific American.* #245:120. August: 1981.

Survival of the Pagan Mysteries

Bonser, Wilfrid. *Survivals of Paganism in Anglo-Saxon England.* monograph. London: John Johnson Press, 1934.

Bord, Colin and Janet Bord.*The Secret Country.* London: Paladin, 1978.

— *Earth Rites In Pre-Industrial England.* London: Paladin, 1977.

Campbell, Joseph.*The Hero with a Thousand Faces.* 1949. Reprint. Cleveland, World Publishing, 1967.

Cumont, Franz *Les Religions orientals dans le paganisme romain.* Paris: fourth ed. Institute Sorbonne, 1929.

Deubner, L. *Attische Feste.* Berlin: Gravure, 1932.

Ferguson, John. *Pelagius, A Historical and Theological Study.* New York: Dutton, 1957.

Meautis, George *The Mystery of Eleusis.* Benares: Theosophy Press, 1932.

Ravenscroft, Trevor. *The Spear of Destiny.* New York: G. P. Putnam's, 1973.

— *The Cup of Destiny, the Quest for the Grail.* London: Rider, 1981.

Robertson, J.M. *Pagan Christs.* New Hyde Park, N.Y.: University.Books, 1967.

Seznic, Jean. *Survival of the Old Gods.* New York: Harper & Row, 1961.

Wind, Edgar. *Pagan Mysteries in the Renaissance.* rev. ed. New York: W. W. Norton, 1968.

The Paleolithic Horizon

Arlette V. "The Archaeology of Lascaux Cave," *Scientific American.* Vol. 246, June 1982.

Bhattacharya, D.K. *Palaeolithic Europe.* Princeton: Humanities Press, 1977.

Gourhan-Leroi, A. *Treasures of Prehistoric Art.* New York: Abrams, 1967.

Hadingham, Evan. *Secrets of the Ice Age*, Walker, New York, 1979.

Marschak, Alexander. "Exploring the Mind of Ice-Age Man." *National Geographic*, CXLVII, January 1975.

— *The Roots of Civilization.* New York: McGraw-Hill, 1972.

— "The Art and Symbols of Ice Age Man," *Human Nature,* #9 September, 1978.

Pfeiffer, John. *The Creative Explosion.* New York: Harper & Row, 1982.

Pyramids and Egyptian Studies

Brunton, Paul. *A Search in Secret Egypt*. London: Ryder, 1969.
Budge, Sir E. A. Wallis *The Egyptian Book of the Dead*. London: 1895. Reprint New York, Harper, 1971.
Fakhry, A. *The Pyramids*. Chicago:University of Chicago Press, 1975.
Lemesurier, Peter. *The Great Pyramid Decoded*. New York: Saint Martin's Press, 1977.
Schwaller de Lubicz. *Sacred Science: The King of Pharonic Theocracy*. Reprint, 1961. New York: Inner Traditions, 1982.
Tompkins, Peter. *Secrets of the Great Pyramids*. New York: Harper & Row, 1973.
— *Mysteries of the Mexican & Mayan Pyramids*. New York: Harper & Row, 1979.
— The Magic of Obelisks. New York: Harper&Row, 1981.
Weissen-Szulmanska, A. *Origines atlantiques des anciens Egyptiens* (The Atlantic Origins of the Ancient Egyptians). Paris: Omnium Litteraire, 1965.

Megalithic Ritual in Christianity

Anitchkof, E."The Grail and the Eucharistic Rite." *Romania,* Vol. 55 1929.
Eliade, M. *Shamanism; Archaic Techniques of Ecstasy*. Princeton: Princeton University Press, 1964.
Every, George. *The Mass*. Dublin: Gill&MacMillan, 1978.
Jungmann, Joseph *The Mass of the Roman Rite*. New York: Grosset, 1959.
Namauchi, Edwin. *Aramaic and Mandaic Bowl Incantations*. New York: American Oriental Society, 1967.
Pulver, Max. "Jesus Round Dance and Crucifixion according to the Acts of Saint John" In: Campbell, Joseph *The Mysteries*. Bollingen Series XXX/.2. Princeton: Princeton University.Press, 1955. 169f.
Williams, Mary. "Some Aspects of the Grail Procession." *Folklore, LXXI*, 1960.

Subject Bibliography

Secret Societies

Allen, Paul. *A Christian Rosenkreutz Anthology*. New York: Biograf Publications, 1973.

Anderson, Flavia. *The Ancient Secret*. London: RKP, 1953.

Angebert, Jean-Michel. trans.*The Occult and the Third Reich*. New York:MacMillan, 1974.

Ashmole, Elias. *History of the Order of the Garter*. 3 vols. Oxford, 1646.

Baigent, M. Leigh, R. and Lincoln, H. *Holy Blood and Holy Grail*. London: Jonathan Cape, 1982.

Begg, Ian *The Cult of the Black Virgin*. London: RKP, 1986.

Cooper-Oakley, Isabel *Masonry and Medieval Mysticism*. London: Theosophical Press, 1977.

Cumont, Franz. *The Mysteries of Mithra*. Reprint. 1902. New York: Dover, 1956.

Daraul, Arkon.*A History of Secret Societies*. New York: Citadel, 1965.

Doresse, Jean *The Secret Book of the Egyptian Gnostics*. London: Hollis and Carter, 1960.

— *Rites and Symbols of Initiation:The Mysteries of Birth and Rebirth*. 1958. Reprint. New York: Harper & Row, 1975.

Evans, A. J. *Shakespeare's Magic Circle*. London: Arthur Barker, 1956.

Feugere, Saint-Maxent and Koker Georges: *Le Serpent Rouge*. Paris: Bibliothèque Nationale, 1887.

Hall, Manly P. *Secret Teachings of All Ages*. Los Angeles: The Philosophical Research Society, 1959.

— *Orders of the Quest*. Los Angeles:The Philosophical Research Society, 1966.

Horne, Alex. *King Solomon's Temple*. Los Angeles: Wilshire Books, 1974.

Jones, Bernard. *Freemasons Guide and Companion*. London: Harrap, 1950.

Lethbridge, T.C. *The Sons of Thunder*. London: RKP,1972.

Lindner, Eric. *Masonry: The Royal Art Illustrated*. Vienna Graz Akademische Druck Verlagsanstalt, 1976.

Lull, Ramon. Caxton, William. trans. & printer. *The Book of the Order of Chyvalry*. London: Reprint 1483-1485. Early English Text Society ed. A.T.R. Byles, 1926.

271

Mackenzie, Norman. *Secret Societies*. New York: Holt, Rinehart & Winston, 1967.

Meautis, George. *The Mystery of Eleusis*. Benares:Theosophy Press, 1932.

Nasr, S.H. "Sufism and the Perenniality of the Mystical Quest," *Studies in Comparitive Religion*, Autumn, 1970.

Philalethes, Eugenius. *The Fame and Confession of the Fraternity of R:C: commonly, of the Rosie Cross, with a Preface annexed thereto and a short Declaration of their Physicall Work*. London: Giles Calvert, Black Spread Eagle, at the west end of Saint Pauls Street, 1652. Reprint facsimile. 1970. Helios, Glastonbury. p.45.

Pike, Albert. *Morals and Dogma*. Philadelphia: The Masonic Press, 1889.

Rothovius, Andrew. "The Adams Family and the Grail." *East-West Journal*, 1975.

Shah, Idres. *The Sufis*. New York: Doubleday, 1965.

Strong, Roy. *The Cult of Elizabeth*. New York: Thames & Hudson, 1977.

Yates, Francis. *The Rosicrucian Enlightenment*. London: RKP, 1974.

— *The Occult In The Elizabethan Age*. London: RKP,1981.

Social Psychology and Anthropology

Canetti, Elais. *Crowds and Power*. New York: Viking, 1963.

Cohane, J. P. *The Key*. New York: Crown, 1969.

Dember, W. *The Psychology of Perception*. New York: Holt, Rinehart & Winston, 1960.

Eliade, M. *Myths,Dreams and Mysteries*. New York: Harper & Row, 1957.

— *The Quest History and Meaning in Religion*. Chicago: University of Chicago Press, 1969.

Finley, M.J. *Democracy — Ancient and Modern*. New York: World Books, 1973.

Gregory, R.L. *The Intelligent Eye*. London: Weidenfeld & Nicolson, 1971.

Hapgood, Charles *Maps of the Ancient Sea Kings*. New York: Chilton, 1966.

Jarrett, Bede. *Mediaeval Socialism*. New York: Dodge, 1913.

Jung, C.G. *Symbols of Transformation.* Princeton, New Jersey: Bollingen Series, Princeton University Press, 1967.
— *Aion.* Bollingen Series, Princeton, 1968.
Maslow, Abraham. *The Further Reaches of Human Nature.* New York: Viking Press, 1973.
— *Religious Values and Peak Experience.* Boston: Brandies University Press, 1965.
Renfrew, Colin. *The Explanation of Cultural Change.* London: Duckworth,1973.
— "The Social Archaeology of Megalithic Monuments" *Scientific American.* Vol. 249, # 5. November,1983.
White, Peter. *The Past is Human.* Edinburgh: Angus & Robertson, 1976.
Yates, Francis. *The Art Of Memory.* London: RKP, 1968.

The Templars and the Crusades

Barber, M. *The Trial of the Templars.* Cambridge: Cambridge University Press, 1980.
Caxton, William trans. & printer. Lull, Ramon. *The Book of the Order of Chyvalry.* London: Reprint 1483-1485. Early English Text Society ed. A.T.R. Byles, 1926. p.141.
Charpentier, John. *The Order of the Templars.* Paris: La Colombe, 1961.
Charroux, Robert. "The Book of the Betrayal of Secrets" *(Le Livre des secrets trahis).* Paris: Laffont, 1965.
Finley, M.J. *Democracy — Ancient and Modern.* New York: World Books, 1973.
Howarth, Stephen. *The Knights Templar.* London: Collins, 1982.
Morizot, Pierre *The Templars.* London: Steiner/Biograf, 1960.
Ormerod, H.A. *Piracy in the Ancient World.* Reprint 1924. Chicago: Argonaut, 1964.
Saint-Loup, M. "The Heretics" *(Les Heritiques).* Paris: Presses de la Cite. 1969.
Turberville, M. C. *Medieval Heresy and Inquisition* London: Crosby, Lockwood & Sons, 1920.

The Dawn People

Bourque, Bruce J. "The Turner Farm Site: A Preliminary Report." *Man in the Northeast*, Vol. II 1976:21-30.

Campbell, Joseph. *The Flight of the Wild Gander*. Chicago: Gateway, 1972.

Fitshugh, William. "Residence Pattern Development in the Labrador Maritime Archaic." In *Archeology of Newfoundland and Labrador 1983*, pp. 6-47.

— Maritime Archaic Cultures of Central and Northern Labrador." *Arctic Anthropology*. Vol. 15 2:61-95, 1978.

— ed *Prehistoric Maritime Adaptations of the Circumpolar Zone*. Mouton Publishers, 1975.

— ed. *Arctic Anthropology*. Vol. 12, # 2, 1975. Papers from a Symposium on Moorehead and Maritime Archaic Problems in Northeastern North America, held at the Smithsonian Institution, February 27-March 2, 1974.

Gardner, Joseph Ed. *Mysteries of Ancient America*. New York: Readers Digest, 1986.

Gunther, Erna. *Indian Life on the Northwest Coast of North America*. University of Chicago Press, 1972.

Hapgood, Charles. *Maps of the Ancient Sea Kings*. New York: Chilton, 1966.

— *The Path of the Pole*. New York: Chilton, 1970 pp.106-122.

Kehoe, Alice. "Small Boats upon the North Atlantic." In: Riley, Carroll & Kelley, Charles eds. *et al: Man across the Sea: Problems of Pre-Columbian Contacts*. Austin: University of Texas Press, 1971 pp. 275-92.

McMann, Jean. *Riddles of the Stone Age, Rock Carvings of Ancient Europe*. London: Thames & Hudson, 1980.

Moorehead, Warren K. *A Report of the Archaeology of Maine*. The Andover Press, 1922.

Rouse, Irving. *Migrations in Prehistory: Inferring Population Movement from Cultural Remains*. Yale University Press, 1986.

Sanger, David. *Discovering Maine's Archaeological Heritage*. Maine Historic Preservation Commission, 1979.

Snow, Dean R. *The Archaeology of New England*. Academic Press, 1980.

Struever, Stuart & Felicia Antonelli Holton.*Koster: Americans in Search of Their Prehistoric Past.* New York: Doubleday, 1979.

Stuart, George E., and Gene S. Stuart *Discovering Man's Past in the Americas.* Washington, D.C.:National Geographic Society, 1969.

Sturtevant, William C. ed. *Handbook of North American Indians, Vol. 6: Subarctic.* Smithsonian Institution Press, 1978.

— ed. *Handbook of North American Indians, Vol. 15: Northeast.* Smithsonian Institution Press, 1978.

Tuck, James A. *Maritime Provinces Prehistory.* National Museums of Man and National Museums of Canada, 1984.

— *Ancient People of Port au Choix.* Memorial University Institute of Social and Economic Studies, # 17. Memorial University of Newfoundland, 1976.

— *Newfoundland Labrador Prehistory.* Ottowa: National Museum of Man, 1976.

— "An Archaic Indian Cemetery in Newfoundland." 1970. In *New World Archaeology: Readings from Scientific American.* W. H. Freeman & Co., 1974.

Tyler, Larry. "Megaliths, Medicine Wheels and Mandalas," *The Midwest Quarterly.* XXI #3 Spring 1980 p. 290-305.

Willoughby, Charles C. *Prehistoric Burial Places in Maine.* Boston: Peabody Museum of American Archaeology and Ethnology, 1898. Also available from Kraus Reprint Co., New York, 1971.

Time and Timelessness

Brown, Frank. "The Clock Timing of Biological Rhythms," *American Scientist*, Nov. 1972.

Briggs, John and F. David Peat. "Times Arrow" in: *Turbulent Mirror.* Harper and Row, San Francisco, 1989.

Burr, H. S. "Electrical Timing of Human Ovulation." *American Journal of Obstetrics & Gynecology,* Vol. 44 #223, 1942.

Eliade, M. *Cosmos and History: The Myth of Eternal Return.* New York: Harper &Row, 1959.

Gauquelin, Michell. *The Cosmic Clocks.* London: Peter Owen, 1969.

Hoyle, Fred. *From Stonehenge to Modern Cosmology.* San Francisco: W.H. Freeman, 1972.

Hawking, Stephen W. *A Brief History of Time.* New York: Bantam, 1989.

Huff, D. *Cycles In Your Life.* London: Gollancz, 1965.

Isikowitz, Karl. *Primitive Views of the World.* New York: Columbia Press,1964.

Jonas, E. "Predetermining the Sex of a Child" In: S. Ostrander S. and Schoeder, L *Psychic Discoveries Behind the Iron Curtain.* New York: Prentice-Hall, 1971.

Munitz, Milton. *Theories of the Universe.* New York: MacMillan, 1979.

Needleman, Jacob. *A Sense of the Cosmos, the Encounter of Modern Science and Ancient Truth.* New York: Doubleday, 1975.

Neugebauer, O. *The Exact Sciences in Antiquity.* 2d ed. New York: Praeger, 1969.

Rose, Kenneth Jon. *The Body in Time.* New York: Wiley & Sons, 1989.

Shuttle, Penelope.*The Wise Wound.* London: Gollencz, 1977.

Troubadours, Cathars and Albigensians

Birkswalter, Gilbert.*The Treasure of Montsegur.* London: Crucible, 1987.

Belperron, Pierre. *The Crusade Against the Albigensians and the Union of Languedoc in France (1209-1249).* Paris: Plon, 1942.

Cantor, Norman. *Medieval Europe.* 2d ed. New York: MacMillan, 1969.

Fox, J.C. "Marie de France." *English Historical Review*, XXV.

Gadel, A. *The Road to the Grail: The Ancient Mysteries of the Cathares.* The Hague: Rosekruiz Press, 1960.

Gorres, J. *Der Heilige Francisckus Assisi, ein Troubadour.* Strassburg, Bibliothèque Nationale, Paris, 1826.

Hueffer, Francis. *The Troubadours.* London: Theology Press, 1878.

Kelly, Amy. *Eleanor of Aquitaine and the Four Kings.* New York, Praeger, 1988.

Madaule, Jaques. *The Albigensian Crusade*. London: Burns and Oates, 1967.

Magre, Maurice.*The Blood of Toulouse,* Paris: Fasquelle, 1931.

— *Magicians and Illuminati,* Paris: Fasquelle, 1932.

— *The Treasure of the Albigensians,* Paris: Fasquelle, 1938.

Nelli, Rene. *Le Phenomene Cathare*. Toulouse: Privat, 1964.

Niel, F *Montsegur, The Mountain of Inspiration*. Paris: Atilier Grenoble, 1967.

Rhan, Otto.*Les Cours de Lucifer*. Paris: Claude Tchou, 1945.

— *The Crusade Against the Grail*. Paris: Stock, 1934.

Saint-Loup, M. "The Heretics" (*Les Heritiques*). Paris: Presses de la Cite. 1969.

Sede, Gerard. *The Treasure of the Cathars*. Paris: Jullier, 1957.

Turberville, M. C. *Medieval Heresy and Inquisition* London: Crosby, Lockwood & Sons, 1920.

Wakefield, Walter. *Heresy in Southern France, 1100-1250*. London: George Allen and Unwin, 1974.

The Healing Witch

Baroja, Julio-Caro. *The World of the Witches*. Chicago: University of Chicago Press, 1964.

Black, G.F. "A Calendar of Cases of Witchcraft in Scotland, 1510-1727." *Bull. New York Public Library.,* xli-xlii 1937-1938.

Hole, Christina. *Witchcraft in England*. New York: Charles Scribners, 1947.

Lethbridge, T. C. *Witches*. London: R.K.P., 1962.

Murray, Margaret.*The Witch Cult in Western Europe*. London: Oxford Clarendon Press, 1921.

— *God of the Witches*. New York: Doubleday, 1962.

— *The Divine King In England,* London: Faber & Faber 1939.

Notestein, Wallace. *A History of Witchcraft in England*. New York: Thomas Cravelle, 1968.

Russell, Jeffrey, Burton. *Witchcraft in the Middles Ages*. New York: Cornell University Press, 1972.

Storms, G. *Anglo-Saxon Magic*. The Hague: Martinus-Nijhoff, 1948.

Thomas, Keith. *Religion and the Decline of Magic*. London:Weidenfeld & Nicolson, 1971.

Manuscript Material

The following references are difficult to locate for the North American scholar, but are usually available in reproduction or on transparencies by writing the institutions listed.

Aroux, Eugene. *Les Mysteres de la Chevalerie*. Paris: mss. Bibliothèque Nationale, 1858.

Aubrey, John. *Monumenta Britannica.,Survey of Stonehenge 1663*. British Museum mss. London: Kings Library,1698.

Bale, J. *Illustrium maioris Britanniae scriptorium summarium.* Being a summary of the major British illustrated scriptoria as of the Tudor period. Ipswich: 1548. In mss: Le Roux de Lincy, *Sur le Abbay de Fecamp*. Vol. 1 p. 292f. Bodliean Library, Oxford.

Baret, Eugene. *Les Troubadours et leur Influence du midi de Europe*. Paris:Bibliothèque Nationale, 1867.

Benoist, Jean. *History des Albigenois et des Vaudois*. 2 vol. Paris: Bibliothèque Nationale. 1691.

Bermant C. and Weitzman M. *Ebla*. New York: Times Books, 1979.

Buttner, H. ed. *Meister Eckhart's Writing and Predictions*. Jena, 1909.

Eisen, Gustavus A. *The Great Chalice of Antioch*. 2 Vol. New York: Kouchakji Press, 1924.

Feugere, Saint-Maxent and Georges Koker. *Le Serpent Rouge*. Paris: Bibliothèque Nationale, 1887.

Gorres, J. *Der Heilige Francisckus Assisi, ein Troubadour*. Strassburg, in: Bibliothèque Nationale, Paris:1826.

Hood, Thomas. *The Use of Both Globes, Celestial and Terrestrial*. Oxford: Ashmolean mss. 1592.

Herodotis. *History*. George Rawlinson trans.London: 1880. Warburg Institute mss.

Laurence, Richard. Archbishop trans.*The Book of Enoch The Prophet*. Oxford: Bodleian mss. 1821. Revised ed. Oxford University Press, 1883.

Morien, L. *Light of Britania, Kimmerian Revelation*. Ashmolean mss. Oxford: 1802.

Oldfather, E. trans. *Diodorus Siculus: Bibliotheca Historica*. London: British Museum mss. Loeb Classic, 1935.

278

Ouvaroff, M. *On the Mysteries of Eleusis.* London: no publisher listed British Museum mss. 1817.

Penn, William. signed mss, *The Seven G's of Ancient Masonry.* London: British Museum mss. 1771. 35 mm slides.

Rogers, John. *"The Displaying of an Horrible secte of grosse and wicked Heretiques naming themselves the Familie of Love."* London: 1578. mss. Warburg Institute and Ashmolean, Oxford.

Rolfe J.C. trans. *Ammianus Marcellinus.* London: British Museum mss. microfilm. 1963.

Rossetti, Dante Gabriel. *Disquisitions on the Anti-Papal Spirit which Produced the Reformation.* London: British Museum. mss. 1834.

Sagger, Martin. *The Path of Enlightenment.* Address to the Department of History in Art, University of Victoria, Victoria, British Columbia. Maltwood Library, 1976.

Sharpe, John. trans. *The History of the Kings of England,* London British Museum mss. 1815.

Sporley, Richard. *Lives of the Abbots-Cosmoti.* London: British Museum mss. Claud, A8, 1460 copy.

Stapel, W. ed. *Parzival by Wolfram von Eschenbach.* Munich: Publisher unknown, 1950.

Stubbs, William R. ed. William of Malmsbury. *Acts of the Kings (DeGestis Regum Anglorum).* London: Rolls, 2 vol. 1887–89.

Stukeley, William. *Stonehenge, a Temple Restored to the British Druids.* British Museum mss.London: 1740.

Tours, Saint Gregory. *Historia Francorum* 10 vol. Paris: Bibliothèque Nationale, Paris.Seventeenth century.

Valeriano, Pierio. *Hieroglyphica.* Latin mss., Bibliothèque Nationale, Paris, 1787.

Vaillant, E. *Les Romes Histoire des Bohemiens. Paris*: Bibliothèque Nationale, 1898.

Warner, G.F. and J.G. Brewer. eds. *Giraldi Cambrensis Opera: (De Instructione Principis et Speculum Ecclesia.* Vol.vi and viii, London: British Museum, Rolls Series, 1861-1891.

Williams, Ithel. *Barddas: Usages of the Bardo-Druidic System in the Isle of Britain.* Caernarvon: Clandovery, 1863. In: Warburg Institute, University of London.

INDEX

O

O'Kelly, Claire 194
O'Kelly, Michael 45-48, 192, 193
Occidental ancestor worship 94
  cultures 151
  religions 74
Og 102, 115
Ogham 115
Ogmios 115
Orcus 106
Origen 75, 136
Orpheus 106
Orphic myth 92
Osborne, Ozzie xviii
Ossian 63, 92
Ovid 101

P

Paleolithic Age 42, 123, 161
  Goddess 149
  hunting rituals 128
  lightbeam God 85
  mask ceremonies 99
  Mother of the Void 116
  Shamanism 133
Paleolithic, Upper 14, 169
Parthelonians 17, 35
Parzival (Wolfram) 3
Passage Tombs xxix, 13, 20
Penobscot Bay (Maine) 30, 31, 169
pentagram 174
Pentatuch 77
Pentecost 99

Perceival 65, 83, 101, 104, 107, 129, 165
perceived time 156
Perlesvaus, The xxi, xxii, 65, 87, 90, 101, 109, 165
Persephone (Goddess of Eleusis) 106-108, 150
Perseus 65, 105, 108, 117
Picts 36
Phanes (light god) 92
Philo of Alexandria 75, 136, 141, 197
Phoenicians 15
  Tammuz 108
Pico della Mirandola 94
Plantagenets, The 92
Plato 142, 163
Plotinus 75
Pluto 106
Poseidon 106
Potato Famine 87
potential Star Temples sites 69
Pravda 40
proto-Grail religion 14, 28, 74, 107
puis (see Fairies) 87
Puritan and Calvinist writers 100
Pyramids 37, 40

Q

Quanterness Cairn 52
Queen of Night, The 99

Strasbourg Cathedral 141,
146, 175
Suess, H.E. (Tree Ring
dating) 40
Sufism 29
Summer Solstice 39, 99, 105
Sun King (Arthur) 84

T

Tain bo Cullainge, The 63, 97
Tain, The (See Cattle Raid on
Cooley)
Tara of Tibet 103
Tara of Ireland 68, 103, 182
Tardenosians (Spain) 38
Tarot xix, 29, 130, 198
Temple of Solomon 143
templum mundi 75
Tetragrammaton 104
Theseus 126
    and Ariadne 84
Thom, Professors Alexander
    and Archibald 67, 155
Tigris 41
time capsules 57
Tir na Og 63, 92
Totenkopf (Deadhead) 138
traditional Trinity 100
Tree of Life 134
trilithon 33, 44-45
troubadours 84, 102, 177-
179
Tuatha de Danann 35

U

Ultima Thule 35
Underwood, Guy (dowser)
123-125
Uther Pendragon (Arthur's
Father) 66

V

Vallancey, Charles 37
Vandenberg, Diana xxvi
Venus of Lascaux 146
Venus 39, 73, 96, 97
Veronica's Veil 2
Vesica Pisces 136
Vinca culture (Danubian) 52
Vinkenoog, Simon xxvi
Virgin Mary 64, 146
Virgo 103, 117
Von Daaniken, Erik xix

W

Warburg Institute xxiii
Washington Post, The 40
Watkins, Alfred 121, 122
Westminster (see Abbeys)
White Goddess 85, 95, 100
William of Malmsbury 141
Winter Solstice 22, 39, 64,
92, 99, 132, 148
Wolfe, Virginia xx
Wolfram von Eschenbach
xxii, 3, 30, 151, 164
Wookey Hole (Glastonbury)
xxi

Index

Y

Yates, Dame Frances xxiii,
  xxvii

Z

Zen Buddhists 123
Zeus 65, 106
Zodiac 83, 104
Zoroastrian 115
Zoser, pyramid of 75

For a free copy of *The Ancient Mysteries* newsletter
and information about the
video tape that accompanies this text, write:

The Archives Press
334 State Street
Dept. HG
Los Altos, California 94022